해양경찰공무원 시험

해사영어 종합 모의고사

임하람 저

해양경찰 필기시험 해사영어 문제 600제!
전체 범위의 모의고사 30회차!
실제 기출문제 및 기출문제와 유사한 유형의 문제 수록!
모든 문제의 정답 및 해설 수록!

cambus 출판사

본 종합모의고사 600제는 단원별 구성이 아닌 실제 해경필기시험과 같이 각 회차가(총30회차) 전범위로 구성되어 있습니다.
제가 집필한 기본이론서인 "올인원 해사영어 기본이론+기출문제(캠버스 출판사)"로 공부를 마치시고 필기시험 응시 전에 본 문제집의 전체 모의고사를 풀어보시는걸 추천 드립니다.
실제 기출문제가 그대로 들어있거나 기출문제 유형의 문제들이 다수 들어가 있고 지엽적이라 여겨지는 아주 과거의 기출문제나 기출예상문제 또한 담았습니다. 가장 최신 해사영어 필기시험의 난이도와 문제구성이 비슷합니다. 시험 직전 실전감각을 키우기에는 더할 나위 없는 교재일겁니다.

여러분의 합격을 위해 기도하겠습니다.

-편저자 임하람-

CONTENTS

PART 01 ▌ 해사영어 종합 모의고사

CHAPTER — 01 모의고사 1회차 ·················6
CHAPTER — 02 모의고사 2회차 ·················13
CHAPTER — 03 모의고사 3회차 ·················22
CHAPTER — 04 모의고사 4회차 ·················29
CHAPTER — 05 모의고사 5회차 ·················36
CHAPTER — 06 모의고사 6회차 ·················43
CHAPTER — 07 모의고사 7회차 ·················51
CHAPTER — 08 모의고사 8회차 ·················58
CHAPTER — 09 모의고사 9회차 ·················65
CHAPTER — 10 모의고사 10회차 ··············73
CHAPTER — 11 모의고사 11회차 ··············81
CHAPTER — 12 모의고사 12회차 ··············89
CHAPTER — 13 모의고사 13회차 ··············97
CHAPTER — 14 모의고사 14회차 ··············105
CHAPTER — 15 모의고사 15회차 ··············113
CHAPTER — 16 모의고사 16회차 ··············121
CHAPTER — 17 모의고사 17회차 ··············129

CHAPTER — 18 모의고사 18회차 ··············137
CHAPTER — 19 모의고사 19회차 ··············144
CHAPTER — 20 모의고사 20회차 ··············151
CHAPTER — 21 모의고사 21회차 ··············158
CHAPTER — 22 모의고사 22회차 ··············166
CHAPTER — 23 모의고사 23회차 ··············174
CHAPTER — 24 모의고사 24회차 ··············181
CHAPTER — 25 모의고사 25회차 ··············188
CHAPTER — 26 모의고사 26회차 ··············195
CHAPTER — 27 모의고사 27회차 ··············202
CHAPTER — 28 모의고사 28회차 ··············209
CHAPTER — 29 모의고사 29회차 ··············217
CHAPTER — 30 모의고사 30회차 ··············223

PART 02 ▌ 정답 및 해설 ··············232

종합 모의고사

해사영어 모의고사

01 다음에 해당하는 용어에 대한 설명으로 옳은 것을 고르시오.

> The speed of a vessel adjusted to that of a pilot boat at which the pilot can safely embark/disembark.

① pilot boat speed ② safe speed
③ manoeuvring speed ④ boarding speed

02 밑줄 친 부분을 옳게 설명한 것은?

> The <u>SSO</u> started security drill at 1630 hours UTC.

① 선박 보안 담당관 ② 항만 보안 담당관
③ 선박 안전 담당관 ④ 선박 보안 순찰자

03 Which is the same meaning as the underlined part?

> 'Captain, the <u>vessel does not answer the wheel,</u> sir!'

① Vessel goes as order.
② Vessel does not as ordered by engine.
③ Vessel has no steerage way.
④ Vessel goes too slow.

04 다음 박스의 질문에 가장 적절한 것은?

> What is the fitting on the deck of a ship which guides the ropes when the ship is being moored?

① accommodation ladder ② bitt
③ Fairway ④ Fair leader

05 다음 빈칸에 들어갈 내용을 고르시오.

> Risk of collision exists when (   ) of an approaching vessel does not appreciably change.

① compass bearing ② speed
③ turing circle ④ track

06 다음 중 SMCP 용어와 그 내용이 알맞게 짝지어진 것의 개수를 구하시오.

> 가. Air draft – The height from the waterline to the highest point of the keel
> 나. Blind sector – An area which can not be scanned by the ship's radar because it is shielded by parts of the superstructure, masts, etc.
> 다. Windward – On or towards the sheltered side of a ship
> 라. Leeward – The general direction from which the wind blows
> 마. COW – Crude Oil Washing
> 바. SBE – Stand By Engine
> 사. BWE – Break Water Entrance

① 3개 ② 4개 ③ 5개 ④ 6개

07 표준해사통신영어(SMCP)의 표현으로 빈칸에 적합한 것을 고르시오.

> SECURITE, repeated 3 times is used to announce an (　　　) message.

① urgency　　　　　② safety
③ distress　　　　　④ medical

08 다음 영문의 밑줄 친 부분과 같은 의미를 가진 단어를 고르시오.

> My vessel is **carrying out** cargo operation.

① commencing　　　② performing
③ keeping　　　　　④ looking

09 다음 중 SMCP 표현으로 올바르지 않은 것을 고르시오.

① What is the length of turning circle?
　: 선회권의 직경은 얼마인가?
② You must stop. Shallow water ahead of you.
　: 정선하라. 당신의 선박 앞에 천수 구역이 있다.
③ my vessel is not under command.
　: 나의 선박은 조종 불능선이다.
④ The cranes are operational.
　: 크레인이 작동한다.

10 빈칸에 들어갈 수 없는 말을 고르시오.

> A : How is the cable growing?
> B : The cable is (   ).

① slack
② going tight
③ tight
④ coming tight

11 다음 괄호 안에 공통적으로 들어가기에 적절치 않은 것은?

> Salvage operation includes;
> - (   ) a vessel which is in danger of running aground.
> - (   ) a vessel which is aground.
> - (   ) a submerged wreck.

① clearing
② towing
③ lowering
④ picking up

12 UNCLOS 상, 빈칸에 들어갈 말을 고르시오.

> The (   ) of coastal State extends, beyond its land territory and internal water and, in the case of an archipelagic State, its archipelagic waters, to adjacent belt of sea, described as the territorial sea.

① sovereignty
② right
③ jurisdiction
④ exclusive jurisdiction

13 다음 빈칸에 들어갈 말로 가장 옳은 것은?

> According to SAR 1979, the colour identification of the contents of droppable containers and packages containing (A) is yellow.

① medical supplies and first aid equipment
② food and water
③ blankets and protective clothing
④ Miscellaneous equipment such as stoves, axes, compasses and cooking utensils

14 다음은(IMO SMCP)상 용어의 정의이다. 가장 옳은 것은?

> An area within defined limits in which one-way traffic is established.

① Waterway
② Traffic clearance
③ Traffic lane
④ Fairway

15 다음은 COLREG RULE 34에 대한 것이다. 빈칸에 순서대로 들어갈 단어로 가장 옳은 것은?

> In a narrow channel, a vessel nearing a bend where other vessels may be obscured shall sound (　　　).
> Such signal shall be answered with (　　　) by any approaching vessel that may be within hearing around the bend or behind the intervening obstruction.

① one prolonged blast, at least 5 short and rapid blast.
② two prolonged blast, two prolonged blast.
③ at least 5 short and rapid blast, at least 5 short and rapid blast.
④ one prolonged blast, one prolonged blast.

16 다음은 CORLEG 상 등화에 대한 설명이다. ㉠㉡㉢에 해당하는 내용으로 가장 옳은 것은?

> ㉠ two all-round light in a vertical line, the upper being red and the lower white, or a shape consisting of two cones with apexes together in a vertical line one above the other.
> ㉡ two all-round red lights in a vertical line where they can best be seen.
> ㉢ at or near the masthead two all round lights in a vertical line the upper white and the lower red.

① ㉠ a vessel engaged in fishing
   ㉡ a vessel not under command
   ㉢ a vessel engaged on pilotage duty
② ㉠ a vessel engaged in fishing
   ㉡ a vessel at anchor
   ㉢ a vessel engaged on pilotage duty
③ ㉠ a vessel engaged in fishing, other than trawling
   ㉡ a vessel not under command
   ㉢ a vessel engaged on pilotage duty
④ ㉠ a vessel engaged in fishing, other than trawling
   ㉡ a vessel engaged on pilotage duty
   ㉢ a vessel not under command

17 다음 COLREG에서 말하는 선박의 등화의 내용으로 올바른 것은?

> A vessel restricted in her ability to manoeuvre shall exhibit : three all-around lights in a vertical line where they can best be seen....

① Red - white - Red
② Red - Red - Red
③ Withe - White - White
④ White - Red - White

18 다음은 IAMSAR MANUAL에 나오는 수색 방식 중 하나이다. 가장 적합한 수색 방식은?

- Most effective when the position of the search is accurately known and the search area is small.
- Used to search a circular area centred on a datum point.
- For vessels, the search pattern radius is usually between 2NM and 5NM, and each turn is 120°, normally turned to starboard.

① Track Line Search ② Expanding Square Search
③ Parallel track Search ④ Sector search

19 Choose the correct one for the blank.

(   ) means a tank specifically designated for the collection of tank drainings, tank washings and other oily mixtures according to MARPOL Convention.

① Sludge tank ② Clean ballast tank
③ Slop tank ④ Bilge tank

20 다음 중 COLREG Rule 18. Responsibility between vessels 에 대한 설명이다. 옳지 않은 것은 몇 개인가?

㉠ A power driven vessel shall keep out of the way of a vessel constrained by her draught.
㉡ A vessel engaged in fishing shall, so far as possible, keep out of the way vessel not under command.
㉢ Hampered vessel shall keep out of the way of vessel constrained by her draught.
㉣ A seaplane on the water shall, keep well clear of all vessels.

① 없음 ② 1개
③ 2개 ④ 3개

해사영어 모의고사

01 다음에 설명하는 용어는 각각 무엇인지 고르시오.

> ⓐ This is the distance travelled in the perpendicular direction of the original course by midship point of a ship from the position at which the rudder order is given to the position at which the heading has changed 90 degree from the original course.
> ⓑ To reverse the windlass to lower the anchor until it is clear of the hawse pipe and ready for dropping.

① Advance, Walk back
② Advance, Walk out
③ Transfer, Walk out
④ Transfer, Walk back

02 다음 중 용어의 정의 중 옳지 않은 것의 개수를 고르시오.

> 가. backing : To run a vessel up on a beach to prevent its sinking in deep water.
> 나. Blind sector : An area which can be scanned by the ship's radar because it is shielded by parts of the superstructure, mast, etc.
> 다. Capsize : To turn over.
> 라. Disabled : Vessel still afloat, abandoned at sea.
> 마. Close up : To decrease the distance to the vessel ahead by increasing one's own speed.

① 1개   ② 2개   ③ 3개   ④ 4개

03 다음 SMCP 상 해석과 표현이 올바르게 짝지어진 것의 개수를 고르시오.

> 가. Keep a sharp lookout.
>   (경계를 철저히 하라.)
> 나. Finished inspection and port officials left her.
>   (점검을 마치고 하역 인부들이 하선함.)
> 다. Filled up No.2 ballast tank with fresh water.
>   (2번 발라스트 탱크에 청수를 채웠다.)
> 라. What are the advance and transfer distance in a crash stop?
>   (기관 정지 시켰을 때의 종거와 횡거의 거리가 어떠한가?)

① 1개　② 2개　③ 3개　④ 4개

04 표준해사통신영어(SMCP)에서 뜻이 알맞게 짝지어진 것의 개수를 고르시오.

> 가. Steady : Steer a steady course on the compass heading indicated at the time of the order.
> 나. Abandon vessel : To evacuate crew and passengers from a vessel following a distress.
> 다. Master's Standing Order : Orders of the Master to the officer of the watch which s/he must comply with.
> 라. SWL : Maximum working load of lifting equipment that should not be exceeded.

① 없음　② 1개　③ 2개　④ 3개

05 괄호 안에 알맞은 것은 무엇인가?

> (　　) means a route within defined limits which has been accurately surveyed for clearance of sea bottom and submerged obstacles as indicated on the chart.

① Traffic lane
② Recommended track
③ Separation zone or line
④ Deep water route (DW)

06 다음 중 옳게 짝지어진 것의 개수를 고르시오.

> 가. I – India
> 나. D – Delta
> 다. Z – Zoo
> 라. M – Milk
> 마. R – Rima
> 바. P – Papa

① 2개 ② 3개 ③ 4개 ④ 5개

07 Which one is not a name of Mooring line?

① spring line
② breast line
③ stern line
④ center line

08 빈칸에 들어갈 가장 적절한 단어는?

> If two more radio waves arrive simultaneously at the same point in space, ( ) results.

① radar interference
② radar refraction
③ radio beacon
④ specular reflection

09 The sentence below is a part of an article from the UNCLOS. Choose the correct one for the blank.

> Article 76
> (   ) of a coastal State comprises the sea-bed and subsoil of the submarine area that extend beyond its territorial sea throughout the natural prolongation of its land territory to the outer edge of the continental margin, or to a distance of 200 nautical miles from the base lines from which the breadth of the territorial sea is measured where the outer edge of the continental margin does not extend up to that distance.

① EEZ
② Contiguous zone
③ Continental shelf
④ land territory

10 "1979년 해상수색 및 구조에 관한 국제협약"에 따를 때 다음에 해당하는 상황은 각각 무엇인가?

> 가. A situation wherein apprehension exists as to the safety of a vessel and of the persons on board.
> 나. A situation wherein there is a reasonable certainty that a vessel or a person is threatened by grave and imminent danger and requires immediate assistance.
> 다. A situation wherein uncertainty exists as to the safety of a vessel and the persons on board.

	가	나	다
①	Alert phase	Distress phase	Emergency phase
②	Alert phase	Distress phase	Uncertainty phase
③	Distress phase	Uncertainty phase	Alert phase
④	Uncertainty phase	Alert phase	Distress phase

11 COLREG에 따라, 빈칸에 들어갈 수 있는 말로 적절하지 않은 것을 고르시오.

> A power-driven vessel underway when towing exhibits (   ).

> 가. side lights
> 나. a stern light
> 다. when the length of tow, measuring from the stern of the towing vessel to the after end of the tow exceeds 200 metres, two mast head lights in a vertical line
> 라. towing light in a vertical line under the stern lights

① 없음   ② 1개   ③ 2개   ④ 3개

12 COLREG 상 아래의 문장이 의미하는 것은 무엇인가?

> A vessel which through some exceptional circumstance is unable to manoeuvre as required by these Rule and is therefore unable to keep out of the way of another vessel.

① vessel under command.
② vessel not under control.
③ vessel constrained in her ability to manoeuvre.
④ vessel not under command.

13 다음 COLREG 음향 신호에 관한 규정 중 옳지 않은 것의 개수는?

> ⓐ A vessel of 12 metres or more in length shall be provided with a whistle.
> ⓑ a vessel of 20 metres or more in length shall be provided with a bell in addition to a whistle.
> ⓒ a vessel of 50 metres or more in length shall be provided with a gong in addition to a whistle and a bell.
> ⓓ the term "short blast" means a blast of about one second's duration.
> ⓔ the term "prolonged blast" means a blast of from two to three second's duration.

① 없음   ② 1개   ③ 2개   ④ 3개

14 다음은 SOLAS 협약 상 Line-throwing appliances에 관한 설명이다. 밑줄 친 단어 중 틀린 것의 개수를 고르시오.

> - be capable of throwing a line with ㉠<u>ambiguous accuracy</u>.
> - include not less than ㉡<u>4 projectiles</u> each capable of carrying the line at least ㉢<u>250m</u> in calm weather.
> - include not less than ㉣<u>4 lines</u> each having a breaking strength of not less than ㉤<u>5kN</u>.
> - have brief instructions or diagrams clearly illustrating the use of the line-throwing appliance.

① 1개   ② 2개   ③ 3개   ④ 4개

15 다음 UNCLOS 상 right of hot pursuit에 대한 내용이다. 틀린 것은 모두 몇 개인가?

ⓐ The hot pursuit of a foreign ship may be undertaken when the competent authorities of the coastal State have no reason to believe that the ship has violated the laws and regulations of the State.
ⓑ It is not necessary that at time when the foreign ship within the territorial sea or the contiguous zone receives the order to stop, the ship giving the order should likewise be within the territorial sea or the contiguous zone.
ⓒ The right of hot pursuit cease as soon as the ship pursued enters the contiguous zone of its own State or of a third State.
ⓓ Where a ship has been stoped or arrested outside the territorial sea in circumstances which do not justify the exercise of the right of hot pursuit, it shall be compensated for any loss or damage that may have been thereby sustained.

① 1개 ② 2개 ③ 3개 ④ 4개

16 다음 중 IAMSAR 상, OSC를 지정하는 과정에서 옳지 않은 것을 고르시오.

① When two or more SAR facilities conduct operations together, the SMC should designate an OSC.
② When deciding how much responsibility to delegate to the OSC, the SMC normally considers the communications and personnel capability.
③ This should be done as early as practicable and preferably before arrival within the search area.
④ Until SAR is over, the first facility arriving at the scene should assume the duties of an OSC.

17 다음은 MARPOL 규정 원문을 발췌한 것이다. 빈칸에 들어갈 말로 가장 옳은 것은?

> An international Oil Pollution Prevention Certificate shall be issued, after survey in accordance with the provisions of Regulation 4 of this Annex, to any oil tanker of ( )tons gross tonnage and above an any other ships of ( )tons gross tonnage and above which are engaged in voyages to ports or off-shore terminals under the jurisdiction of the Parties to the Convention.

① 400 10000   ② 400 150   ③ 150 400   ④ 150 300

18 다음에 해당하는 것을 고르시오.

> ( ) means that in any sea condition water will not penetrate into the ship.

① Weathertight   ② Bulkhead   ③ Packing   ④ Uppermost deck

19 다음은 MARPOL기름 배출 규제에 관한 내용이다. 옳지 않은 것은?

> Any discharge into the sea of oil or oily mixtures from ship of 400 gross tonnage and above shall be prohibited except when all the following conditions are satisfied.

① the ship is not within a special area.
② the ship is proceeding en route.
③ the oil content of the effluent without dilution does not exceed 25 parts per million.
④ the oily mixture does not originate from cargo pump room bilges on oil tankers.

20 다음은 Anchor 운용에 관련한 도선사와 선장 간의 대화이다. 빈칸에 들어갈 말로 가장 알맞은 것은?

> Pilot : Is the vessel ready to heave up anchor?
> Captain : Yes, (   ).

① The windlass is in gear.
② ready to let go anchor.
③ The anchor is secured.
④ ready to walk out.

3회차 해사영어 모의고사

01 다음은 Log Book에 기재된 사항이다. 빈칸에 들어갈 말로 올바른 것을 순서대로 고르시오.

> Collided ( ) a fishing boat which carried no light. Stopped engine immediately to pick ( ) the fishermen of the collided boat.

① with, up　　② with, in
③ at, up　　　④ at, in

02 다음 밑줄 친 부분과 바꾸어 쓸 수 있는 것을 각각 고르시오.

> 가. **Keep** well clear of the towing line.
> 나. Pilotage **started again** for all vessels.

① remove, retarded　　② remove, resumed
③ stand, retarded　　④ stand, resumed

03 빈칸에 들어갈 알맞은 말을 고르시오.

> After we discovered the ( ) of the fire, immediately we reduced speed in order to avoid the fire spreading.

① outline　　　　② taking
③ extinguishing　④ outbreak

04 UNCLOS의 제89조에 따라, 빈칸에 들어갈 알맞은 용어를 고르시오.

> No state may validly purport to subject any part of the high seas to its ( ).

① sovereignty ② right ③ jurisdiction ④ freedom

05 다음 중 빈칸에 들어갈 말을 순서대로 고르시오.

> 가. When possible, the ( ) transmitter power of VHF Radio necessary for satisfactory communication should be used.
> 나. Incheon VTS, this is MV Alice. My maximum draught is 10.5 meters and I was informed that the tide is Ebb now. Is there sufficient ( ) to proceed by the fairway?

① lowest, depth of water
② lowest, draught
③ highest, draught
④ highest, depth of water

06 다음 SMCP 표현 중 문장과 해석이 올바르게 연결되어 있지 않은 것을 고르시오.

① Ice-breaker service suspected until 1st October.
   (쇄빙선 서비스가 10월 1일까지 일시 중단되었다.)
② Prepare emergency plan for first aid.
   (응급 처치를 위해 비상계획을 준비하라.)
③ There are enough life saving appliance for everyone on board.
   (선상의 모든 사람에게 충분한 구명설비가 있음.)
④ I am maneuvering with difficulty.
   (본선은 조종에 어려움이 있음.)

07 'Underway'가 아닌 상태의 개수를 고르시오.

> 가. S.B.E. & prepared unmooring.
> 나. Single up fore & aft and prepared for sea.
> 다. Proceeding at manoeuvring speed.
> 라. F.W.E. Pilot & tug away and dismissed the station.
> 마. Cleared out of Canal, R/up eng. and dismissed the station.
> 바. Anchor aweigh form the bottom.
> 사. Put the windlass in gear to heave anchor.

① 2개   ② 3개   ③ 4개   ④ 5개

08 다음 VTS에 관한 용어에 대한 설명 중 옳지 않은 것의 개수를 고르시오.

> 가. Fairway : Navigable part of a waterway
> 나. Fairway speed : Minimum speed in a fairway
> 다. Traffic clearance : VTS authorization for a vessel to proceed under conditions specified
> 라. Reporting point : A mark or place at which a vessel comes under obligatory entry, transit, or escort procedure
> 마. Manoeuvring speed : A vessel's increased speed in restricted waters such as fairway or harbours

① 1개   ② 2개   ③ 3개   ④ 4개

09 SMCP의 숫자 사용 중 잘못된 것의 개수를 고르시오.

> 가. Steady on 200 : Steady on two hundreds
> 나. Starboard 10 : Starboard one-zero
> 다. 3.2 degree : three decimal two degree
> 라. My present course is 300 : My present course is three-zero-zero

① 1개   ② 2개   ③ 3개   ④ 4개

10 다음 용어 및 통신부호의 설명이 옳은 것의 개수를 고르시오.

> 가. Ship capability : The ability of the ship to return to the upright when slightly inclined.
> 나. ANSWER : This indicates that the following message is the reply to previous question.
> 다. QUESTION : This indicates that the following message is of interrogative character.
> 라. ADVICE : This indicates that the following message implies the intention of the sender to inform others about danger.

① 1개　② 2개　③ 3개　④ 4개

11 IAMSAR MANUAL 상 아래의 절차에 따라 행하는 'Scharnov turn'에서 밑줄 친 부분 중 옳지 않은 것의 개수를 고르시오.

> (ⓐTo be used in an "immediate action" situation.)
> 1. ⓑRudder hard over.
> 2. After deviation from the original course by ⓒ60°, ⓓrudder hard over to the opposite side.
> 3. When ⓔheading 20° short of opposite course, rudder to ⓕmidship position so that ship will turn to opposite course.

① 없음　② 1개　③ 2개　④ 3개

12 다음 약어 중 옳지 않은 것의 개수를 고르시오.

> 가. SRU - Search and Rescue Unit
> 나. SMC - Search and Rescue On scene coordinator
> 다. SRR - Search and Rescue Region
> 라. OSC - On Scene Co-ordinator
> 마. ACO - Alter Course

① 1개　② 2개　③ 3개　④ 4개

13 다음은 COLREG 상, 제한 시계 내에서의 음향신호에 관련된 내용이다. 제한 시계에서 다음의 음향신호를 하는 선박으로 옳지 않은 것의 개수를 고르시오.

> Sound at intervals of not more than 2 minutes three blasts in succession, namely one prolonged followed by two short blasts.

> 가. A vessel not under command
> 나. A power-driven vessel underway but stopped and making no way through the water
> 다. A vessel restricted in her ability to manoeuvre
> 라. A vessel constrained by her draught
> 마. A sailing vessel
> 바. A vessel towed
> 사. A vessel engaged in fishing

① 1개   ② 2개   ③ 3개   ④ 4개

14 다음 빈칸에 들어갈 말을 순서대로 고르시오.

> 가. (   ) means a white light placed as nearly as practicable at the stern showing an unbroken light over an arc of the horizon of 135 degrees and so fixed as to show the light 67.5 degrees from right aft on each side of the vessel.
> 나. (   ) means a white light placed over the fore and aft centreline of the vessel showing an unbroken light over an arc of the horizon of 225 degrees and so fixed as to show the light from right ahead to 22.5 degrees abaft the beam on either side of the vessel.

① masthead light, stern light
② stern light, side light
③ stern light, masthead light
④ side light, masthead light

15 'man-over-board' 상황에서 당직 항해사가 해야 할 'simultaneous actions'으로 알맞은 것의 개수를 고르시오.

> 가. To stop engine
> 나. To transmit a general urgency signal to all ships in the vicinity
> 다. To order the helm midships
> 라. To release a life buoy to which a self-igniting light

① 1개　② 2개　③ 3개　④ 4개

16 야간의 head-on situation 상황에서 식별할 수 있는 등화 상태의 개수는 보기 중 몇 개인가?

> 가. you can see the masthead lights of the other in a line or nearly in a line by night.
> 나. you can see both sidelights by night.
> 다. You can see the stern light by night.
> 라. You see only a red light on your starboard bow.

① 1개　② 2개　③ 3개　④ 4개

17 다음 SMCP 표현 중 해석과 문장이 올바르게 연결되지 않은 것을 고르시오.

① Read standing order and sign on it.
　(당직근무수칙을 읽고 서명하시오.)
② Is the radar operational?
　(레이더가 작동됩니까?)
③ Yes, M/V Dotori, this is Busan VTS. Go ahead.
　(네, 도토리호, 여기는 부산VTS입니다. 전진하십시오.)
④ We have radio contact with rescue craft.
　(우리는 구조선과 통신을 하고 있음.)

18 다음 중 밑줄 친 it에 해당하는 것은 무엇인가?

> Chart and light lists should be checked to see that they have been corrected through the latest it.

① Notice To Mariners
② Sea chart
③ Sailing direction
④ Mercator chart

19 What is not appropriate navigational watch?

① keep the watch on the bridge.
② in no circumstances leave the bridge until properly relieved.
③ continue to be responsible for the safe navigation, despite the presence of the master on the bridge.
④ preferably, notify the C/O when you are in doubts.

20 ISPS에 따라 다음의 빈칸에 들어갈 것을 순서대로 고르시오.

> 가. (   ) means the qualification of the degree of risk that a security incident will be attempted or will occur in the ISPS Code.
> 나. (   ) means the level for which minimum appropriate protective security measures shall be maintained at all time.

① Security incident, Security level 1
② Security incident, Security level 2
③ Security level, Security level 1
④ Security level, Security level 2

해사영어 모의고사

01 빈칸에 들어갈 말을 순서대로 고르시오.

> (　) tug's line (　) the center fairlead.
> : 예인선의 줄을 센터 페어레더 쪽으로 잡아라.

① take, on　　　　　　② take, through
③ put, on　　　　　　④ put, through

02 다음은 UNCLOS의 Territorial sea에 관한 내용이다. 옳지 않은 것은 모두 몇 개인가?

> - The sovereignty of a coastal state extends, beyond its land territory and ㉠international waters and, in the case of an ㉡archipelagic state, its archipelagic waters, to an adjacent belt of sea, described as the territorial sea.
> - This sovereignty extends to the ㉢land space over the territorial sea as well as to its ㉣bed and ㉤subsoil.
> - The sovereignty over the territorial sea is exercised subject to this Convention and to other rules of ㉥internal law.

① 2개　② 3개　③ 4개　④ 5개

03 다음 COLREG에 대한 내용 중 옳지 않은 것을 고르시오.

① Vessel of less than 20metres in length, sailing vessels and vessels engaged in fishing may use the inshore traffic zone.
② A vessel using a traffic separation scheme shall so far as practicable keep clear of a traffic separation line or separation zone.
③ A vessel not using a traffic separation scheme shall avoid it by as wide a margin as is practicable.
④ A vessel shall use an inshore traffic zone when she can safely use the appropriate traffic lane within the adjacent TSS.

04 ISPS에 따라, 다음의 내용 이후에 나올 것으로 옳지 않은 것을 고르시오.

> Where a risk of attack has been identified, the Contracting Government concerned shall advise the ships concerned and their Administrations of :

① the mandatory speed of the vessel.
② the current security level.
③ any security measures that should be put in place by the ships concerned to protect themselves from attack, in accordance with the provisions of part A of the ISPS Code.
④ security measures that the coastal State has decided to put in place, as appropriate.

05 다음 중 SOLAS 적용 제외 선박은 몇 개인가?

> 가. Wooden ships of primitive build
> 나. Cargo ships of less than 5000 tons gross tonnage
> 다. Pleasure yachts engaged in trade
> 라. Ships not propelled by mechanical means
> 마. Ships of war and troopships
> 바. Fishing vessels

① 3개　② 4개　③ 5개　④ 6개

06. 다음 SMCP 용어에 대한 설명이다. ㉠㉡㉢㉣에 해당하는 내용으로 가장 옳은 것은?

> ㉠ Vessel still afloat, abandoned at sea.
> ㉡ A vessel damaged or impaired in such a manner as to be incapable of proceeding on its voyage.
> ㉢ Uncontrolled movement at sea under the influence of current tide or wind.
> ㉣ A Vessel which has been destroyed or sunk or abandoned at sea.

	㉠	㉡	㉢	㉣
①	Derelict	Disabled	Adrift	Wreck
②	Disabled	Derelict	Adrift	Wreck
③	Derelict	Wreck	Adrift	Disabled
④	Wreck	Adrift	Disabled	Derelict

07. 다음은 Master's Standing Order(당직근무수칙)의 일부분이다. 빈칸에 순서대로 들어갈 말을 고르시오.

> - The officer of the watch shall keep a proper (   ).
> - Do not hand (   ) the duty to the relieving officer who is not good condition.

① look in, over ② look out, over ③ look out, in ④ look out, on

08. IAMSAR Manual 상 수색패턴(Search pattern)들 중 확대 사각 수색 법에 대한 내용을 발췌한 것이다. 아래 내용 중 옳지 않은 것은 몇 개인가?

> ㉠Parallel Sweep Search (PS)
> - Most effective when the location of the search object is ㉡known within relatively close limits.
> - The commence search point is ㉢always the datum position.
> - Often appropriate for vessels or small boats to use when searching for persons in the water or other search object with ㉣big leeway.

① 없음 ② 1개 ③ 2개 ④ 3개

09 빈칸에 들어갈 가장 적절한 단어는?

> Your draft is more than the available depth of water. Your vessel is ( ).

① altering ② aground
③ adrift   ④ sunken

10 COLREG 제27조의 원문이다. 옳지 않은 것의 개수를 고르시오.

> (a) A vessel not under command shall exhibit :
> (i) ⓐthree all-round ⓑred lights in a vertical line where they can best be seen.
> (ii) ⓒthree ⓓballs or similar shapes in a vertical line where they can best be seen.
> (iii) when making way through the water, in addition to the lights prescribed in this paragraph, ⓔsidelights, a stern light and masthead light.

① 1개 ② 2개 ③ 3개 ④ 4개

11 다음은 SOLAS 상 증서의 유효 기간 및 효력에 관한 규정이다. 옳은 것은 모두 몇 개인가?

> A Passenger Ship Safety Certificate shall be issued for a period not exceeding ㉠6 months. A Cargo Ship Safety Construction Certificate, Cargo Ship Equipment Certificate, Cargo ship Safety Radio Certificate shall be issued for a period specified ㉡by the Administration which shall not exceed ㉢12 months. An Exemption Certificate ㉣shall not be Valid for longer than the period of the certificate to which it refers.

① 없음 ② 1개 ③ 2개 ④ 3개

12 표준해사통신용어 상 사용되는 글자의 철자이다. 옳지 않은 것은 모두 몇 개인가?

	ⓐ	ⓑ	ⓒ	ⓓ	ⓔ
Letter	S	R	F	T	J
Code	Sierra	Radar	Foxtro	Tango	Julu

① 1개   ② 2개   ③ 3개   ④ 4개

13 SMCP 상 ship routing System에 대한 설명이다. 가장 옳지 않은 것은?

① Inshore traffic zone : A designated area between the landward boundary of traffic separation scheme and adjacent coast, intended for local traffic.

② Two-way route : A route within defined limits inside which two-way traffic is established, aimed at providing safe passage of ships through waters where navigation is difficult or dangerous.

③ Area to be avoided : A routing measure comprising an area within defined limits in which either navigation is particularly hazardous or it is exceptionally important to avoid casualties and which should be avoid by all ship; or certain classes of ship.

④ Recommended track : A routing measure comprising an area within defined limits where ships must navigate with particular caution and within which the direction of traffic flow may be recommended.

14 다음 빈칸에 들어갈 말로 가장 적합한 것은?

> This is Busan VTS. Navigational information follow (   ) VHF CH. 72

① of   ② to   ③ on   ④ with

15 다음은 COLREG 상 용어의 정의에 대한 설명이다 옳지 않은 것은 모두 몇 개인가?

> 가. Power-driven vessel : Any vessel propelled by machinery.
> 나. Vessel : Includes every description of water craft and seaplane used or transportation on water.
> 다. Sailing vessel : Any vessel under sail provided that propelling machinery, if fitted, is not being used.
> 라. WIG craft : Includes any aircraft designed to manoeuvre on the water.

① 없음 ② 1개 ③ 2개 ④ 3개

16 다음은 SOLAS(International Convention for the Safety of Life at Sea) chapter III Life-saving appliances and arrangements에 관한 내용이다. 빈칸에 알맞은 수를 모두 합한 값은?

> - for passenger ships on voyages less than 24h, a number of infant life jackets equal to at least (   )% of the number of passengers on board shall be provided;
> - for passenger ships on voyages 24h or greater, infant life jackets shall be provided for each infant onboard;
> - a number of life jackets suitable for children equal to at least (   )% of the number of passengers on board shall be provided or such greater number as may be required to provide a life jacket for each child;

① 10 ② 12.5 ③ 15 ④ 17.5

17 UNCLOS 제19조에 따라 빈칸에 들어갈 것으로 올바른 것을 고르시오.

> Passage is innocent so long as it is not (   ) to the peace, good order or security of the coastal State.

① harmless ② prejudicial
③ good   ④ justify

18 다음 빈칸에 들어갈 말로 가장 적합한 것은?

> If a shipowner registers his ships in a country other than his own to escape paying some home taxations, to employ labour cheaper than that at home, or to benefit financially in any similar way, his ships are said to fly a (   ).

① flag of convenience
② flag
③ flag of discrimination
④ flag of destination

19 다음 중 〈COLREG(국제해상충돌예방규칙)〉상 "Action to avoid collision"에 대한 설명으로 옳지 않은 것을 고르시오.

① Action to avoid collision shall be positive.
② Action to avoid collision shall be a succession of small alterations of course.
③ Action to avoid collision shall be taken with due regard to the observance of good seamanship.
④ Action to avoid collision shall be made in ample time.

20 다음 표준해사통신용어(Standard Marine Communication Phrases) 표현 중 옳지 않은 것의 개수를 고르시오.

> 가. 엔진을 정지하라. : Put engine(s) Crash stop.
> 나. 본선이 귀선의 풍하측이 되게 해 달라. : make a lee for your boat.
> 다. 선박의 횡경사를 수정하라. : Correct the trim of the vessel.
> 라. 하선이 불가능하다. : Embarkation is not possible.

① 모두   ② 1개   ③ 2개   ④ 3개

01 다음 ship's log book 기사에 중 빈칸에 들어갈 말을 알맞게 짝지은 것을 고르시오.

- Crossed the meridian of 180° into east longitude at Lat.43°N, July 12 was (   )
- (   ) the ship's clock from GMT-9 to GMT-8

① repeated, Advanced
② repeated, Retarded
③ skipped, Advanced
④ skipped, Retarded

02 UNCLOS 상 표기가 적절하게 연결된 것의 개수를 고르시오.

가. Right of hot pursuit - 추적권
나. Right of visit - 임검권
다. Right of innovation passage - 무해통항권
라. Archipelago - 군도국가

① 1개   ② 2개   ③ 3개   ④ 4개

03 다음은 COLREG 제9조 "Narrow Channels"에 대한 설명이다. 빈칸에 알맞은 것을 고르시오.

A vessel proceeding along the course of a narrow channel or fairway shall keep as near to the (   ) limit of the channel or fairway which lies on her starboard side as is safe and practicable.

① inner   ② middle   ③ end   ④ outer

04 다음 중 빈칸에 들어갈 단어로 가장 옳은 것은?

> When her stern draft is higher than bow draft, it is ( ).

① even keel
② trim by the head
③ trim by the stern
④ trim

05 COLREG 상, 빈칸에 들어갈 용어를 고르시오.

> A vessel constrained by her draught may, in addition to the lights prescribed for power-driven vessels in Rule 23, exhibit where they can best be seen three all-round red lights in a vertical line, or ( ).

① two black balls
② three black balls
③ one black ball
④ a cylinder

06 VHF radio의 사용에 대한 설명 중 틀린 것의 개수를 고르시오.

> 가. Transmitting without correct identification should be avoided.
> 나. If communications on a channel are unsatisfactory, indicate change of channel and do not await confirmation.
> 다. Any distress call/message should be recorded in the ship's log and passed to the master.
> 라. Instructions given on communication matters by shore station which authority was given should be obeyed.

① 없음　② 1개　③ 2개　④ 3개

07 다음 중 SMCP 표현으로 가장 자연스러운 것을 고르시오.

① What is your ETA from BUSAN?
② What is your ETA at BUSAN?
③ What is your ETD on BUSAN?
④ What is your ETD to BUSAN?

08 다음 표준해사통신용어(Standard Marine Communication Phrases) 표현과 가장 관련이 깊은 것은?

> MV CAMBUS proceeds by narrow channel and detects a fishing vessel crossing ahead of her in close distance. MV CAMBUS let go anchor to avoid a collision.

① Anchoring   ② emergency stop   ③ Dragging   ④ Dredging

09 "1979년 해상수색 및 구조에 관한 국제협약"에 따를 때, 다음 용어에 대한 설명 중 옳지 않은 것은 모두 몇 개인가?

> 가. Search : An operation to retrieve persons in distress, provide for their initial medical or other needs, and deliver them to a place of safety.
> 나. EPIRB : A survival craft transponder that, when activated, sends out a signal automatically when a pulse from a nearby radar reaches it. The signal appears on the interrogating radar screen and gives the bearing and distance of the transponder from the interrogating radar for search and rescue purposes.
> 다. SART : A device, usually carried aboard maritime craft, that transmit a signal that alert search and rescue authorities and enables rescue unit to locate the scene of the distress.
> 라. Search and Rescue unit : A unit composed of trained personnel and provided with equipment suitable for the expeditious conduct of search and rescue operations.
> 마. to ditch : in the case of an aircraft, to make a forced landing on water.

① 2개   ② 3개   ③ 4개   ④ 5개

10 다음에 해당하는 용어를 고르시오.

> The state of a tidal current when it's speed is near zero, especially the moment when a current changes direction and its speed is zero.

① Flood tide ② Stand of tide ③ Ebb tide ④ Slack

11 빈칸에 들어갈 용어를 올바르게 짝지은 것을 고르시오.

> The SMCP is divided into ( ) Communication Phrases and ( ) Communication Phrases.

① External, Distress
② Distress, On board
③ External, On board
④ External, Internal

12 STCW에 따라 다음 중 옳지 않은 것을 고르시오.

> The officer in charge of the navigational watch shall :

① keep the watch on the bridge.
② notify the master when in any doubt as to what action to take in the interest of safety.
③ continue to be responsible for the safe navigation of the ship, despite the presence of the master on the bridge, until informed specifically that the master has assumed that responsibility and this is mutually understood.
④ be assigned or undertake any duties which would interfere with the safe navigation of the ship.

13 VTS에서 제공하는 서비스 중에서 다음 빈칸에 들어갈 말로 가장 적절한 것은?

> (　　　　　　) is especially important in difficult navigational or meteorological circumstances or in case of defects or deficiencies. This service is normally rendered at the request of a vessel or by the VTS when deemed necessary.

① Navigational assistance service
② Information service
③ Traffic organization service
④ General information service

14 다음 중 빈칸에 들어갈 말로 가장 옳은 것은?

> The distress traffic controlling station/other station may impose radio (A) on any interfering stations by using the term : "(B)" unless the latter have messages about the distress.

① A. silence   B. Interference
② A. silence   B. Seelonce Mayday
③ A. switch off B. Interference
④ A. switch off B. Seelonce Mayday

15 Choose suitable answer in the blank.

> Any action to avoid collision shall be taken in accordance with the Rules of this Part and shall, if the circumstances of the case admit, be positive, made in ample time and with due regard to the (　　　　　).

① recognizing the turing circle
② observance of good seamanship
③ observance of seamanship
④ early time

16 SMCP 상 각각의 빈칸에 들어갈 말로 가장 옳은 것은?

- Two-way route : A route within defined limits inside which two-way traffic is established, aimed at (　　) of ships through water where navigation is difficult or dangerous.
- (　　) : route which has been specially examined to ensure so far as possible that it is free of danger and along which ships are advised to navigate.

① providing safe passage, Recommended track
② providing fast passage, Precautionary area
③ providing safe passage, Precautionary area
④ providing fast passage, Recommended track

17 다음 내용 중 빈칸에 순서대로 들어갈 말로 가장 옳은 것은?

- Traffic lane : An area within defined limits inside which (　　) traffic is established. Natural obstacles, including those forming separation zones, may constitute a boundary.
- Precautionary area : An area within defined limits where ship must navigate (　　) particular caution and within which the direction of flow of traffic may be recommended.

① two-way, with
② one-way, with
③ one-way, to
④ one-way, within

18 다음 빈칸에 들어갈 말로 가장 옳은 것은?

If the ship is to discharge at more than one port, the cargo for the first port of discharge is stowed in the upper part of the hold. In other words, cargo to be discharged at the first discharging port should be (　　).

① delivered last
② loaded first
③ loaded last
④ stowed first

19 다음 빈칸에 공통적으로 들어갈 말로 가장 적절한 것은?

- Every State has the right to establish the breath of its territorial sea up to a limit not exceeding 12 nautical miles, measured from (　　)s determined in accordance with its convention.
- The contiguous zone may not extend beyond 24 nautical miles from the (　　)s from which the breath of the territorial sea is measured.
- The exclusive economic zone shall not extend beyond 200 nautical miles from the (　　)s.

① base line　　② horizontal line
③ straight baseline　　④ normal baseline

20 다음 UNCLOS중 무해통항(Innocent passage) 조항에서 외국선박이 연안국의 평화, 공공질서 또는 안전을 해치는 활동으로 규정한 것은 모두 몇 개인가?

가. any fishing activity
나. the landing any aircraft
다. stopping vessel to avoid collision
라. any drills onboard

① 1개　　② 2개　　③ 3개　　④ 4개

해사영어 모의고사

01 빈칸에 들어갈 말을 순서대로 고른 것은?

> - ( ) : To reverse the action of a windlass to ease the cable (of anchors).
> - ( ) : Services, designed to improve safety and efficiency of vessel traffic and to protect the environment.
> - ( ) : To regulate the motion of a cable, rope or wire when it is running out too fast.
> - ( ) : to increase the distance from the vessel ahead by reducing one's own speed.

① walk out-VTS-pooping down-Drop Back
② walk out-AIS-check-Close up
③ walk back-VTS-check-Drop Back
④ walk back-AIS-check-Close up

02 표준해사통신용어 상 사용되는 글자의 철자이다. 옳지 않은 것은 모두 몇 개인가?

	ⓐ	ⓑ	ⓒ	ⓓ	ⓔ
Letter	G	L	M	T	X
Code	Golf	Lomeo	Mike	Tango	X-ray

① 1개 ② 2개 ③ 3개 ④ 4개

03 다음 용어 설명 중 올바르지 않은 것의 개수를 고르시오.

> ㉠ Embarkation Ladder : Ladder attached to plat form at vessel's side with flat steps and handrails enabling persons to embark/disembark from the water.
> ㉡ Backing : Shift of the wind direction in anti-clockwise manner, for example from north to east.
> ㉢ General emergency alarm : A sound signal of seven long blasts and one short blast given with the vessel's sound system.
> ㉣ Jettison : Throwing overboard of goods accidently.
> ㉤ Leeward : On or towards the sheltered side of a ship.
> ㉥ Leeway : Vessels sideways drift leeward of the desired course.

① 1개   ② 2개   ③ 3개   ④ 4개

04 다음 중 옳지 않은 것은 몇 개인가?

> ㉠ Make Water : Major uncontrolled flow of seawater into the vessel.
> ㉡ Flooding : Seawater flowing into the vessel due to hull damage or hatches awash and not properly closed.
> ㉢ Leaking : Escape of liquid such as water, oil etc., out of pipes boilers, tanks etc., or a minor inflow of seawater into the vessel due to damage to hull.
> ㉣ Spill : The accidental escape of oil, etc from a vessel, container, etc into the sea.
> ㉤ Overflow : Escape of oil or liquid from a tank because of a two-fold condition as a result of overflowing, thermal expansion, change in vessel trim or vessel movement.

① 1개   ② 2개   ③ 3개   ④ 4개

05 다음은 UNCLOS 상 접속수역에 대한 설명이다. 밑줄 친 보기 중 옳지 않은 것을 고르시오.

> In a zone ①contiguous to its territorial sea, described as the contiguous zone, the ②coastal state may exercise the control necessary to : prevent ③infringement of its custom, fiscal, immigration or sanitary laws and regulation within its ④contiguous zone.

06 다음은 UNCLOS 원문이다. 밑줄 친 단어와 연관하여 빈칸에 알맞은 말을 순서대로 고른 것은?

> Ships have the nationality of the State whose <u>flag</u> they are entitled to fly. Ships shall sail under the flag of (   ) and, save in exceptional cases expressly provided for in international treaties or in this Convention, shall be subject to its <u>exclusive jurisdiction</u> on the (   ).

① two States or more - high seas
② one State only - territorial sea
③ two States or more - internal water
④ one State only - high seas

07 다음에서 설명하는 것은 무엇인가?

> Telegraphy system for transmission of maritime safety information, navigation and meteorological warnings, and urgent information to ships by using MF Frequencies.

① EGC   ② NAVTEX   ③ SART   ④ EPIRB

08 다음 조타와 관련된 내용 중 옳지 않은 것의 개수를 고르시오.

> ㉠ All wheel orders given should be repeated by the helmsman.
> ㉡ All wheel orders should be held until countermanded.
> ㉢ When there is concern that the helmsman is attentive he should be questioned "What is your heading?"
> ㉣ When the helmsman report the course corresponded to wheel order, s/he should call out the number combined.

① 1개   ② 2개   ③ 3개   ④ 4개

09 다음 SMCP 표현 중 옳지 않은 것은 몇 개인가?

> ㉠ I am on fire. : 본선에 화재가 발생하였음.
> ㉡ I am flooding below the water line.
>   : 수선 하부에서 침수가 발생하고 있음.
> ㉢ I have has dangerous stranding by port.
>   : 본선 좌현으로 위험한 좌초가 발생.
> ㉣ Is the fire on control?
>   : 화재는 진압되었나?
> ㉤ Are you trimmed by the head?
>   : 선수 트림이 발생했는가?
> ㉥ Which side must I hang the pilot ladder?
>   : 어느 현에 파일럿 사다리를 설치해야하는가?

① 1개   ② 2개   ③ 3개   ④ 4개

10 다음 중 해석이 잘못된 것은 무엇인가?

① Checked gyro compass error by transit line, found no error.
   (중시선에 의하여 자이로 컴퍼스 오차를 점검하였다. 오차가 없었다.)
② It is dangerous to alter course to port.
   (좌현으로 변침하는 것은 위험하다.)
③ I have located you on my radar.
   (나는 레이더에서 귀선을 포착했다.)
④ turn in cable.
   (닻줄을 감으시오.)

11 다음 중 약어와 해석이 올바르게 짝지어진 것은 몇 개인가?

> ㉠ DSC : Digital Satellite Calling (디지털위성호출)
> ㉡ E.P : Estimated Position (추측위치)
> ㉢ P/STN : Pilot Station (도선사 승선지점)
> ㉣ K.O : Knocked off (작업 시작)
> ㉤ ELT : Emergency locator transmitter (비상위치탐사발신기)
> ㉥ TEU : Twenty Foot Equivalent Unit (컨테이너 규격의 단위)

① 2개   ② 3개   ③ 4개   ④ 5개

12 다음 SMCP의 정의 중 빈칸에 들어갈 수 없는 말을 고르시오.

> ㉠ Damage control team : A group of crew members trained for fighting (　　) in vessel.
> ㉡ Beach : to run a vessel up on a beach to prevent its (　　) in deep water.
> ㉢ Refloat : to pull a vessel off after (　　); to set afloat.

① flooding   ② capsizing
③ grounding   ④ sinking

13 다음 빈칸에 들어갈 숫자를 모두 합한 것은?

> ㉠ Every crew member shall participate in at least one abandon ship drill and one fire drill every month. the drill of the crew shall take place within (　　)hours of the ship leaving a port if more than 25% of the crew have not participated in abandon ship and fire drills on board.
> ㉡ When vessels are in sight of one another, a power driven vessel underway.
>   (1) (　)short blast to mean "I am altering my course to port."
>   (2) (　)short blast to mean "I am operating astern propulsion."
> ㉢ In restricted visibility, in case of "A sailing vessel" sound at intervals of not more than (　　)minutes three blasts in succession, namely one prolonged followed by two short blasts.

① 29   ② 30   ③ 31   ④ 32

14 Choose the best one for the blank.

> Approaching a dock, you will throw (　　) first to pier to send a hawser.

① heaving line　　② towing line
③ mooring line　　④ spring line

15 부두 접안 과정의 순서대로 나열한 것은?

> (a) Pilot on board & Took tug
> (b) F.W.E & all station dismissed
> (c) First line to pier
> (d) S.B.E to reduce speed
> (e) All line made fast

① (d)-(e)-(c)-(b)-(a)
② (d)-(a)-(c)-(e)-(b)
③ (d)-(a)-(b)-(c)-(a)
④ (d)-(c)-(b)-(e)-(a)

16 다음 물음에 답하시오.

> Your vessel is proceed at sea when a man falls overboard on the port side. As the man on watch you should first :

① put the rudder midship position.
② put the engine full astern.
③ turn the wheel hard right.
④ turn the wheel hard left.

17 다음은 Right of innocent passage에 관한 설명이다. 밑줄친 보기 중 틀린 것을 고르시오.

> Passage shall be ①safe and relieve. However, passage includes stopping and anchoring, but only in so far as the same are ②incidental to ordinary navigation or are rendered necessary by ③force majeure or distress or for the purpose of ④rendering assistance to persons, ships or aircraft in danger or distress.

18 다음은 IAMSAR Manual에 나오는 수색 방식 중 Sector Search에 관한 내용이다. 옳지 않은 것은 몇 개인가?

> Most effective when the position of the search object is ①accurately known and the search area is ②big. Used to search a ③circular area centered on a datum point. For vessels, the search pattern radius is usually between ④5NM and 20NM and each turn is 120, normally turned to ⑤port.

① 1개 ② 2개 ③ 3개 ④ 4개

19 다음 중 IAMSAR에서 규정하는 Scharnov turn에 대한 설명으로 옳지 않은 것의 개수를 고르시오.

> (a) ㉠can be carried out effectively unless the time elapsed between occurrence of the incident and the commencement of the manoeuvre is known.
> (b) ㉡less distance is covered, saving time.
> (c) ㉢Not proper in an immediate action situation.
> (d) (1) Rudder hard over.
>   (2) After deviation from the original course by ㉣230, rudder hard over to the opposite side.
>   (3) When heading 20 short of opposite course, ㉤rudder hard over to the opposite side.
> (e) ㉥Will take vessel back into her wake.

① 없다. ② 1개 ③ 2개 ④ 3개

20 다음은 SOLAS규정 중 Rescue boat에 관한 규정의 일부이다. 빈칸에 들어갈 숫자의 합을 고르시오.

> ㉠ The rescue boat embarkation and launching arrangements shall be such that the rescue boat can be boarded and launched in the shortest possible time.
> ㉡ all rescue boats shall be capable of being launched, where necessary utilizing painters, with the ship making headway at speeds up to ( )knots in calm water.
> ㉢ Recovery time of the rescue boat shall be not more than ( )min in moderate sea conditions when loaded with its full complement of persons and equipment.

① 6   ② 8   ③ 10   ④ 12

7회차 해사영어 모의고사

01 다음 중 해양 관련 국제협회 또는 국제조직의 명칭과 설명이 틀린 것은?

① IALA(국제항로표지협회) :
   International association of lighthouse authority
② IHO(국제수로기구) :
   International hydrographic organization
③ INMARSAT(국제해사위성기구) :
   International maritime satellite organization
④ ICS(국제해운회의소) :
   International committee of shipping

02 다음은 길이 20m 미만의 선박, 범선, 어로종사 중인 어선이 진입 할 수 있는 Ships routing system에 대한 설명이다. 빈칸에 들어갈 말로 알맞은 것은?

> A routing measure comprising a designated area between the (   ) boundary or a traffic separation scheme and the adjacent coast, where local special rules may apply, and normally not to be used by through traffic.

① TSS   ② Seaward   ③ Land   ④ Landward

03 다음 용어 설명 중 올바르지 않은 것의 개수를 고르시오.

> ㉠ Veering – Clockwise change in the direction of the wind.
> ㉡ Way point – A mark or place at which a vessel come under obligatory entry, transit, or escort.
> ㉢ berthing : The action of bringing your vessel alongside a jetty or dock.
> ㉣ point line : an imaginary line on which a ship at sea must lie to satisfy certain data obtained by the observations of territorial or celestial object.

① 없음   ② 1개   ③ 2개   ④ 3개

04 빈칸에 순서대로 들어갈 알맞은 말을 고르시오.

> A vessel nearing a ( ) or an area of an channel or fairway where other vessels may be obscured by an intervening obstruction shall sound ( ) blast.

① bend, one prolonged
② narrow channel, one prolonged
③ bend, one short
④ narrow channel, one short

05 다음은 추적권에 대한 설명이다. 빈칸에 들어갈 말을 순서대로 고른 것은?

> ㉠ The pursuit may only be commenced after a ( ) signal to stop has been given at a distance which enables it to be seen or heard by the foreign ship.
> ㉡ The release of a ship arrested within the jurisdiction of a State and escorted to a port of that State for the purpose of an inquiry before the competent authorities ( ) be claimed solely on the ground that the ship, in the course of its voyage, was escorted across a portion of the exclusive economic zone or the high seas, if the circumstances rendered this necessary.

① proper, may not
② visual and auditory, may not
③ proper, may
④ visual and auditory, may

06 다음은 SOLAS 상의 규정 일부이다. 빈칸에 들어갈 숫자로 올바른 것을 고르시오.

> Muster stations shall be provided close to the embarkation stations. Each muster station shall have sufficient clear deck space to accommodate all persons assigned to muster at that station, but at least ( )m² per person.

① 0.15　② 0.25　③ 0.35　④ 0.45

07 COLREG 상 아래 빈칸에 들어갈 단어는?

> Every vessel which is directed by these Rule to keep out of the way of another vessel shall, so far as possible, take (　　　) action to keep well clear.

① early and substantial
② positive and good timing
③ good seamanship
④ early, good

08 SMCP 상 freeboard의 의미로 알맞은 것은?

① The height from water surface to upper deck at a midship.
② The height from water surface to the highest point of keel.
③ The height from load water line in winter to upper deck.
④ The height from water surface to the most highest point of vessel.

09 다음은 IAMSAR Manual에 나오는 수색패턴에 대한 설명이다. 옳지 않은 것은 모두 몇 개인가?

> ㉠ Expanding Square Search(SS) : Most effective when the location the object is known within relatively close limits.
> ㉡ Sector Search(VS) : Most effective when the position of the search object is unknown.
> ㉢ Parallel Track Search : Used to search a large area when survivor location is certain.
> ㉣ Contour Search : Normally used when an aircraft or vessel has disappeared without a trace along a known route.
> ㉤ Track Line Search(TS) : It is used around mountains and in valleys when sharp changes in elevation make other patterns not practical.

① 1개　② 2개　③ 3개　④ 4개

10 다음 중 약자와 원어가 올바르게 짝지어진 것은?

① IMO – International Maritime Organization
② A/Co – Apparent Course
③ TMAS – Merchant Assistance
④ R/Up – Road Up

11 Choose an answer in the blank.

> The characteristic on which bearing resolution depends is to distinguish an echo which is on the similar distance and different bearing, affected by (   ).

① vertical beam width
② horizontal beam width
③ distance resolution
④ super-refraction

12 다음은 COLREG 상 등화에 대한 설명이다. 등화 색상에 대한 설명이 옳지 않은 것은 모두 몇 개인가?

> ㉠ "Sidelights" means a green light on the starboard side and a red light on the port side.
> ㉡ Fishing vessel other than trawling : two all-round lights in a vertical line, the upper being green and the lower white.
> ㉢ Vessel Not Under Command : two all-round red light in a vertical line where they can best be seen.
> ㉣ Pilot vessels not engaged on pilotage duty : at or near the masthead, two all-round lights in a vertical line, the upper being white and the lower red.

① 1개   ② 2개   ③ 3개   ④ 4개

13 다음은 SOLAS 상 화재 훈련, 퇴선훈련에 관한 규정이다. 내용이 옳지 않은 것은?

> Every crew member shall participate in at least ①one abandon ship drill and one fire drill ②every month, the drill of the crew shall take place within ③12h of the ship leaving a port if more than ④25% of the crew have not participated in abandon ship and fire drills on board that particular ship in the previous month.

14 다음은 항해 당직 및 업무와 관련한 내용이다. 가장 옳지 않은 것은 무엇인가?

① The officer in charge of the navigational watch shall hand over the watch to the relieving officer if there is reason to believe that the latter is not capable of carrying out the watchkeeping duties effectively, in which case the master shall be notified.
② prior to taking over the watch relieving officers shall satisfy themselves as to the ship's estimated or true position and confirm its intended track, course and speed, and UMS controls as appropriate.
③ if at any time the navigational officer is to be relieved when a manoeuvre or other action to avoid any hazard is taking place, the relief of that officer shall be deferred until such action has been completed.
④ The master of every ship is bound to ensure that watchkeeping arrangements are adequate for maintaining a safe navigational watch.

15 표준해사통신용어 상 사용되는 글자의 철자이다. 옳지 않은 것은 모두 몇 개인가?

	ⓐ	ⓑ	ⓒ	ⓓ	ⓔ
Letter	B	D	O	V	Z
Code	Bravo	Devo	Oscar	Victory	Zulu

① 1개   ② 2개   ③ 3개   ④ 4개

16 다음은 MARPOL 상 용어에 대한 설명이다. 빈칸에 들어갈 단어로 가장 옳은 것은?

> (   ) menas any thank adjacent to the side shell plating.

① Slop tank   ② Center tank   ③ Wing tank   ④ Tank

17 COLREG 상 용어에 대한 설명으로 옳지 않은 것을 고르시오.
① power-driven vessel : any vessel propelled by machinery.
② seaplane : any aircraft designed to manoeuvre on the water.
③ restricted visibility : any condition in which visibility is restricted.
④ Sailing vessel : Any vessel under sail provided that propelling machinery, if fitted, is being used.

18 SMCP 상 ship routing System에 대한 설명이다. 가장 옳지 않은 것은?
① Inshore traffic zone : A designated area between the landward boundary of traffic separation scheme and adjacent coast, intended for local traffic.
② Two-way route : A route within defined limits inside which two-way traffic is established, aimed at providing safe passage of ships through waters where navigation is difficult or dangerous.
③ Precautionary area : A routing measure comprising an area within defined limits in which either navigation is particularly hazardous or it is exceptionally important to avoid casualties and which should be avoid by all ship; or certain classes of ship.
④ Recommended track : A route which has been specially examined to ensure so far as possible that it is free of dangers and along which ship are advised to navigate.

19 통상 기선의 올바른 표현은?

① Common base line
② Normal base line
③ Base line
④ Natural base line

20 아래 지문은 MARPOL에서 규정하는 Sewage 배출에 대한 조항이다. 다음 중 옳지 않은 것은?

> The ship is discharging comminuted and disinfected sewage using system approved by the ①Administration at a distance of more than ②6 nautical miles from the nearest land or sewage which is not comminuted or disinfected at a distance of more than ③12 nautical miles from the nearest land, provided that in any case, the sewage that has been stored in holding tanks shall not be discharged instantaneously but at a moderate rate when the ship is en route and proceeding at not less than ④4knots; the rate of discharge shall be approved by the Administration.

8회차 해사영어 모의고사

01 아래 상황에서 가장 바람직한 통신 절차는 무엇인가?

> Your vessel found a dangerous wreck located in position two nautical mile from Hongdo light house. You may use SMCP phrases following.

① Mayday, Mayday, Mayday. I need help.
   I have been in collision.
② Pan-Pan, Pan-Pan, Pan-Pan. I have problems with engines.
③ Securite Securite Securite. Dangerous wreck located in position two nautical mile from Hongdo light house. Navigate with caution.
④ Securite Securite Securite. I am on fire after explosion.

02 다음 중 괄호 안에 들어갈 말로 올바른 단어는 무엇인가?

> The angle-caused between the (　　) and Compass North is Compass error.

① True North　　② Magnetic North
③ Variation　　　④ Deviation

03 빈칸에 들어갈 말로 알맞은 것을 고르시오.

> When you hearing Distress calls/messages all other transmissions should (　　) and a listening watch should be (　　).

① cease, kept　　　② cease, put off
③ keep, go on　　　④ keep, continue

04. 다음 중 외국 선박에 대한 '임검권(right of visit)'에 대한 설명 중 가장 옳지 않은 것은?

① A warship can purport right of visit to foreign ship on the high sea, though flying a foreign flag or refusing to show its flag, the ship is in reality, of the same nationality as the warship.
② if the suspicions prove to be unfounded, and provided that the ship boarded has not committed any act justifying them, it shall be compensated.
③ These provisions apply 'mutatis mutandis' to military aircraft.
④ These provisions apply only to warship or military air craft.

05. 다음은 SMCP를 사용하는 일반적 원칙에 대한 내용이다. 옳지 않은 것은 모두 몇 개인가?

> ㉠ If the geographical names on the chart or in sailing direction are not understood, latitude and longitude should be given.
> ㉡ Speed is to be expressed in knots. Without further notation meaning speed over the ground.
> ㉢ Distance is preferably to be expressed in nautical miles or cables, and the unit may be omitted in case it is understood each other.
> ㉣ The numbers are to be spoken in separate digits except when rudder angles are given.
> ㉤ When the position is related to a mark, the mark shall be a well-defined charted object.

① 1개   ② 2개   ③ 3개   ④ 4개

06 다음은 MARPOL 원문을 발췌해 온 것이다. 빈칸에 들어갈 말로 가장 옳은 것은?

> Any ship of ( ) gross tonnage and above shall be provided with oil filtering equipment, and with arrangements for an alarm and for automatically stopping any discharge of oily mixture when the oil content in the effluent exceeds 15 parts per million.

① 150 tons   ② 400 tons   ③ 10,000 tons   ④ 20,000 tons

07 다음 보기 중 투묘 작업의 순서로 올바른 것을 고르시오.

> 가. Brought up anchor.
> 나. Let go port anchor.
> 다. Walk out the port anchor.
> 라. Stand by port anchor for letting go.

① 라-다-나-가   ② 라-나-다-가
③ 다-나-라-가   ④ 나-라-가-다

08 다음 빈칸에 들어갈 말로 가장 적합한 것을 고르시오.

> ( ) is the first water tight bulkhead in the ship.

① bulkhead   ② compartment
③ bulbous bow   ④ collision bulkhead

09 Choose an answer in the blank.

> A helicopter (   ) is a point at which it is safe for a helicopter to land. (   ) is marked by H painted on the ship's a deck.

① Helicopter point
② hoisting point
③ hovering point
④ landing point

10 다음 설명 중 옳지 않은 것을 고르시오.

① The advantage of mercator chart is the fact that a vessel's course can be presented on it as a straight line.
② In SMCP, drop back means to increase the distance from the vessel ahead by reducing one's own speed.
③ If there is a marked temperature inversion or a sharp decrease in water vapor content with increased height, a horizontal radio duct may be formed. It is super-refraction.
④ indirect reflection may be caused by radiowaves reflected by water surface or windows, building.

11 표준해사통신영어(SMCP)의 표현으로 빈칸에 적합한 것을 고르시오.

> When the information requested cannot be obtained, say (   ).

① Stand by
② No information
③ Advice
④ Correction

12 다음 빈칸에 들어갈 말로 가장 적합한 것을 고르시오.

> (　　　　　) of the Republic of Korea is the area of the sea which extends up to 200 nautical miles from the baseline provided for in Article 2 of the Territorial Sea and Contiguous Zone Act, excluding the territorial sea of the Republic of Korea.

① The contiguous zone
② The exclusive economic zone
③ The continental shelf
④ The high seas

13 IAMSAR 상 구명용품의 용기 색채 식별에 따라, 용기의 색이 'Black'인 내용물에 해당하는 것의 개수를 고르시오.

> 가. food
> 나. water
> 다. blankets
> 라. first aid equipment
> 마. axes
> 바. cooking utensils

① 2개　② 3개　③ 4개　④ 5개

14 STCW에 따라, 다음 빈칸의 내용을 순서대로 고르시오.

> The officer in charge of the navigational watch shall not (　　　) the watch to the (　　) if there is any reason to believe that the latter is not capable of carrying out the watchkeeping duties effectively, in which case the master shall be notified.

① hand over, relieved officer
② hand over, relieving officer
③ take over, relieving officer
④ take over, relieved officer

15 다음 중 표준해사통신영어(SMCP)의 목적으로 가장 옳은 것은?

① To supplant international Regulations for Preventing Collision at Sea.
② To supresede the International Code of Signals.
③ To contradict special rules or recommendations made by IMO concerning ship's routing.
④ To assist in the greater safety of navigation and of the conduct of the ship.

16 다음은 STCW의 원문이다. 빈칸에 들어갈 적절한 말을 고르시오.

> The master of every ship is bound to ensure that (   ) are adequate for maintaining a safe navigational watch.

① watchkeeping arrangements ② steering
③ continuous radio watch ④ look-out

17 COLREG에 따라, 다음 빈칸에 들어갈 말로 가장 적절한 것을 고르시오.

> According to COLREG'72, every vessel shall (   ) proceed at a "safe speed". Safe speed is defined as that speed which you can take proper and effective action to avoid collision.

① at emergency circumstances ② at all times
③ at distress circumstances ④ in restricted visibility

18 다음 중 MARPOL에서 정의하는 "Oil"에 속하지 않는 것은?

① oily mixture ② sludge ③ refined products ④ Crude oil

19 다음 중 약어로 옳지 않은 것의 개수를 고르시오.

> ㉠ SART - Search and rescue radar transponder
> ㉡ SRR - Search and rescue range
> ㉢ SMC - Search and rescue mission co-ordinator
> ㉣ NBDP - Narrow-band direct printing
> ㉤ SRU - Search and Rescue Unit
> ㉥ UTC - Universal Time Co-ordinated

① 없음 ② 1개 ③ 2개 ④ 3개

20 SMCP 상 ship routing System에 대한 설명이다. 가장 옳지 않은 것은?

① Recommended track : A route which has been specially examined to ensure so far as possible that it is free of dangers and along which ship are advised to navigate.
② Traffic lane : An area within defined limits in which two-way traffic is established. Natural obstacles, including those forming separation zones, may constitute a boundary.
③ Area to be avoided : A routing measure comprising an area within defined limits in which either navigation is hazardous or it is exceptionally important to avoid casualties and which should be avoid by all ship; or certain classes of ship.
④ Inshore traffic zone : A designated area between the landward boundary of traffic separation scheme and adjacent coast, intended for local traffic.

해사영어 모의고사

01 다음 SMCP 표현 중 해석과 문장이 올바른 것은 무엇인가?

① I have collided to M/T Romeo.
   (본선은 탱커선 로미오 호와 충돌했음)
② Is it safe to fire a rocket?
   (귀선은 로켓을 발사해도 안전합니까?)
③ Maximum speed is 12 knots.
   (항로상 제한속력은 12노트입니다.)
④ Keep the sea under your port bow.
   (좌현 선미에 파도를 받으시오.)

02 다음 중 약어가 올바르게 짝지어진 것은 몇 개인가?

┌───┐
│ ㉠ PPM : part(s) per minute   │
│ ㉡ S.B.E : Stand By Engine   │
│ ㉢ F.W.T : Fresh Water Tank   │
│ ㉣ ETA : Estimated Time of Arrival   │
│ ㉤ MSI : Mobile Safety Information   │
│ ㉥ MMSI : Maritime Mobile Safety Information number │
│ ㉦ VTS : Vessel Traffic Separation   │
└───┘

① 1개   ② 2개   ③ 3개   ④ 4개

03 다음 용어 설명 중 올바르지 않은 것을 고르시오.

① "Safe Speed" means that speed of a vessel allowing the minimum possible time for effective action to be taken to avoid a collision and to be stopped within an appropriate distance.
② "Reference line" means a line displayed on the radar screens in VTS Centers and/or electronic sea-charts separating the fairway for inbound and outbound vessels so that they can safely pass each other.
③ "Traffic Clearance" means VTS authorization for a vessel to proceed under conditions specified.
④ "Manoeuvring Speed" means a vessel's reduced speed in circumstances where it may be required to use the engines at short notice.

04 다음은 COLREG 상 Action to avoid collision의 원문이다. 빈칸에 들어갈 것을 순서대로 고른 것은?

> Any action taken to avoid collision shall, if the circumstances of the case admit, be (   ), made in (   ) and with due regard to the observance of good seamanship. Any alteration of course and/or speed to avoid collision shall, if the circumstances of the case admit, (   ) enough to be readily apparent to another vessel observing visually or by radar.
> A (   ) of course and/or speed should be avoided.

① affirmative - ample time - accurate - succession of small alternations
② positive - ample time - be large - succession of small alternations
③ affirmative - pressing time - accurate - rapid alternation of steering
④ positive - ample time - be small - rapid alternation of steering

05 다음 중 빈칸에 들어갈 말은 무엇인가?

> A vessel aground shall exhibit the lights of vessel at anchor and in addition, (　　) in a vertical line, (　　) in a vertical line.

① three all-round red lights, three black balls
② two all-round red lights, two black ball
③ three all-round red lights, two black balls
④ two all-round red lights, three black balls

06 COLREG에 따라 TSS항법이 바르게 설명되지 않은 것의 개수를 고르시오.

> ㉠ normally join or leave a traffic lane at the termination of the lane, but when joining or leaving from either side shall do so at as right angle to the general direction of traffic flow as practicable.
> ㉡ so far as practicable, avoid crossing traffic lanes but if obliged to do so shall cross on a heading as nearly as practicable at as small angle to the general of traffic flow.
> ㉢ so far as practicable keep clear of a traffic separation line or traffic separation zone.
> ㉣ A vessel shall not use an inshore traffic zone when she can safely use the appropriate traffic lane within the adjacent traffic separation scheme. However, vessels of less than 12m in length, sailing vessel and vessels engaged in fishing may use the inshore traffic zone.

① 없다.　　② 1개　　③ 2개　　④ 3개

07 다음 보기의 괄호 안에 들어갈 말을 순서대로 고른 것은?

㉠ We ( ) Singapore a month ago. : 한 달 전에 싱가폴을 기항하였습니다.
㉡ As weather getting threatening, we ( ) recommended route of sailing direction.
   : 기상이 악화되어 항로지의 추천항로를 따라 항해하였습니다.
㉢ M/V Sarah is ( ) Jin-do.
   : 사라호가 진도를 향해 가고 있습니다.

① called at – proceed by – bound for
② called in – proceed at – bound for
③ called at – proceed at – bound for
④ called in – proceed by – bound to

08 빈칸에 들어갈 말을 순서대로 고른 것은 무엇인가?

㉠ ( ) : make rudder angle to zero degrees and put rudder fore and aft.
㉡ ( ) : check the movement or swing of the ship's bow.
㉢ ( ) : steer a steady course on the compass heading indicated at the time of the order.
㉣ ( ) : Reduce the swing as rapidly as possible.

① meet her – midships – steady – steady as she goes
② midships – meet her – steady as she goes – steady
③ steady – midships – steady as she goes – meet her
④ midships – steady – steady as she goes – meet her

09 다음은 COLREG 상 "Sound signal" 장비에 관한 규정이다 빈칸에 들어갈 숫자의 합을 고르시오.

A vessel of less than ( )metres in length shall not be obliged to give the above-mentioned signals(a whistle , a bell, a gong) but, if she does not, shall make some other efficient sound signal at intervals of not more than ( ) minutes.

① 22   ② 21   ③ 14   ④ 13

10 SOLAS 규정에 따라 옳은 것을 고르시오.

① On passenger ships, an abandon ship drill and fire drill shall take place monthly.
② Every passenger ship shall carry additional life jackets for not less than 15% of the total number of persons on board.
③ Inspection of the life-saving appliances, including life boat equipment, shall be carried out monthly using the checklist required by regulation.
④ Same groups of life boats should be used at successive boat drills and every lifeboat shall be swung out and, if practicable and reasonable, lowered at least once every 3months.

11 빈칸에 들어갈 알맞은 말을 고르시오.

> International Maritime Dangerous Goods CODE is belong to (   ).

① The MARPOL convention
② The STCW convention
③ The SOLAS convention
④ The ISPS Recommendation

12 UNCLOS 제27조 "Criminal jurisdiction on board a foreign ship"에서 외국선박에 대한 형사 관할권을 행할 수 있는 경우로 알맞은 것의 개수는?

> ㉠ if the consequences of the crime extend to the coastal state.
> ㉡ if the crime is of a kind to conserve the peace of the country or the good order of the territorial sea.
> ㉢ if such measures are necessary for the suppression of illicit traffic in narcotic drugs or psychotropic substances.
> ㉣ if the assistance of the local authorities has been requested only by the diplomatic agent of the Flag State.

① 1개   ② 2개   ③ 3개   ④ 4개

13 The advantage of mercator chart is the fact that a vessel's course can be presented on it as a (   ).

① straight line   ② Circle   ③ curve line   ④ right angle

14 다음은 MARPOL 원문의 일부이다. 다음 빈칸에 들어갈 것을 순서대로 고른 것은?

> Any Ship of (   )tons gross tonnage and above shall be provided with oil filtering equipment. Any Ship of (   )tons gross tonnage and above in addition to oil filtering equipment, has to be provided with (   ) any discharge of oily mixture when the oil content in the effluent exceeds (   ) parts per million and alarm system.

① 400, 1000, automatically examined, 15
② 400, 10000, automatically stopped, 30
③ 300, 10000, automatically stopped, 30
④ 400, 10000, automatically stopped, 15

15 다음 중 COLREG 상 용어의 정의에 대한 설명으로 옳지 않은 것의 개수를 고르시오.

> ㉠ The word 'underway' means that a vessel is not anchor, or made fast the shore, or stop.
> ㉡ The word 'length of a vessel' means her L.O.A(length over all) and the word 'breadth of a vessel' means her greatest Breadth.
> ㉢ The term 'restricted visibility' means any condition in which visibility is restricted by fog, mist or any other causes.
> ㉣ 'Vessel making way' is a moving vessel using own engine.

① 없다.   ② 1개   ③ 2개   ④ 3개

16 다음 지문의 빈칸에 들어갈 말에 대한 올바른 대답을 고르시오.

> The vessel was proceeding in the fairway at 8knots through the water. Her speed over the ground was 4knots, which was caused by (ⓐ).
> Captain was asked from the VTS as "What is your present speed?" In this case, the answer is "(ⓑ)".

① ⓐ counter current,
　ⓑ My present speed is 8knots.
② ⓐ counter current,
　ⓑ My present speed is 4knots.
③ ⓐ with current,
　ⓑ My present speed is 8knots.
④ ⓐ with current,
　ⓑ My present speed is 4knots.

17 다음 용어의 설명이 옳지 않은 것의 개수를 고르시오.

> ㉠ QUESTION : This indicates that the following message is asking for action from others with respect to the vessel.
> ㉡ REQUEST : this is preferably used for navigational and traffic information etc.
> ㉢ INSTRUCTION : This means that the sender, e.g. a VTS – Station or a naval vessel, must have the full authority to send such a message.
> ㉣ ANSWER : this may contain another question.

① 1개　　② 2개　　③ 3개　　④ 4개

18 다음 빈칸에 들어갈 적절한 것을 순서대로 적은 것은?

> When deciding how much responsibility to delegate to the (　　), the (　　) normally considers the endurance, communication and (　　).

① SMC, OSC, personnel capabilities
② OSC, SMC, personnel capabilities
③ OSC, CSS, turning characteristics
④ SMC, SCC, turning characteristics

19 다음 중 ISPS의 SSAS(The Ship Security Alert) system의 작동원칙에 대한 설명으로 옳은 것의 개수를 고르시오.

> The SSAS, when activated, shall :
> ㉠ initiate and transmit a ship-to-shore security alert identifying the ship, its location and indicating that the security of the ship is under threat or it has been compromised.
> ㉡ Send the ship security alert to any other ships.
> ㉢ Raise any alarm on-board the ship.
> ㉣ Continue the ship security alert until deactivated and / or reset.
> ㉤ the ship security alert system shall be capable of being activated only from the navigation bridge.

① 2개　② 3개　③ 4개　④ 5개

20 다음 SOLAS의 보조 조타기에 대한 규정 중 잘못된 것은 몇 개인가?

> Capable of putting the rudder from ㉠15°on one side to 15°on the other side in not more than ㉡60s with the ship at its ㉢lowest seagoing draught and running ahead at one half of the maximum ahead service speed or ㉣6knots, which ever is the ㉤lower.

① 1개　② 2개　③ 3개　④ 4개

10 해사영어 모의고사

01 다음 중 SMCP의 원칙대로 올바르게 짝지어진 것은 몇 개인가?

> ㉠ Bearing of the mark or vessel concerned, in the 360 degrees notation from north(magnetic north unless otherwise stated).
> ㉡ Relative Bearing can be expressed in degrees relative to the vessel's head.
> ㉢ Position : When latitude and longitude are used, theses shall be expressed in degrees and minutes.
> ㉣ Distances : to be expressed in nautical miles or cables, the unit can be omitted.

① 없다.   ② 1개   ③ 2개   ④ 3개

02 다음 중 항로지정에 대한 설명 중 옳은 것은 무엇인가?

① "Routing System" means any system of one or more routes or routing measures aimed at increasing the risk of casualties.
② "Separation Zone or Line" means a routing measure comprising a separation point or circular traffic lane within defined limits.
③ "Inshore Traffic Zone" means a routing measure comprising a designated area between the landward boundary of a traffic separation schemes and the adjacent coast, where local special rules may apply, and normally not to be used by through traffic.
④ "Recommended track" means a routing measure comprising an area within defined limits which either navigation is particularly hazardous or it is exceptionally important to avoid casualties.

03 다음 중 SMCP 예문과 그 해석이 올바르지 않은 것은 무엇인가?

① Stand well clear of the spring line.
   -〉 스프링 라인을 제거하라.
② Give one prolonged blast on the whistle.
   -〉 기적 장음 1회를 울려라.
③ The Safety Working Load of the crane is 200 tones.
   -〉 그 크레인의 안전작업하중은 200톤이다.
④ You are required to comply with traffic regulations. Fairway speed is 4knots.
   -〉 귀선은 교통 규정을 준수 해야만 한다. 항로내 제한 속력은 4노트이다.

04 다음 중 빈칸에 들어갈 단어로 가장 옳은 것을 순서대로 고른 것은?

> ㉠ She is said to have (   ) when her speed is sufficient for her rudder to take effect.
> ㉡ "(   )" is standard wheel order to avoid allowing the vessel's head to go to starboard.

① headway, Hard a starboard
② headway, Nothing to starboard
③ steerageway, Hard a starboard
④ steerageway, Nothing to starboard

05 다음 중 COLREG Rule 18. Responsibility between vessels 에 대한 설명이다. 옳지 않은 것은 몇 개인가?

> ㉠ A sailing vessel shall keep out of the way of a fishing vessel not engaged in fishing.
> ㉡ A vessel engaged in fishing when shall, so far as possible, keep out of the way a sailing vessel.
> ㉢ A vessel not under command shall keep out of the way of a vessel constrained by her draught.
> ㉣ A power driven vessel shall keep out of the way of a vessel constrained by her draught.

① 없다.   ② 1개   ③ 2개   ④ 3개

06 다음 대화문을 읽고 빈칸에 들어갈 말을 순서대로 고른 것은 무엇인가?

> T/S HANBADA : HANNARA, this is T/S HANBADA.
>   How do you ( ) me, over?
> T/S HANNARA : HANBADA, this is T/S HANNARA.
>   change ( ) channel 08. Over.
> T/S HANBADA : Roger that.
>   I wish to overtake you on your starboard side, Over.
> T/S HANNARA : HANBADA, This is HANNARA. Do not overtake me.
>   ( ). Do not overtake me. A fishing vessel group is on my starboard bow. Over.

① read - to - Say again
② read - on - Repeat
③ read - to - Repeat
④ hear - to - INSTRUCTION

07 다음은 ISPS CODE에 관한 사항이다. 다음 밑줄 친 부분 중 틀린 부분을 고르시오.

> ISPS code means the international code for the ①Safety of ships and of port facilities consisting of part A(the provisions of which shall be treated as ②mandatory) and Part B(the provisions shall be treated as ③recommendatory) as adopted, on 12 December 2002, by resolution 2 of the Conference of Contracting Governments ④to the international Convention for the Safety of Life at Sea, 1974.

08 빈칸에 들어갈 말을 순서대로 고른 것은 무엇인가?

> (㉠) : means the hours spent on voyage from up and down anchor to let go anchor.
> (㉡) : means the distance that a propeller will move the vessel in one revolution.
> (㉢) : of radar is the discrimination between two objects at the same bearing but on different ranges.

	㉠	㉡	㉢
①	Hours underway	Pitch	Range Resolution
②	Hours propelling	R.P.M	Bearing Resolution
③	Hours underway	R.P.M	Range Resolution
④	Hours propelling	Pitch	Bearing Resolution

09 다음에 해당하는 용어는 무엇인지 순서대로 고르시오.

> ㉠ (　　) : This is the situation standing by anchor and about to let go anchor.
> ㉡ (　　) : this is turning rotation when ship's bow is pushed first to port and than to starboard.

① Walk back - Rolling　　② Walk out - Yawing
③ Cock bill - Yawing　　④ Cock bill - Rolling

10 다음은 Log book의 출항 준비 기사 중 일부이다. 빈칸에 들어가기에 적절한 단어를 고르시오.

> Tested steering gear, whistle, means of communications. All in good order. (　　) bridge & E/R clocks.

① made course　　② Synchronized
③ steered　　④ Stationed

11 다음은 urgency 통신문의 예문이다. 다음 중 옳은 것의 개수를 고르시오.

> ㉠ Mayday x3 , This is M/T GLORY.
> ㉡ MMSI number, 1-2-3-4-5-6.
> ㉢ Call sign, D3FS.
> ㉣ I have lost a man overboard. I require Search and rescue units.

① 1개　② 2개　③ 3개　④ 4개

12 다음은 STCW의 내용이다. 옳지 않은 것은?

> Every officer in charge of a navigational watch serving on a seagoing ship of ①500gross tonnage or more shall hold an appropriate certificate.
> - Every candidate for certification shall :
>   (i) be not less than ②18years of age
>   (ii) have approved seagoing service of not less than ③6 months as part of an approved training programme which includes on-board training which meets the requirements of section A-I1/1 of the STCW Code and is documented in an approved training record book, or otherwise have approved seagoing of not less than ④three years.

13 다음은 IAMSAR Manual 수색패턴(Search pattern) 중 'Expanding Square Search'에 대한 설명이다. 옳지 않은 것은 무엇인가?

① Most effective when the location of the search object is known within relatively close limits.
② The commence search point is always the datum position.
③ Often appropriate for vessels or small boats to use when searching for persons in the water or other search objects with big or huge leeway.
④ It is difficult for fixed wing aircraft to fly legs close to datum if S is less than 2NM.

14 Choose the correct one for the blank.

> If a vessel goes from fresh water to salt water, (   ).

① her draft will not changed
② her draft will be increased
③ her freeboard will be decreased
④ her freeboard will be increased

15 빈칸에 들어갈 용어로 올바른 것을 고르시오.

> (   ) are vertical partitions of walls. All ships must have a specified number depending on their length. By dividing the ship into watertight divisions, they reduce the danger of sinking if one compartment is holed.

① Bulkheads
② Compartments
③ Deadweight tonnage
④ collision bulkhead

16 다음 보기 중 다음 빈칸에 들어갈 수 있는 말로 옳지 않은 것은 무엇인가?

> As navigational and safety communications from ship to shore and vice versa, ship to ship, and on board ships must be (   ), so as to avoid confusion and error, there is a need to standardize the language used.

① continuous   ② simple   ③ precise   ④ unambiguous

17 다음은 SOLAS 상 선교 안전설비 규정이다. 빈칸에 들어갈 숫자로 옳은 것은?

> Not less than (   ) rocket parachute flares shall be carried and be stowed on or near the navigation bridge.

① 2   ② 4   ③ 6   ④ 12

18 다음 빈칸에 들어갈 적절한 것을 순서대로 적은 것은?

> When two power-driven vessels are crossing so as to involve risk of collision, the vessel which has the other on her own port side shall (　　　). And the give way vessel shall avoid crossing (　　　) of the other vessel.

① keep course and speed, astern
② keep course and speed, ahead
③ keep out of the way, ahead
④ keep out of the way, astern

19 다음 중 외국 선박에 대한 추적권(Right of hot pursuit)에 대한 설명 중 옳지 않은 것의 개수를 고르시오.

> ㉠ The release of a ship arrested within the jurisdiction of a State and escorted to a port of that State for the purposes of an inquiry before the competent authorities cannot be claimed solely on the ground that the ship, in the course of its voyage, was escorted across a portion of the exclusive economic zone or the high seas, if the circumstances rendered this necessary.
> ㉡ The right of hot pursuit ceased when the ship pursued enters the territorial sea of its own State or of a third state.
> ㉢ Where a ship has been stopped or arrested outside the territorial sea in circumstances which do not justify the exercise of the right of hot pursuit, it shall not be compensated for any loss or damage that may have been thereby sustained.

① 1개　　② 2개　　③ 3개　　④ 없음

20 다음 중 빈칸에 들어갈 말을 순서대로 고른 것은?

> A vessel at anchor not less than 50m shall exhibit where it can be best be seen :
> ⅰ) in the fore part, a(n) (㉠) or (㉡).
> ⅱ) at or near the stern and at a(n) (㉢) level than the light prescribed in (ⅰ), (㉣).

① ㉠ masthead
　㉡ one ball
　㉢ higher
　㉣ masthead

② ㉠ all round white light
　㉡ two ball
　㉢ lower
　㉣ all round white light

③ ㉠ all round white light
　㉡ one ball
　㉢ lower
　㉣ all round white light

④ ㉠ masthead
　㉡ one ball
　㉢ lower
　㉣ masthead

해사영어 모의고사

01 다음 중 SMCP문구에서 괄호 안에 들어갈 내용으로 가장 옳은 것은?

> Use (   ) when position is unconfirmed, and use (   ) when position has been confirmed by survey or other means.

① LOCATED – REPORTED
② REPORTED – LOCATED
③ TRUE POSITION – ESTIMATED POSITION
④ ESTIMATED POSITION – TRUE POSITION

02 다음 빈칸에 들어갈 문구로 가장 적절하지 않은 것은?

> A : When do you expect to refloat?
> B : M/V Victory expects to refloat (   ).

① when tide goes high
② when weather improves
③ when draft increases
④ at 0900 UTC.

03 빈칸에 가장 알맞은 말을 고르시오.

> (   ) Chart available should always be used when coastal navigation, since errors are reduced to a minimum and detail is shown.

① The largest-scale
② The world-scale
③ The smallest-scale
④ The medium-scale

04 Select the correct one for the blank.

> When considering the turing circle it must be remembered that the whole vessel does not follow the same path, but that the turn will center about the (   ) which lies about one third of the vessel's length from the stern.

① center of gravity
② midship
③ pivoting point
④ diameter

05 UNCLOS 상 형사관할권에 대한 내용이다. 다음 중 빈칸에 들어갈 문장으로 옳지 않은 것은?

> The criminal jurisdiction of the coastal State should not be exercised on board a foreign ship passing through the territorial sea to arrest any person or to conduct any investigation in connection with any crime committed on board the ship during its passage, save only in the following cases : (   ).

① If the crime is of a kind to disturb the peace of the country or the good order of the territorial sea.
② If the correspondences of the crime extend to the flag State.
③ If the assistance of the local authorities has been requested by the master of the ship or by a diplomatic agent or consular of the flag State.
④ If such measures are necessary for the suppression of illicit traffic drugs or psychotropic substances.

06 다음은 VHF통신기 운용 중 규율에 대한 내용이다. 옳은 것은 모두 몇 개인가?

> VHF equipment should be used correctly and in accordance with the radio regulations. The following in particular should be avoided :
> ㉠ calling on channel 16 for purpose of other than distress, urgency and very brief safety communications.
> ㉡ communications related to safety and navigation on port operation channels.
> ㉢ non-essential transmissions, e.g needless and superfluous signals and correspondence.
> ㉣ transmitting without correct identification.

① 모두   ② 1개   ③ 2개   ④ 3개

07 "In case of ordinary leakage it should be remembered that the ship should not be given up till she shows evident signs of <u>foundering</u>" The underlined part means...

① seeking
② capsizing
③ sinking
④ sounding

08 다음 COLREG의 일부분을 발췌한 내용이다. ㉠㉡㉢에 각각 들어갈 표현으로 옳은 것은?

> I. When two power driven vessels are meeting on reciprocal or nearly reciprocal courses so as to involve risk of collision each shall alter her course to (㉠) so that each shall pass on the port side of the other.
> II. When two-power driven vessels are crossing so as to involve risk of collision, the vessel which has the other on her own (㉡) side shall keep out of the way and shall, if the circumstances of the case admit, avoid crossing ahead of the other vessel.
> III. Every vessel which is directed by these Rules to keep out of the way of another vessel shall, so far as possible, take (㉢) and substantial action to keep well clear.

	㉠	㉡	㉢
①	starboard	starboard	early
②	port	port	positive
③	port	starboard	early
④	starboard	starboard	positive

09 다음 COLREG 상 등화에 대한 설명으로 옳지 않은 것은?

① The two green lights or two balls of a vessel engaged in minesweeping operations indicate that it is dangerous for another vessel to approach within 1000 meters of the minesweeping vessel
② A vessel when engaged in trawling shall exhibit two all-round lights in a vertical line, the upper being green and the lower white.
③ A vessel engaged in fishing, other than trawling, shall exhibit two all-round lights in a vertical line, the upper being red and the lower white.
④ A vessel engaged on pilotage shall exhibit two all-round lights in a vertical line, the upper being white and the lower red.

10 다음 중 빈칸에 들어갈 말을 올바르게 짝 지은 것을 고르시오.

> (가) Relative bearings can be expressed in degrees relative to the vessel's (　　　).
> (나) (　　　) is a whistle signal made by the vessel.

① bow – P.A system　　② bow – blast
③ center line – P.A system　　④ center line – blast

11 다음은 UNCLOS의 원문이다. 빈칸에 들어갈 것을 순서대로 고르시오.

> In (　　　) the Coastal State may exercise the control necessary to prevent (　　　) of its customs, fiscal, immigration or sanitary laws and regulations within its territory or territorial sea.

① the contiguous zone, infringement
② the contiguous zone, observance
③ the exclusive economic zone, observance
④ the exclusive economic zone, infringement

12 MARPOL에 따라 빈칸에 들어갈 수 없는 것의 개수를 고르시오.

> Sewage means (　　　).
> ㉠ drainage and other wastes from any form of toilets and urinals.
> ㉡ drainage and other oily mixtures from slop tank.
> ㉢ drainage from spaces containing living animals.
> ㉣ drainage from bilge tank.
> ㉤ drainage from medical premises.

① 없다.　　② 1개　　③ 2개　　④ 3개

13 괄호에 들어가기 적합한 통신부호(Message marker)는?

( ). Do not cross the fairway, you are in danger of collision.

① Information   ② Instruction   ③ Request   ④ Intention

14 What is the meaning "out" in wireless conversation?

① I am off the house.
② I have completed my transmission.
③ I am terminating whole conversation.
④ I am ready to receive your message.

15 보기는 COLREG 상 제한시계(restricted visibility) 내에서의 변침만으로의 피항 중 하지 말아야하는 동작에 대한 설명이다. 빈칸에 들어갈 말을 고르시오.

I. an alteration of course to ( ) for a vessel forward of the beam, other than for vessel being overtaken.
II. an alteration of course towards a vessel abeam or abaft the beam.

① starboard   ② port   ③ ahead   ④ astern

16 보기가 설명하는 단어를 고르시오.

The angle the ship's keel, or center line, makes with the wake of the vessel, or track through the water.

① Leeward   ② Wind blow   ③ Leeway   ④ drifting

17 다음 국제항공 및 해상수색 구조 편람의 용어 설명 중 틀린 것은 모두 몇 개인가?

> ㉠ To ditch : The distance the waves have been driven by a wind blowing in a constant direction, without obstruction
> ㉡ CES : Coast Earth Satellite
> ㉢ AMVER : A world-wide ship reporting system for search and rescue
> ㉣ Datum : A geographic point, line, or area used as a reference in search planning
> ㉤ IMO : International Maritime Organization
> ㉥ GMDSS : A global communications service based upon automated systems, both satellite-based and terrestrial to provide distress alerting and promulgation of maritime information to mariners

① 1개   ② 2개   ③ 3개   ④ 4개

18 다음은 COLREG의 원문 일부이다 빈칸에 들어갈 말을 순서대로 고르시오.

> When, from any cause, the vessel required to keep her course and speed finds herself so (   ) that collision cannot be avoided by the action of the (   ) alone, she shall take action as best aid to avoid collision.

① sufficient, give way vessel
② sufficient, stand-on vessel
③ close, stand-on vessel
④ close, give way vessel

19 COLREG 상 Rule.13의 내용 중 아래 빈칸에 순서대로 들어갈 단어는?

> Any subsequent alteration of the bearing between the two vessels shall not make the (   ) vessel a crossing vessel within the meaning of these Rules or relieve her of the duty of keeping clear of (   ) vessel until she is finally past and clear.

① overtaking - overtaken
② overtaken - overtaking
③ overtaking - crossing
④ crossing - overtaking

20 MARPOL 내용에 따라, 빈칸에 들어갈 적절한 용어를 순서대로 고르시오.

> 1. (   ) means a ship designated to carry either oil or solid cargoes in bulk.
> 2. (   ) means the ballast water introduced into tank which is completely separated from the cargo oil and oil fuel system.

① Combination carrier − clean ballast
② Oil tanker − Segregated ballast
③ Combination carrier −Segregated ballast
④ Oil tanker − clean ballast

해사영어 모의고사

01 다음은 STCW의 선장이 적절한 당직 배치를 위해 확인해야할 사항이다. 옳지 않은 내용을 고르시오.

① Officer in charge of the navigational watch are responsible for navigating the ship safely during their periods of duty, when they shall be physically present on the navigating bridge or in a directly associated location such as the chartroom or bridge control room at all times.
② radio operators are responsible for maintaining a continuous radio watch on appropriate frequencies during their periods of duty;
③ officers in charge of an engineering watch shall be immediately available and on call to attend the machinery spaces.
④ an appropriate and effective watch or watches do not need to be maintained for the purpose of safety at all times, while the ship is at anchor or moored.

02 다음 중 약어의 표현이 잘못 연결된 것은 몇 개인가?

> ㉠ PA system : Public Address system (확성 방송 장치)
> ㉡ MMSI : Maritime Mobile Service Identity number (해상 이동 업무 식별 번호)
> ㉢ UKC : Upper Keel Clearance (용골 상 여유수심)
> ㉣ LMT : Local Maritime Transit (지방 해상 통과시)
> ㉤ ISM : International Security Management Code
> ㉥ Lat. : Latitude (경도)

① 1개 ② 2개 ③ 3개 ④ 4개

03 빈칸에 들어갈 말을 순서대로 고른 것은?

㉠ (　　　　) can be defined as the ability of the ship to return to the upright when slightly inclined.
㉡ When heading on a course, you put your rudder hard over. The distance traveled in the right angle direction of the original course from when you put your rudder over until your heading differs by 90 is known as : (　　　　).
㉢ (　　　　) is vertical distance from the uppermost deck to the center of the disc which is marked on the vessel's sides and which indicates the position of the load water line in summer.

① Ship stability - Advance - load line
② Ship stability - Transfer - Freeboard
③ Ship capability - Tactical Diameter - Air draft
④ Ship capability - Advance - Freeboard

04 다음 중 anchoring 용어로 잘못 연결된 것은 몇 개인가?

㉠ A cock bill state : To reverse the action of a windlass to lower the anchor until it is clear of the hawse pipe and ready for dropping.
㉡ Walk out : The situation standing by anchor and about to let go anchor.
㉢ Walk back : To let out a greater length of cable.
㉣ Dragging : Moving of an anchor over the sea bottom voluntarily because it is no longer preventing the movement of the vessel.
㉤ Dredging : Moving of an anchor over the sea bottom to control the movement of the vessel.

① 1개　　② 2개　　③ 3개　　④ 4개

05 다음 중 빈칸에 들어갈 말로 가장 적절한 것은?

(　　) mean uncontrolled movement at sea under the influence of current, tide or wind.

① leeway　　② adrift　　③ draft　　④ derelict

06 Pilot boat와 일반 Vessel 간의 도선업무 관련 통신 중 "Pilot boat 측"에서 사용할 수 있는 표현으로 가장 적절한 것을 고르시오.
① I will make a lee for your vessel.
② Request, rig the pilot ladder on the lee-side.
③ Which side must I rig the pilot ladder?
④ My ETA at P/STN is 1230LT.

07 UNCLOS 상 Archipelagic baseline에 대한 설명이다. 빈칸에 들어갈 수 없는 단어를 고르시오.

> An archipelagic State may draw straight archipelagic baseline joining the outermost points of the outermost ( ) and ( ) or the ( ).

① islands
② drying reef
③ archipelago
④ low-tide elevation

08 다음은 COLREG 중 일부를 발췌한 것이다. ㉠ 선박을 고르고, ㉡에 들어갈 단어를 고르시오.

> ⓐ (i) Where by any of these Rules one of two vessels is to keep out of the way the other shall keep her course and speed.
> (ii) (㉠) may however take action to avoid collision by her manoeuvre alone, as soon as it becomes apparent to her that the vessel required to keep out of the way is not taking appropriate action in compliance with these Rules.
> ⓑ A power-driven vessel which takes action in a crossing situation in accordance with subparagraph (a)(ii) of this Rule to avoid collision with another power-driven vessel shall, if the circumstances of the case admit, not alter course to (㉡) for a vessel on her own port side.

① ㉠ : stand-on vessel ㉡ : port
② ㉠ : give-way vessel ㉡ : port
③ ㉠ : stand-on vessel ㉡ : starboard
④ ㉠ : give-way vessel ㉡ : starboard

09 다음 COLREG 상 Narrow channel에 대한 내용 중 옳지 않은 것을 고르시오.

① A vessel proceeding along the course of a narrow channel or fairway shall keep as near to the outer limit of the channel or fairway which lies on her starboard side as is safe and practicable.

② A vessel of less than 12 meters in length or a sailing vessel shall not impede the passage of a vessel which can safely navigate only within a narrow channel or fairway.

③ A vessel engaged in fishing shall not impede the passage of any other vessel navigating within a narrow channel or fairway.

④ Any vessel shall, if the circumstances of the case admit, avoid anchoring in a narrow channel.

10 다음 SMCP 상 표현에 들어갈 빈칸으로 가장 올바른 것을 고르시오.

> ① (㉠) 2 short blasts (on the whistle).
>   : 2 회의 단음을 울려라.
> ② (㉡) 2 shackles in the water.
>   : 닻줄을 2 샤클 만큼 풀어주시오.
> ③ (㉢) the windlass in gear.
>   : 양묘기 사용 준비.

	㉠	㉡	㉢
①	Give	turn	put
②	Horn	turn	pick
③	Give	put	pick
④	Give	put	put

11 다음 SMCP 단어의 내용 중 옳은 것은?

① DANGER : This indicates that the following message implies the intention of the sender to inform others about danger.

② REQUEST : This indicates that the following message is of interrogative character.

③ ADVICE : The decision whether follow the message does stay with recipient.

④ INSTRUCTION : This indicates that the following message is restricted to observed facts, situations, etc.

12 다음은 SOLAS에서 정하는 구명부환에 관한 규정이다. 옳지 않은 것의 개수는?

> Not less than ㉠5% of the total number of life-buoys shall be provided with life-buoy ㉡self-igniting light complying with the requirements of paragraph 2.1.2 of the Code; not less than ㉢one half of these shall also be provided with life buoys ㉣self-activating smoke signals complying with the requirements of paragraph 2.1.3 of the Code and be capable of quick release from the ㉤accommodation.

① 1개   ② 2개   ③ 3개   ④ 4개

13 다음은 SOLAS에서 정하는 구명정의 일반장비에 관한 규정이다. 빈칸에 들어갈 말은?

> The normal equipment of every lifeboat shall consist of (㉠) rocket parachute flares complying with the requirement of regulation and (㉡) hand flares complying with requirements of regulation and (㉢) buoyant smoke signal complying with the requirements of regulation.

	㉠	㉡	㉢
①	4	6	4
②	2	6	2
③	6	4	2
④	4	6	2

14 다음은 UNCLOS 상 무해통항권에 위배되는 행위중 하나이다. 빈칸으로 알맞은 것은?

> ⅰ. any act of (㉠) pollution contrary to this convention
> ⅱ. any (㉡) activities

	㉠	㉡
①	wilful and serious	fishery
②	wilful or negligent	fishing
③	wilful and serious	fishing
④	wilful or negligent	fishery

15 다음은 형사적 관할권 조항에 관한 내용이다. ㉠㉡㉢으로 알맞은 것을 고르시오.

> The criminal jurisdiction of the coastal State should not be exercised on board foreign ship passing through the territorial sea to arrest any person or to conduct any investigation in connection with any crime committed on board the ship during its passage, save only in the following cases;
> - if the crime is of a kind to disturb (㉠) of the country or the good order of the (㉡).
> - if such measures are necessary for the suppression of (㉢) traffic in narcotic drugs or psychotropic substances.

	㉠	㉡	㉢
①	peace,	contiguous zone,	illicit
②	peace,	territorial sea,	illicit
③	conservation,	territorial sea,	legal
④	conservation,	contiguous zone,	legal

16 다음 중 UNCLOS 상 틀린 것은 무엇인가?

① The hot pursuit of a foreign ship undertaken when the competent authorities of the coastal State have good reason to believe that the ship has violated the laws and regulations of that State.

② The right of hot pursuit may be exercised by warships or military aircraft.

③ It is necessary that, at the time when the foreign ship within the territorial sea or the contiguous zone receives the order to stop, the ship giving the order should likewise be within the territorial sea or the contiguous zone.

④ The right of hot pursuit ceases as soon as the ship pursued enters the territorial sea of its own State or of a third State.

17 IAMSAR 용어 상 설명으로 옳은 것은 몇 개인가?

> ㉠ Craft : Any air or sea surface vehicle, or submarine of any kind of or size
> ㉡ Datum : Point, normally specified by the SMC, where a SAR facility is to begin its search pattern
> ㉢ NAVTEX : The system for the broadcast and automatic reception of maritime safety information by means of narrow-band direct-printing telegraphy
> ㉣ Rescue unit : An operation to retrieve persons in distress
> ㉤ False Alert : Distress alert received from any source, including communications equipment intended for alerting, when no distress situation actually exists, and a notification of distress should not have resulted

① 1개 ② 2개 ③ 3개 ④ 4개

18 다음은 IAMSAR Manual 중 Parallel Sweep Search에 대한 설명이다. 옳지 않은 항목의 개수를 고르시오.

> ㉠ Used to search a large area when survivor location is certain
> ㉡ Most effective over mountain or water
> ㉢ Usually used when a large search area must be divided into sub-areas for assignment to individual search facilities on-scene at the same time
> ㉣ Search legs are vertical to each other and to long sides of the sub-area

① 1개 ② 2개 ③ 3개 ④ 4개

19 All of the following are distress signal except :

① red flare ② orange smoke
③ international AA ④ rising and lowering arms

20 SOLAS 규정에 따를 때, 다음 빈칸에 들어갈 숫자를 고르시오.

> Manually operated call points complying with the Fire Safety Systems Code shall be installed throughout the accommodation spaces, service spaces and control stations. One manually operated call point shall be located at each exit. Manually operated call points shall be readily accessible in the corridors of each deck such that no part of the corridor is more than ( )m from a manually operated call point.

① 12　　② 20　　③ 22　　④ 24

13 해사영어 모의고사

01 다음 SMCP 표현 중 해석과 문장이 올바르게 적히지 않은 것을 고르시오.

① I will jettison cargo to stop skinking.
　→〉 본선은 전복을 막기 위해 화물을 투하할 것이다.
② Are you ready to underway?
　→〉 귀선은 항해할 준비가 되었는가?
③ Are the cranes operational?
　→〉 크레인이 작동가능 합니까?
④ Fishing gear has fouled my propeller.
　→〉 어구가 본선 프로펠러에 꼬였다.

02 다음 중 SMCP 표현이 어색한 것을 고르시오.

① I am making way through the water.
② You must drop back to the vessel astern of you.
③ We called at Busan a week ago.
④ Pilotage is in operation for all vessels.

03 선박이 한쪽 현으로 회두를 하던 도중 타수가 Midships 명령을 받고 타를 중립으로 놓았다. 이 시점에서 사용할 수 있는 조타명령의 개수를 고르시오.

　㉠ steady
　㉡ hard a starboard
　㉢ Ease to ten
　㉣ port ten

① 1개　② 2개　③ 3개　④ 4개

04 다음 내용 중 옳은 것의 개수를 고르시오.

> ㉠ Inshore Traffic Zone : A routing measure comprising designated area between landward boundary of a TSS and the adjacent coast
> ㉡ Destination : The most probable position of a search target at a given time
> ㉢ Blast : A whistle signal made by the vessel
> ㉣ last port of call : port which a vessel is bound for
> ㉤ Announcement : Loudspeaker in the vessel's cabins, mess room, etc. and on deck through which important information can be broadcast from a central point, mostly from the navigation bridge

① 1개   ② 2개   ③ 3개   ④ 4개

05 다음은 STCW중 Pilot 승무에 관한 사항 중 일부이다. 옳지 않은 것은?

① Despite the duties and obligations of pilot, his presence on board dose not relieve the master or officer in charge of the watch.
② The master and the pilot need to exchange information regarding navigation procedures, local conditions and the ship's characteristics.
③ The master and officer of navigational watch shall co-operate closely with the pilot and maintain an accurate check on the ships position and movement.
④ if in any doubt as to the pilot's action or intentions, the officer in charge of the navigational watch shall not seek clarification from the pilot.

06 다음 SMCP 표현 중 옳지 않은 것의 개수를 고르시오.

> ㉠ Put engine ahead. : 기관 전진하라.
> ㉡ I will make a lee for your boat.
>   : 본선을 귀선의 풍하측으로 오게 하라.
> ㉢ Correct the list of the vessel.
>   : 선박의 경사를 수정하라.
> ㉣ Embarkation is not possible.
>   : 승선이 불가능하다.

① 없다.   ② 1개   ③ 2개   ④ 3개

07 SMCP 상 화재 시 사용하는 표현이다. 빈칸으로 옳은 것은?

> If you detect a fire, smell, fume or smoke, act immediately as follows :
> (ⓐ) "Fire"
> (ⓑ) the nearest fire alarm.
> (ⓒ) a member of the crew.
> (ⓓ) the navigation bridge.

	ⓐ	ⓑ	ⓒ	ⓓ
①	Call out	Operate	Inform	Telephone
②	Shout out	Break	Search	Assembly
③	Call out	Operate	Search	Go to
④	Shout out	Cancel	Tell	Contact

08 다음 빈칸에 들어갈 가장 알맞은 말을 순서대로 고르시오.

> 가) Attention! the cargo operation (ⓐ).
>   (주목, 화물 작업이 시작됩니다.)
> 나) Vessel (ⓑ), frequent rounds (ⓒ) for lines.
>   (선박 대기 중, 계류줄 순찰이 수시로 진행됨.)

	ⓐ	ⓑ	ⓒ
①	turn to	idle	made
②	knock off	depart	go
③	turn to	clear	go
④	resume	idle	made

09 IAMSAR에서 규정하는 수색 법에 대한 설명 중 옳지 않은 것의 개수를 고르시오.

> ㉠ Sector Search – An aircraft and a vessel may be used together to perform independent sector searches of the same areas
> ㉡ Parallel Sweep Search – Most Effective over water or flat terrain
> ㉢ Expanding Square Search – The commence search point is always the datum position
> ㉣ One turn – difficult because approach to person is straight
> ㉤ Scharnove turn – will not take vessel back into her wake
> ㉥ Williamson turn – fast procedure

① 1개 ② 2개 ③ 3개 ④ 4개

10 보기가 설명하는 IAMSAR용어를 고르시오.

> A service of Inmarsat enhanced group call (EGC) system specifically designed for promulgation of maritime safety information (MSI) as a part of the GMDSS.

① SafetyNET ② Navtex ③ EPIRB ④ SART

11 UNCLOS에 따라 배타적 경제수역에서의 관할권에 해당하는 것의 개수를 고르시오.

> ㉠ jurisdiction with regard to the establishment and use of artificial islands, installations and structures.
> ㉡ prevent infringement of its customs, fiscal, immigration or sanitary laws and regulations within its territory or territorial sea.
> ㉢ jurisdiction with regard to marine scientific research.
> ㉣ punish infringement of the its customs, fiscal, immigration or sanitary laws and regulations committed within its territory or territorial sea.
> ㉤ jurisdiction with regard to the protection and preservation of the marine environment.

① 2개 ② 3개 ③ 4개 ④ 5개

12 UNCLOS 상의 권리 중 다음 설명에 해당하는 권리(right)는?

( ) means the exercise in accordance with this Part of the freedom of navigation and overflight solely for the purpose of continuous and expeditious transit of the strait between one part of the high seas or an exclusive economic zone and another part of the high seas or an exclusive economic zone.

① Right of innocent passage
② Right of visit
③ Right of transit passage
④ Right of hot pursuit

13 다음 밑줄 친 내용 중 옳지 않은 것의 개수는 몇 개인가?

When two sailing vessels are approaching one another, so as to involve risk of collision, one of them shall keep out of the way of the other as follows.
(1) when each has the wind on a different side the vessel which has the wind on the ㉠starboard side shall keep out of the way of the other.
(2) when both have the wind on the same side, the vessel which is to ㉡leeward shall keep out of the way of the vessel which is to ㉢windward.
(3) if a vessel with the wind on the ㉣port side sees a vessel to windward and cannot determine with certainty whether the other vessel has the wind on the port or on the starboard side, she shall keep out of the way of the other.

① 1개   ② 2개   ③ 3개   ④ 4개

14 다음 SMCP 표현 중 문장과 해석이 올바르게 연결되지 않은 것을 고르시오.

① All tanks are fully inerted.
   모든 탱크가 완전히 불활성화 되었다.
② Write all checks into the log book.
   모든 점검사항을 항해일지에 기재하시오.
③ Have a periodical fire watch.
   주기적인 화재 당직을 유지하시오.
④ How many persons are on board?
   몇 명의 선내 인원이 당직중입니까?

15 조타명령이 "Steady"와 "Steady as she goes"를 옳게 설명한 것은 몇 개인가?

> ㉠ 명령 후 선박이 가는 침로의 결과는 같다.
> ㉡ Steady as she goes 명령어는 명령 당시의 선수방향으로 선박을 다시 정침하라는 의미이다.
> ㉢ Steady는 선박의 회두를 줄이라는 의미이다.
> ㉣ Steady는 Steady as she goes를 줄인 표현이다.

① 1개   ② 2개   ③ 3개   ④ 4개

16 다음 중 가장 옳은 것을 고르시오.

① "Bearing" can be expressed in degrees relative to the vessel's head or head bow. More frequently this is in relation to the port or starboard bow.
② The angle caused between the axis of the compass and magnetic meridian is called "variation".
③ When sailing along a coast, to avoid sunken rocks, shoals, or dangerous obstructions at or below the surface of the water, and which are marked on the chart, the navigator may pass these at any desired distance by using what is known as "sounding".
④ "collision bulkhead" are vertical partitions of walls. All ships must have a specified number of compartments depending on their length.

17 다음 SOLAS 내용 중 밑줄 친 항목의 틀린 개수를 고르시오.

> The view of the sea surface from the conning position of ships of not less than ㉠50m in length shall not be obscured by more than two ship lengths, or ㉡500m, whichever is the ㉢greater, forward of the bow to ㉣15° on either side under all conditions of draught, trim and deck cargo.

① 1개   ② 2개   ③ 3개   ④ 4개

18 다음은 COLREG 상 일반적인 항법에 관한 설명이다. 빈칸에 들어갈 말을 고르시오.

> When vessels in sight of one another are approaching each other and from any cause either vessel fails to understand the intentions or actions of the other, or is in doubt whether sufficient action is being taken by the other to avoid collision, the vessel in doubt shall immediately indicate such doubt by giving (   ) blasts in the whistle.

① at least 3 short and rapid
② at least 4 short and rapid
③ at least 5 short and rapid
④ at least 6 short and rapid

19 다음은 MARPOL 원문 중 기름기록부에 관한 규정 일부를 발췌해 온 것이다. 다음 중 옳지 않은 것의 개수는?

> Every oil tanker of ㉠150 tons gross tonnage and above and every ship ㉡400 tons gross tonnage and above other than oil tanker shall be provided with an Oil Record Book whether as part of this ship's ㉢unofficial log book or otherwise in the form specified in appendix 3 to this Annex the Oil Record Book shall be kept in such place as to be ㉣readily available for inspection at all reasonable times and except in the case of unmanned ships under tow, shall be kept on board the ship. it shall be preserved for a period of ㉤five years after the last entry has been made.

① 1개   ② 2개   ③ 3개   ④ 4개

20 SOLAS에서 규정하는 Life Jacket의 추가 비치 규정이다. 빈칸에 알맞은 숫자를 고르시오.

> Every passenger ship shall carry life jackets for not less than ( )% of the total number of persons on board. These life jackets shall be stowed in conspicuous places on deck or at muster stations.

① 5
② 10
③ 15
④ 20

14 해사영어 모의고사

01 다음 중 SMCP 표현으로 옳은 것은?

① I read you six.
② I am under fire.
③ I will proceed by fairway.
④ Which side must I hang the pilot ladder?

02 다음 중 SMCP표현이 어색한 것을 고르시오.

① Report me your position to assist identification.
② M/V GLORY will turn my vessel at the quay ahead of you. You must stay clear of the fairway.
③ You must not close up on the container vessel ahead of you.
④ What is your ETA from BUSAN Port?

03 다음 중 SMCP 단어와 설명이 옳지 않은 것은 몇 개인가?

> ㉠ Derelict – A vessel which has been destroyed or sunk or abandoned at sea
> ㉡ Veering – Clockwise change in the direction of the wind
> ㉢ Transit Speed – Speed of a vessel required for the passage through a canal, fairway, etc.
> ㉣ Recover – To pull a vessel off after grounding to set afloat again
> ㉤ Refloat – To pick up shipwrecked persons
> ㉥ Flooding – Major uncontrolled flow of seawater into the vessel
> ㉦ Course – The horizontal direction of the vessel's bows at a given moment measured in degrees clockwise from the north
> ㉧ Drifting – Being driven along by the wind, tide or current

① 1개   ② 2개   ③ 3개   ④ 4개

04 다음 SMCP 예문과 해석이 잘못 연결된 것은 무엇인가?

① How many shackles are to come in?
묘쇄를 얼마나 더 감아 들여야 하는가?
② How is the cable growing?
닻줄의 장력은 어떠한가?
③ Fairway Speed is 6kts.
항로 내 권고속력은 6노트이다.
④ Arrange two tug boats for me.
본선을 위해 두 대의 예인선을 준비하라.

05 다음 빈칸에 들어갈 가장 적절한 말은 무엇인가?

> When the GMDSS Radio Operator on watch hears "SECURITE" spoken three times, he can expect to receive the message concerning the (   ).

① any parts of the message considered sufficiently important for safeguarding.
② immediate and very important for escaping from dangerous situation.
③ safety of navigation or important meteorological warnings.
④ message appropriate to RCC for contacting through a shore station and the distress alert.

06 다음 빈칸에 알맞은 말을 각각 고르시오.

> ㉠ The master of ship on receiving a wireless distress signal from any other ships is bound to proceed with all speed to the (   ) of the persons in distress.
> ㉡ Whoever is in charge of a navigational watch shall not be assigned or undertaken any duties which would (   ) the safe navigation of the ship.

① avoidance - interfere with
② assistance - protect
③ avoidance - protect
④ assistance - interfere with

07 다음 중 외국선박에 대한 추적권에 대한 설명 중 옳은 것은 몇 개인가?

> ㉠ The right of hot pursuit may be exercised only by warships or military aircraft, or other ships or aircraft clearly marked and identifiable as being on government service and authorized to that effect.
> ㉡ The right of hot pursuit ceases although the ship pursuing enters the territorial sea of its own State or of a third State.
> ㉢ Where a ship has been stopped or arrested outside the territorial sea in circumstances which do not justify the exercise of the right of hot pursuit, it shall not be compensated for any loss or damage that may have been thereby sustained.
> ㉣ The release of a ship arrested within the jurisdiction of a State and escorted to a port of that State for the purposes of an inquiry before the competent authorities may be claimed solely on the ground that the ship, in the course of its voyage, was escorted across a portion of the exclusive economic zone or the high seas, if the circumstances rendered this necessary.

① 1개　② 2개　③ 3개　④ 4개

08 다음은 UNCLOS 상 Article11의 내용을 발췌한 것이다. 이것은 무엇에 관한 설명인가?

> (　　　) which are normally used for the loading and anchoring of ships, and which would otherwise be situated wholly or partly outside the outer limit of the territorial sea, are included in the territorial sea.

① Roadsteads
② Reefs
③ EEZ
④ Contiguous zone

09 다음은 COLREG의 음향신호에 관한 규정이다. ㉠㉡㉢㉣중 틀린 것의 개수는?

> when in sight of one another in a narrow channel or fairway
> (i) A vessel intending to overtake another shall in compliance with rule9 (e)(i) indicate her intention by the following signals on her whistle ;
>   – ㉠<u>one</u> prolonged blast followed by ㉡<u>one</u> short blast to mean "I intend to overtake you on your starboard side."
>   – ㉢<u>one</u> prolonged blast followed by ㉣<u>two</u> short blasts to mean "I intend to overtake you on your port side."
> (ii) the vessel about to be overtaken when acting in accordance with Rule9 (e)(i) shall indicate her agreement by the following signal on her whistle:
>   – ㉤<u>five</u> short blasts rapidly.

① 1개   ② 2개   ③ 3개   ④ 4개

10 다음 UNCLOS 상, 공해의 자유에 해당하는 것의 개수를 고르시오.

> ㉠ freedom of navigation
> ㉡ freedom of overflight
> ㉢ freedom of propaganda
> ㉣ freedom of lay submarine cables and pipelines
> ㉤ freedom of scientific research
> ㉥ freedom of fishing
> ㉦ freedom of pollution

① 3개   ② 4개   ③ 5개   ④ 6개

11 다음은 COLREG RULE 35 'Sound signals in restricted visibility'의 원문 일부이다. 밑줄 친 부분 중 옳지 않은 것의 개수를 고르시오.

> In or near an area of restricted visibility, a vessel towed or if more than one vessel is towed the ㉠<u>first vessel</u> of the tow, if manned, shall at intervals of not more than ㉡<u>2minutes</u> sound ㉢<u>one prolonged</u> followed by ㉣<u>two short</u> blasts. When practicable, this signal shall be made immediately ㉤<u>before</u> the signal made by the towing vessel.

① 1개 ② 2개 ③ 3개 ④ 4개

12 SMCP 상, 약어로 올바르지 않은 것의 개수를 고르시오.

> ㉠ SART – Search and Rescue radar transponder
> ㉡ VHF – Very High Frequency
> ㉢ SMC –Search and rescue mission co-ordinator
> ㉣ NBDP – Narrow Band Direct Printing
> ㉤ SRU – Search and Rescue Unit
> ㉥ LMT – Local Mean Time

① 없다. ② 1개 ③ 2개 ④ 3개

13 다음 IAMSAR 매뉴얼 상, 용어에 대한 설명으로 가장 옳은 것을 순서대로 고른 것은?

> ㉠ A unit subordinate to a rescue co-ordination centre established to complement within a specified area within a search and rescue region.
> ㉡ A unit responsible for promoting efficient organization of search and rescue services and for co-ordinating the conduct of search and rescue operations within a search and rescue region.

① SRU, RCC ② SRU, RSC
③ RSC, RCC ④ RCC, RSC

14 다음의 상황에 해당하는 것을 고르시오.

> When ship A is coming up with ship B from a direction more than two points abaft her beam at night, the only visual indication to ship A of the presence of ship B will be the stern light of the latter.

① Ship A and B are crossing each other.
② Ship B is overtaking ship A.
③ Ship A is followed by ship B.
④ Ship A is overtaking ship B.

15 다음 중 UNCLOS에 따라 임검권(Right of visit)을 행할 수 있는 경우로 옳은 것의 개수는?

> ㉠ the ship is engaged in piracy.
> ㉡ the ship is engaged in the slave trade.
> ㉢ the ship is engaged in unauthorized broadcasting and the flag State of the warship has jurisdiction.
> ㉣ the ship is engaged in fishing.
> ㉤ the ship is engaged in research operation.
> ㉥ the ship is without nationality.
> ㉦ though flying a foreign flag or refusing to show its flag, the ship is, in reality, of the same nationality as the warship.

① 4개   ② 5개   ③ 6개   ④ 7개

16 다음 중 SMCP단어와 설명이 옳은 것을 고르시오.

① Stand on : To keep out of the way of another vessel
② Knock off : To start work
③ Icing : To reduce the oxygen in a tank by inert gas to avoid an explosive atmosphere
④ helicopter landing point : A point at which it is safe for a helicopter to land, It is marked by H painted on the ship's deck

17 다음 중 SMCP 상 용어와 그 정의에 대한 내용이다. 옳게 짝지어진 것을 모두 고르시오.

> ㉠ INTENTION : This indicates that the following message is of interrogative character.
> ㉡ ANSWER : This indicates that the following message is to reply to previous question.
> ㉢ ADVICE : This indicates that the following message implies the intention of the sender to inform others about danger.
> ㉣ REQUEST : This indicates that the following message is asking for action from others with respect to the vessel.

① 1개　② 2개　③ 3개　④ 4개

18 COLREG에 따라 충돌의 위험이 있을 때, 두 선박이 해야 하는 규칙으로 옳지 않은 것의 개수를 고르시오.

> ㉠ Except in narrow channels, traffic separation scheme, and when overtaking, a power-driven vessel must give way to a sailing vessel.
> ㉡ When two power-driven vessels are crossing, the vessel which has the other on the port side must give way.
> ㉢ When two power-driven vessels are meeting head-on both must alter course to starboard so that they pass on the port side of the other.
> ㉣ When two sailing vessels approaching one another, and each has the wind on a different side, the vessel which has the wind to port must give way.

① 없음　② 1개　③ 2개　④ 3개

19 다음 중 MARPOL Annex(부속서) 1~6에 포함되는 내용으로 옳지 않은 것은?

① Pollution control by ship's sewage
② Pollution control by noxious liquid substances
③ Pollution control by discharge of ship's ballast water
④ Pollution control by ship's harmful substances carried by sea in packaged form

20 다음은 MARPOL의 원문이다. 빈칸에 들어갈 숫자를 모두 합한 것은 얼마인가?

> The ship is discharging comminuted and disinfected sewage using a system approved by the Administration at a distance of more than (　) nautical miles from the nearest land or seawage which is not comminuted or disinfected at a distance of more that (　) nautical miles from the nearest land, provided that in any case, the sewage that has been stored in holding tanks shall not be discharged instantaneously but at a moderate when the ship is en route and proceeding at not less than (　) knots. the rate of discharge shall be approved by the Administration based upon standards developed by the Organization.

① 15　　② 17　　③ 19　　④ 21

15 회차 해사영어 모의고사

01 다음은 COLREG 상 등화의 시인거리에 대한 내용이다. 다음의 밑줄 친 수치들 중 옳지 않은 항목은?

(A) In vessel of ①<u>50meters</u> or more in length
  ②<u>– a masthead light, 6miles</u>
  – a sidelight 3miles
  – a stern light, 3miles
  – a towing light, 3miles
  – a white, red, green or yellow all-round light, 3miles
(B) In vessel of 12meters or more in length but less than 50 meters in length:
  ③<u>– a masthead light, 5miles; except that where the length of the vessel is less than 20meters, 3miles</u>
  – a sidelight 2miles
  – a stern light, 2miles
  – a towing light, 2miles
  – a white, red, green or yellow all-round light, 2miles
(C) In vessel of less than 12 meters in length:
  – a masthead light, 2miles
  ④<u>– a sidelight 2miles</u>
  – a stern light, 2miles
  – a towing light, 2miles

02 다음은 항로 지정에 사용되는 용어들에 관한 설명이다. 틀린 것은 몇 개인가?

> ⓐ Recommended Track : A route which has been specially examined to ensure so far as possible that it is free of dangers and along which ships are advised to navigate.
> ⓑ Traffic Lane : An area within defined limits in which one-way traffic is established. Natural obstacles, including those forming separation zones, may constitute a boundary.
> ⓒ Separation Zone or Line : A zone or line separating the traffic lanes in which ships are proceeding in opposite or nearly opposite direction, or separating a traffic lane from the adjacent inshore traffic zone.
> ⓓ Precautionary Area : A routing measure comprising an area within defined limits where ships must navigate with particular caution and within which the direction of traffic flow may be recommended.
> ⓔ Routing System : A scheme which separates traffic proceeding in opposite or nearly opposite direction by the use of a separation zone or line, traffic lanes or by other means.

① 없다. ② 1개 ③ 2개 ④ 3개

03 다음 중 SMCP 단어와 설명이 옳지 않은 것은 몇 개인가?

> ⓐ Fire patrol : A member of the watch going around the vessel at certain intervals so that an outbreak of fire may be promptly detected. *mandatory in vessels carrying more than 36 passengers.
> ⓑ Make Water(to) : Sea water flowing into the vessel due to hull damage or hatches awash and not properly closed.
> ⓒ Initial Course : On or towards the sheltered side of a ship, opposite of windward.
> ⓓ Stripping : Final pumping of tank's residues.
> ⓔ Retreat signal : Sound, visual or other signal to a team ordering it to return to its base.
> ⓕ Shackle : Length of chain cable measuring 15 fathoms.
>   * 1fathom : 1.82m

① 1개 ② 2개 ③ 3개 ④ 4개

04 빈칸에 들어갈 알맞은 말은 무엇인가?

> (   ) means a vessel which from the nature of her work is restricted in her ability to manoeuvre as required by these Rules and is therefore unable to keep out of the way of another vessel.

① Vessel restricted in her ability to manoeuvre
② Vessel engaged in fishing
③ Vessel constrained by her draught
④ Vessel not under command

05 다음 용어에 대한 설명 중 옳지 않은 것은 몇 개인가?

① Rescue – an operation to retrieve persons in distress, provide for their initial medical or other needs, and deliver them to place of safety.
② Alert Phase – A situation wherein apprehension exists as to the safety of a vessel and the persons on board.
③ Uncertainty Phase – A situation wherein uncertainty exists as to the safety of a vessel and the persons on board.
④ Distress Phase – A generic term meaning, as the case may be, uncertainty phase, alert phase or distress phase.

06 다음 중 VHF 무선 통신 사용에 대해 잘못 설명한 것은?

① When possible, the lowest transmitter power necessary for satisfactory communication should be used.
② Transmitting without correct identification should be avoided.
③ Where the information isn't immediately available but soon will be, say "Stand by."
④ If communications on a channel are unsatisfactory, indicate change of channel and do not await confirmation.

07 다음은 일반 선박과 도선사와의 대화이다. IMO 표준해사통신영어로 ㉠,㉡,㉢에 가장 알맞은 것은?

> A : This is M/V SARAH. How do you read me?
> B : Read you good. Good morning M/V SARAH. This is ULSAN pilot. What is your (㉠)?
> A : My (㉠) is 0900UTC.
> B : Roger that. Please approach to the (㉡) with dead slow ahead.
> A : Roger that. Which side should I (㉢) the pilot ladder?
> B : Lee-side please.

    ㉠   ㉡   ㉢
① ETA - break water - hang
② ETA - pilot station - rig
③ ETD - No. buoy - rig
④ ETD - pilot station - hang

08 다음은 UNCLOS Article13의 내용을 발췌한 것이다. 빈칸에 들어갈 말로 적절한 것은?

> (　　) is a naturally formed area of land which is surrounded by and above water at low tide but submerged at high tide.

① straight line　　② low tide elevation
③ port　　④ artificial island

09 다음 중 아래에서 설명하고 있는 내용상 빈칸에 들어갈 단어를 고르시오.

> (　　) is a craft capable of sustaining the lives of persons in distress from the time of abandoning the ship.

① Life raft　　② Rescue boat
③ Life boat　　④ Survival craft

10 다음 SMCP의 약자에 대한 설명이다. ㉠㉡㉢㉣에 해당하는 내용으로 가장 옳은 것은?

㉠ Very High Frequency
㉡ Ultra High Frequency
㉢ Medium Frequency
㉣ High Frequency

	㉠	㉡	㉢	㉣
①	UHF	VHF	MF	HF
②	VHF	UHF	MF	HF
③	VHF	UHF	HF	MF
④	VHF	UTC	MF	HF

11 빈칸에 들어갈 알맞은 말을 고르시오.

When sailing along the coast, to avoid sunken rocks, shoals, or dangerous obstruction at or below the surface of the water, and which are marked on the chart, the navigator may pass these at any desired distance by using what is known as (   ).

① danger
② sounding
③ transit
④ cross bearing

12 다음은 ISPS에 관한 설명이다. 가장 적절하지 않은 것은?

① "ISPS code" means the international code for the Security of ships and of port facilities consisting of part A(shall be treated as mandatory) and part B(shall be treated as recommendatory)as adopted, on 12 December 2002, by SOLAS.
② "Security Incident" means the qualification of the degree of risk that a security incident will be attempted or will occur.
③ "Security level 2" means the level for which appropriate additional protective security measures shall be maintained for a period of time as a result of heightened risk of a security incident.
④ "Port Facility" means a location, as determined by the contracting government or by the designated Authority, where the ship/port interface takes place.

13 다음 중 빈칸에 들어갈 말로 가장 적절한 것은?

> All the distances given on the charts for the visibility of lights are calculated for (　　) of 5 metres.

① a minimum height of eye
② a height of observer's eye
③ a standard height of a light
④ a height of standard light

14 다음 빈칸에 들어갈 말은 무엇인가?

> In case the temperature is decreasing at constant quantity of air and humidity, the humidity will be increased relatively and the moisture in the air shall begin to be liquefied at some point of temperature that is called at (　　).

① dew point
③ absolute humidity
② relative humidity
④ freezing point

15 다음 설명 중 옳은 것의 개수를 고르시오.

> ⓐ If two more radio waves arrive simultaneously at the same point in space, result in multiple reflection.
> ⓑ radar interference can be created by reflection between own ship and an object before the scanner finally collects its energy. we will see a line of targets on the same bearing and with equal distance between them.
> ⓒ Super refraction may be caused by radio-waves reflected by water surface or windows, buildings.
> ⓓ Blind Sector is an area which can not be scanned by the ship's radar because it is shielded by parts of the superstructure, etc.

① 1개　② 2개　③ 3개　④ 4개

16 다음 중 COLREG 상 규정하는 Safe Speed를 결정하기 위한 요소로 알맞지 않은 것을 고르시오.

① the characteristics, efficiency and limitations of the radar equipment
② the state of visibility
③ the state of wind, sea and current, and the proximity of navigational hazards
④ the officer's good seamanship

17 다음 중 SMCP 용어 설명 중 옳지 않은 것은 무엇인가?

① dredging of anchor : A movement of an anchor over the sea bottom to control the movement of the vessel.
② Abandon vessel : To evacuate crew and passengers from a vessel following a distress.
③ Rescue Signal : a kind of signal with sound, visual or other methods to a team ordering it to return to its base in the search and rescue operation.
④ Casualty : Case of death in an accident or shipping disaster.

18 다음 중 빈칸에 들어갈 단어를 순서대로 고른 것은?

> ⓐ Light house are built on dangerous rocks in the sea. Lantern in theses houses throw light over the dark water to help sailors (   ).
> ⓑ The direction of the current is true, not magnetic, and is the direction (   ) which the current is setting, while the wind given is in the direction (   ) which it is blowing.

① keep their ships from being wrecked, toward, from
② keep their ships from being wrecked, from, toward
③ judge how deep the sea is, from, toward
④ judge how deep the sea is, toward, from

19 다음은 구명정 진수방식에 대한 정의이다. 진수 타입을 알맞게 연결한 것을 고르시오.

> ⓐ (   ) launching is that method of launching a survival craft whereby the craft is automatically released from a sinking ship and is ready for use.
>
> ⓑ (   ) launching is that method of launching a survival craft whereby the craft with its complement of persons and equipment on board is released and allowed to fall into the sea without any restraining apparatus.

① Free-fall, Float-free
② Float-free, Free-fall
③ Inflatable, Free-fall
④ Inflated, Float-free

20 SMCP에서 사용하는 표현으로 문장이 어색한 것은?

① Vessels are advised to keep clear of this area.
② Vessels must navigate by caution.
③ My vessel is under pirate attack.
④ You must alter your course to port side.

16 회차 해사영어 모의고사

01 빈칸에 들어갈 말을 순서대로 고른 것은?

ⓐ ( ) : means that in any sea conditions water will not penetrate into the ship.
ⓑ ( ) : means having scantlings and arrangements capable of preventing the passage of water in any direction under the head of water likely to occur in intact and damaged conditions. In the damaged condition, the head of water is to be considered in the worst situations at equilibrium, including intermediate stages of flooding.

	ⓐ	ⓑ
①	waterproof	watertight
②	watertight	weathertight
③	weathertight	watertight
④	weathertight	waterproof

02 다음 괄호에 알맞은 말을 순서대로 고르시오.

- You must ( ) up anchor.
  귀선은 양묘하시오.
- The tide is ( ) you.
  조류가 순조이다.
- The tide is ( ) you.
  조류가 역조이다.
- You are ( ) into danger.
  귀선은 위험 지역으로 향하고 있다.

① heave - with - against - running
② heave - for - past - running
③ heaving - with - against - running
④ heaving - for - past - running

03 COLREG 20조에서 빈칸에 순서대로 들어가기에 가장 적절한 것을 고르시오.

> The Rules concerning lights shall be complied with from ( ) to ( ).

① sunrise, sunset   ② morning, evening
③ sunset, sunrise   ④ evening, morning

04 다음은 COLREG의 선박의 조종 및 경고신호에 관한 내용이다. 빈칸으로 적절한 것은?

> If whistles are fitted on a vessel at a distance apart of more than ( )m, one whistle only shall be used for giving manoeuvring and warning signals

① 100   ② 55   ③ 200   ④ 50

05 Choose a proper word to a blank each.

> When ship's balance between gravity and ( ) is broken, ship will lose her ( ) and be capsized in a result.

① attraction – hull   ② reaction – movement
③ buoyancy – stability   ④ density – pitching

06 IAMSAR 상의 단어와 설명이 잘못된 것의 개수를 고르시오.

> ⓐ Alert phase : A situation wherein apprehension exists as to the safety of an aircraft or marine vessel and of the persons on board.
> ⓑ Global satellite system : A satellite system designed to detect and locate activated distress beacons transmitting in the frequency of 406.0–406.1 MHz.
> ⓒ Distress phase : A situation wherein there is reasonable certainty that a vessel or other craft, including an aircraft or a person, is threatened by grave and imminent danger and requires immediate assistance.
> ⓓ Cospas-sarsat : An organization which operates a system of geostationary satellites and other emergency communications system.

① 1개   ② 2개   ③ 3개   ④ 모두 맞다.

07 다음 정의에 부합하는 통신의 종류로 옳은 것은?

> (   ) : Operational and public correspondence, traffic other than distress, urgency and safety messages, transmitted or received by radio.

① Safety Communication   ② Urgent Communication
③ Distress Communication   ④ General Communication

08 ISPS 상 (a),(b),(c)에 들어갈 말을 고르시오.

> - Security level (a) means the level for which minimum appropriate protective security measures shall be maintained at all times.
> - Security level (b) means the level for which further specific protective security measures shall be maintained for a limited period of time when a security incident is probable or imminent.
> - Security level (c) mean the level for which appropriate additional protective security measures shall be maintained for a period of time as a result of heightened risk of a security incident.

① (a) 1 – (b) 3 – (c) 2   ② (a) 1 – (b) 2 – (c) 3
③ (a) 2 – (b) 1 – (c) 3   ④ (a) 3 – (b) 1 – (c) 2

09 다음 COLREG와 관련된 내용에서 빈칸에 들어갈 수 없는 사람을 고르시오.

> Rule 2 Responsibility
> (a) Nothing in these Rules shall exonerate (   ) from the consequences of any neglect to comply with these Rules or of the neglect of any precaution which may be required by the ordinary practice of seamen, or by the special circumstances of the case.

① the crew
② the owner of the ship
③ the port control officer
④ the master

10 다음 COLREG 상 Safe Speed에 대한 내용 중 틀린 것을 고르시오.

> Every vessel shall at all times proceed at a safe speed so that she can take proper and effective action to avoid collision and be stopped within a distance appropriate to the prevailing circumstances and conditions. In determining a safe speed the following factors shall be among those taken into account by all vessels :
> (i) the state of visibility;
> (ii) the ㉠traffic density including concentrations of fishing vessels or any other vessels;
> (iii) the ㉡manoeuvrability of the vessel with special reference to stopping distance and turning ability in the prevailing conditions;
> (iv) at night the presence of ㉢side direction light such as from shore lights or from back scatter of her own lights;
> (v) the state of wind, sea and current, and the ㉣proximity of navigational hazards;
> (vi) the draught in relation to the available depth of water.

① ㉠   ② ㉡   ③ ㉢   ④ ㉣

11 다음 COLREG 상의 용어 설명 중 틀린 것은?

① <u>vessel not under command</u> : a vessel which through some exceptional circumstance is unable to manoeuvre as required by these Rules and is therefore unable to keep out of the way of another vessel.
② <u>length and breadth</u> : length overall and greatest breadth.
③ <u>vessel constrained by her draught</u> : a power-driven vessel which because of her draught in relation to the available depth and width of navigable water, is severely restricted in her ability to deviate from the course she is following.
④ <u>vessel engaged in fishing</u> : any vessel fishing with nets, lines, trawls or other fishing apparatus which do not restrict maneuverability.

12 다음 SOLAS의 내용 설명 중 빈칸에 들어갈 말로 올바른 것은?

> (   ) is protective suit for use by rescue boat and marine evacuation system parties.

① Immersion suit
② life jacket
③ thermal protective aids
④ Anti-exposure suit

13 다음 빈칸에 들어갈 내용을 고르시오.

> Risk of collision exists when (   ) of an approaching vessel does not appreciably change.

① compass bearing
② speed
③ turing circle
④ track

14 다음은 STCW의 일부 내용이다. 빈칸에 들어갈 숫자의 합은 무엇인가?

> All person who are assigned duty as officer in of a watch or as a rating forming part of a watch shall be provided with a rest period of not less than a minimum of ( ) hours of rest in any 24 hour period.
> The hours of rest may be divided into no more than two periods, one of which shall be at least ( ) hours in length, and the intervals between consecutive periods of rest shall not exceed ( ) hours.

① 24　　② 26　　③ 28　　④ 30

15 다음 MARPOL의 용어가 의미하는 것은?

> A tank used for the collection and stowage of seawage

① slop tank　　　　② ballast tank
③ holding tank　　　④ bilge tank

16 다음 중 MARPOL 상 틀린 것은 무엇인가?

① 'Oil' means petroleum in any form including crude oil, fuel oil, sludge, oil refuse and refined products.
② 'Oil tanker' means a ship designed to carry either oil or solid cargoes in bulk.
③ 'Oil fuel' means any oil used as fuel in connection with the propulsion and auxiliary machinery of the ship in which such oil is carried.
④ 'Oily mixture' means a mixture with any oil content.

17 다음은 MARPOL 상 '분리 평형수'에 대한 정의 부분이다. 다음 빈칸의 알맞은 용어를 고르시오.

> Segregated ballast means the ballast water introduced into a ( ) which is completely separated from the cargo oil and oil fuel system and which is permanently allocated to the carriage of ballast.

① ballast
② tank
③ oil
④ cargo

18 다음 SOLAS 상 빈칸에 들어갈 말로 가장 옳은 것은?

> The main steering gear rudder stock shall be capable of putting the rudder from (a) on either side (b) on the other side in not more than 28 seconds at its deepest seagoing draught and running ahead at (c) ahead service speed.

① (a) 30° / (b) 30° / (c) 7 knots
② (a) 30° / (b) 35° / (c) one half of maximum
③ (a) 35° / (b) 30° / (c) maximum
④ (a) 35° / (b) 35° / (c) minimum

19 다음 빈칸에 들어가기에 가장 적절한 말은?

> I have a man overboard at the Singapore strait, please help ( ).

① medical assistance
② I am adrift
③ to emergency anchorage
④ with search and rescue assistance

20 다음은 STCW 상의 각종 당직 및 당직 교대에 관한 규정들이다. 옳지 않은 것을 고르시오.

① The duties of the look-out and helmsperson are gathered and helmsperson shall be considered to be the look-out while steering.
② If at any time the officer in charge of the navigational watch is to be relieved when a manoeuvre or other action to avoid any hazard is taking place, the relief of that officer shall be deferred until such action has been completed.
③ The officer in charge of the navigation watch shall in no circumstances leave the bridge until properly relieved.
④ Radio operator are responsible for maintaining a continuous radio watch on appropriate frequencies during their periods of duty.

17 해사영어 모의고사

01 빈칸에 들어갈 말을 순서대로 고른 것은?

> ⓐ (　　　) : a place assigned to a vessel when anchored or lying alongside a pier, etc.
> ⓑ (　　　) : ladder attached to platform at vessel's side with flat steps and handrails enabling persons to embark/disembark from water or shore.
> ⓒ (　　　) : a sea room to be kept for safety around a vessel, rock, platform, etc.

① space - embarkation ladder - berth
② berth - accommodation ladder - berth
③ berth - embarkation ladder - clearance
④ space - accommodation ladder - clearance

02 SMCP에 따라 다음 문장들을 말할 때, 빈칸에 들어갈 message marker로 알맞은 것은?

> - (　　　). Do I have permission to enter the fairway?
> - (　　　). I will alter my course to 225°.
> - (　　　). You are running into danger.

① QUESTION - ADVICE - MAYDAY
② ADVICE - ADVICE - WARNING
③ QUESTION - INTENTION - WARNING
④ QUESTION - INFORMATION - WARNING

03 다음 IAMSAR의 용어 중 틀린 것은?

① ACO : Aircraft commander
② CSS : Co-ordinator surface search
③ OSC : On-scene coordinator
④ RCC : Rescue co-ordination centre

04 다음 UNCLOS의 무해통항권의 '통항'에 관한 규정 내용 중 잘못된 부분의 개수를 고르시오.

> (Part2. Section3. Article18 - Meaning of passage)
>
> 1. Passage means navigation through the territorial sea for the purpose of :
> - traversing that sea without entering ⓐ<u>external waters</u> or calling at a roadstead or port facility outside internal waters; or
> - proceeding to or from ⓑ<u>internal waters</u> or a call at such roadstead or port facility.
>
> 2. Passage shall be ⓒ<u>continuous and expeditious</u>. However, passage includes stopping and anchoring, but only in so far as the same are incidental to ordinary navigation or are rendered necessary by ⓓ<u>force majeure</u> or distress or for the purpose of rendering assistance to persons, ships or aircraft in danger or distress.

① 1개   ② 2개   ③ 3개   ④ 4개

05 다음은 COLREG 'action to avoid collision'에 대한 내용이다. 밑줄 친 단어 중 옳지 않은 것은 모두 몇 개인가?

> Ⅰ. A succession of small alternations of course and/or speed should be ㉠avoided.
> Ⅱ. if there is ㉡sufficient sea room ㉢alteration of course alone may be the most effective action to avoid a close-quarters situation provided that it is made in good time, is substantial and does not result in another close-quarters situations.
> Ⅲ. If necessary to avoid collision or allow more time to assess the situation, a vessel shall ㉣increase her speed or take way off by stopping or reversing her means of propulsion.
> Ⅳ. A vessel the passage of which is not to be impeded remains fully ㉤recommended to comply with the rules of this part when the two vessels are approaching one another so as to involve risk of collision.

① 1개   ② 2개   ③ 3개   ④ 4개

06 표준해사통신용어 상 사용되는 글자의 철자이다. 옳지 않은 것은 모두 몇 개인가?

	ⓐ	ⓑ	ⓒ	ⓓ	ⓔ
Letter	G	L	M	T	X
Code	Golf	Lomeo	Mike	Tango	X-ray

① 1개   ② 2개   ③ 3개   ④ 4개

07 아래 빈칸에 들어갈 수 없는 말은?

> "내일 아침으로 출항이 연기되었다."
> "( ) her departure till tomorrow morning."

① Put off
② Put on
③ Postponed
④ Delayed

08 ISPS 적용 선박이 아닌 것은?

① passenger ships engaged in international voyage
② cargo ship of 500 gross tonnage and upwards engaged on international voyage
③ Warships, naval auxiliaries or other ships owned or operated by Contracting Government
④ mobile offshore drilling units

09 Choose similar meaning with underlined word.

> When our vessel is stranded to shallow water, we jettison of cargo to make ship afloat.

① burn   ② shift   ③ transfer   ④ lighten

10 다음 COLREG 상 Risk of Collision에 대한 내용 중 틀린 것을 고르시오.

> Rule 7 Risk of Collision
> - Every vessel shall use all available means appropriate to the prevailing circumstances and conditions to determine if risk of collision exists. If there is any doubt such risk shall be deemed to exist.
> - Proper use shall be made of radar equipment if fitted and operational, including ①long-range scanning to obtain early warning of risk of collision and radar plotting or equivalent systematic observation of detected objects.
> - Assumptions ②shall be made on the basis of scanty information, especially scanty radar information.
> - In determining if risk of collision exists the following considerations shall be among those taken into account :
> i. Such risk shall be deemed to exist if the ③compass bearing of an approaching vessel does not appreciably change;
> ii. such risk may sometimes exist even when an appreciable bearing change is evident, particularly when approaching a ④very large vessel or a tow or when approaching a vessel at close range.

11 다음 COLREG 상의 용어 설명 중 틀린 것은?

① vessel : includes every description of water craft, including non-displacement craft, WIG craft and seaplanes, used or capable of being used as a means of transportation on water.
② power-driven vessel : any vessel propelled by machinery.
③ sailing vessel : any vessel under sail provided that propelling machinery, if fitted, is not being used.
④ seaplane : includes any craft designed to manoeuvre under the water.

12 다음 SMCP 표현 중 빈칸에 들어갈 올바른 단어를 고르시오.

- Send (㉠) the 00 spring(s) forward/aft.
  : 선수 선미의 스프링 라인을 00줄 내어주시오.
- Heave (㉡) the fore breast line.
  : 선수 옆 줄을 계속 감으시오.
- pick (㉢) the slack on the bow line.
  : 선수 줄의 늘어짐을 팽팽하게 하시오.

	㉠	㉡	㉢
①	out	down	over
②	out	on	up
③	into	down	over
④	into	on	up

13 다음 SOLAS 내용 상 빈칸에 들어갈 것은?

- Sea area (   ) means an area within the radiotelephone coverage of at least one VHF coast station in which continuous DSC alerting is available, as may be defined by a Contracting Government.
- Sea area (   ) means an area, excluding sea area A1, within the radiotelephone coverage of at least one MF coast station in which continuous DSC alerting is available, as may be defined by a Contracting Government.

① A1 - A2   ② A1 - A3   ③ A2 - A1   ④ A3 - A1

14 다음은 MARPOL Garbage 처리 규정이다. ⓐ의 숫자로 옳은 것은?

> Discharge of the following garbage into the sea outside special areas shall only be permitted while the ship is en route and as far as practicable from the nearest land, but in any case not less than :
> 3 nautical miles from the nearest land for food wastes which have been passed through a comminuter or grinder. Such comminuted or ground food wastes shall be capable of passing through a screen with openings no greater than (ⓐ)mm.

① 10 ② 15 ③ 20 ④ 25

15 다음 MARPOL에서 설명하는 것은 무엇인가?

> any substance which, if introduced into the sea, is liable to create hazards to human health, to harm living resources and marine life, to damage amenities or interface with other legitimate uses of the sea, and includes any substances subject to control by the present Convention.

① Harmful substances ② Oil fuel
③ Oil Mixture ④ Oil

16 다음 Seawage 배출규정 중 틀린 것은?

> Annex IV / Reg. 9 Sewage Systems
> the ship is discharging comminuted and disinfected sewage using a system approved by the Administration at a distance of more than ①6 nautical miles from the nearest land or sewage which is not comminuted or disinfected at a distance of more than ②12 nautical miles from the nearest land, provided that in any case, the sewage that has been stored in ③holding thanks shall not be discharged instantaneously but at a moderate rate when the ship is en route and proceeding at not less than ④4 knots; the rate of discharge shall be approved by the Administration based upon standards developed by the Organization.

17 다음 MARPOL 상 "Holding tank capacity" 에 관한 내용이다. ⓐ,ⓑ에 순서대로 들어갈 수 있는 것으로 옳은 항목은?

> A holding tank of the capacity to the satisfaction of the Administration for the retention of all sewage, having regard to the operation of the ship, the (ⓐ) on board and other relevant factors. The holding tank shall be constructed to the satisfaction of the Administration and shall have a means to indicate (ⓑ) the amount of its contents.

	ⓐ	ⓑ
①	number of person	invisibly
②	number of person	visually
③	amount of cargo	visually
④	amount of cargo	invisibly

18 UNCLOS 상 빈칸에 순서대로 들어갈 말을 고르시오.

> An archipelagic State may draw straight archipelagic baseline joining the outermost points of the outermost islands and drying reefs of the archipelago provided that within such baselines are included the main islands and an area in which the ratio of the area of the water to the area of the land, including atolls, is between (   ) and (   ).

① 1 to 1 / 8 to 1 ② 1 to 1 / 1 to 9
③ 1 to 1 / 9 to 1 ④ 1 to 1 / 2 to 1

19 다음 중 밑줄 친 부분의 가장 가까운 의미는?

> Large vessel is leaving. <u>Keep clear of</u> approach channel.

① close ② pass ③ Avoid ④ Go by

20 다음 빈칸에 가장 알맞을 말을 고르시오.

> When the general emergency alarm is sounded with seven short blasts and one prolonged blast, all passengers have to go to their (   ).

① mess room
② bridge
③ muster station
④ embarkation ladder

18 회차 해사영어 모의고사

01 빈칸에 들어갈 말을 순서대로 고른 것은?

> ⓐ (　　　) : A sound signal made with the whistle of the vessel.
> ⓑ (　　　) : Areas which cannot be scanned by the radar of the vessel because they are shielded by parts of its superstructure, masts, etc, or shore obstructions.
> ⓒ (　　　) : Turning of a vessel upside down while on water.

① whistle - blind sectors - capsizing
② bell - blind center - listing
③ blast - blind center - sinking
④ blast - blind sectors - capsizing

02 다음 괄호에 알맞은 말을 순서대로 고르시오.

> - I am (ⓐ) attack by pirates.
>   본선은 해적에게 공격받고 있다.
> - I am (ⓑ).
>   본선은 좌초되었다.
> - I (ⓒ) tug assistance.
>   본선은 예인원조를 요청한다.
> - I am (ⓓ).
>   본선은 조종불능상태이다.

　　　　ⓐ　　　ⓑ　　　ⓒ　　　ⓓ
① on / adrift / have / not under control
② on / aground / have / not under control
③ under / adrift / require / not under command
④ under / aground / require / not under command

03 다음 중 빈칸에 들어갈 단어로 가장 옳은 것은?

> You estimate that you will depart from Hamburg port at 2130 hours. 2130 is your (　　).

① ETA　　② ETD　　③ TCPA　　④ ETB

04 빈칸에 알맞은 숫자를 모두 합한 것은?

> - Exclusive Economic Zone of the Republic of Korea is the area of the sea which extends up to (　　) nautical miles from the baseline provided for in Article 2 of the Territorial Sea and Contiguous zone Act, excluding the territorial sea of the Republic of Korea.
> - A vessel shall not use an inshore traffic zone when she can safely use the appropriate traffic lane within the adjacent traffic separation scheme. However, vessels of less than (　)metres in length, sailing vessel and vessels engaged in fishing may use the inshore traffic zone.
> - Every oil tanker of (　)tons gross tonnage and above and every ship (　)tons gross tonnage and above other than an oil tanker shall be provided with an Oil Record Book Part 1.

① 770　　② 800　　③ 870　　④ 900

05 다음 IAMSAR의 용어 중 틀린 것은?

① Emergency Position Indicating Radar Beacon (EPIRB)
② Search And Rescue (radar) Transponder (SART)
③ Search and Rescue Unit (SRU)
④ SAR Mission Coordinator (SMC)

06 다음 중 수색목표물의 위치를 가장 정확히 알고 있을 때 효과적인 수색방식에 해당하는 것은 모두 몇 개인가?

> ⓐ Due to the small area involved, this procedure must not be used simultaneously by multiple aircraft at similar altitudes or by multiple vessels.
> ⓑ Most effective when the position of the search object is accurately known and the search area is small.
> ⓒ Normally used when an aircraft or vessel has disappeared without a trace along a known route.
> ⓓ Used to search a large area when survivor location is uncertain.
> ⓔ Search may be along the intended track and once on each side, then search facility continues on its way and does not return.

① 1개   ② 2개   ③ 3개   ④ 4개

07 다음 중 UNCLOS 상 영해에서 Criminal Jurisdiction on board a foreign ship의 지원을 요청할 수 있는 사람의 개수를 고르시오.

> 가. master of the ship
> 나. diplomatic agent of the port state
> 다. consular office of the flag state
> 라. consular office of the coastal state

① 1개   ② 2개   ③ 3개   ④ 4개

08 다음 빈칸에 들어갈 말로 가장 적절한 것은?

> According to COLREG'72, every vessel shall at all time proceed at a "safe speed". Safe speed is defined as that speed which (   ).

① you can stop within your visibility range.
② you are travelling at a slower speed than surrounding vessels.
③ you can take proper and effective action to avoid collision.
④ no wake comes from your vessel.

09 다음 중 빈칸에 들어갈 가장 알맞은 말을 순서대로 고른 것은?

- Every vessel shall at all times maintain a proper (ⓐ) by sight and hearing as well as by all available means appropriate in the prevailing circumstances and condition so as to make a full appraisal of the situation and of (ⓑ).
- (ⓒ) shall be continuous and expeditious. However, (ⓒ) includes stopping and anchoring, but only in so far as the same are incidental to ordinary navigation, force majeure or distress or for the purpose of rendering assistance to persons, ships of aircraft in danger or distress.

	ⓐ	ⓑ	ⓒ
①	safe speed	the risk of aground	navigation
②	safe speed	the risk of collision	navigation
③	look out	the risk of collision	passage
④	look out	the risk of aground	passage

10 유엔해양법 협약 상 ( ) 안에 들어갈 적절한 말은?

In the territorial sea, submarines and other underwater vehicles are required to navigate (   ).

① under the water and to show their flag
② on the surface and to show their flag
③ on the surface and to show their bridge
④ under the water and to show bridge

11 다음 COLREG 관련 용어 설명 중 틀린 것은?

① Vessel Making-way : a moving vessel by wind or sea.
② Wing-In-Ground (WIG) craft : a multimodal craft which, in its main operational mode, flies in close proximity to the surface by utilizing surface-effect action.
③ restricted visibility : any condition in which visibility is restricted by fog, mist, falling snow, heavy rainstorms, sandstorms or any other similar causes.
④ underway : means that a vessel is not at anchor, or made fast to the shore, or aground.

12 choose the correct one for the blank.

> In Standard Maritime Navigation Vocabulary, the height of a vessel is defined as the height of highest point of vessel's structure (   ).

① under masthead
② above waterline
③ over keel
④ beyond deck line

13 Select the best answer at blank.

> Started (   ) for destruction of vermin & rodents.

① observation
② fumigation
③ ventilation
④ immigration

14 보기 중 UNCLOS 상 연안국의 "territorial sea"에서 행사될 수 있는 것의 개수를 고르시오.

> ⓐ the sovereignty
> ⓑ right of hot pursuit
> ⓒ the right of innocent passage
> ⓓ exclusive jurisdiction
> ⓔ criminal jurisdiction
> ⓕ right of visit

① 2개   ② 3개   ③ 4개   ④ 5개

15 빈칸에 들어갈 알맞은 단어를 고르시오.

> "(   )" means any noxious liquid substance which remains for disposal.

① residue   ② sewage   ③ oil   ④ oil fuel

16 UNCLOS 상 무해통항에 대한 설명 중 옳지 않은 것의 개수를 고르시오.

> ⓐ Passage is innocent so long as it is not prejudicial to the peace, good order or security of the coastal State.
> ⓑ Passage shall be expeditious.
> ⓒ Passage shall be continuous.
> ⓓ Passage of a foreign ship shall be considered to be prejudical to the peace, good order, or security of the Coastal state, if in the territorial sea it engages in the launching, landing or taking on board of any aircraft.

① 없다.　② 1개　③ 2개　④ 3개

17 다음 COLREG 상 조종신호의 보충 시 사용되는 발광신호(flashing light)에 대한 설명으로 옳지 않은 것은?

> (ii) The duration of each flash shall be about ⓐone second, the interval between flashes shall be about ⓑtwo seconds, and the interval between successive signals shall be not less than ⓒtwo minutes.
> (iii) the lights used for this signal shall, if fitted, be an all-round white light, visible at a minimum range of ⓓ5 miles, and shall comply with the provisions of Annex I.

① 없음　② 1개　③ 2개　④ 3개

18 다음 내용 중 밑줄 친 it이 의미하는 것은?

> Chart and light list should be checked to see that they have been corrected through the latest it.

① Notice To Mariner　② Mercator chart
③ Navigation chart　④ Light list

19 다음 SOLAS협약 일부의 빈칸에 들어갈 말을 고르시오.

> Passenger ship muster of crew for boat drill shall take place (   ) when practicable.

① daily
② weekly
③ monthly
④ within 24 hours after departure

20 다음 용어들의 설명 중 틀린 개수를 고르시오.

> ⓐ Convoy : A group of vessels which sail together, e.g. through a canal or ice.
> ⓑ Course made good : That course of which a vessel makes good through the water after allowing for the effect of currents, tidal streams, and leeway caused by wind and sea.
> ⓒ Crash stop : An emergency reversal operation of the main engine to avoid a collision.
> ⓓ Close up : To decrease the distance to the vessel ahead by increasing one's own speed.

① 없음   ② 1개   ③ 2개   ④ 3개

19 해사영어 모의고사

01 빈칸에 들어갈 말을 순서대로 고른 것은?

> ⓐ (　　　) : Major uncontrolled flow of seawater into the vessel.
> ⓑ (　　　) : Often harmful gas produced by fires, chemicals, fuel, etc.
> ⓒ (　　　) : List of crew, passengers, and all on board and their functions in a distress or drill.

① Sinking - Fume - Crew list
② Flooding - Petroleum - Muster list
③ Flooding - Fume - Muster list
④ Sinking - Petroleum - Crew list

02 다음 괄호에 알맞은 말을 순서대로 고르시오.

> - Received your (　　).
>   귀선의 조난통보를 수신하였다.
> - I will (　　) vessel at 1200UTC.
>   본선은 세계시 1200에 퇴선 할 것이다.
> - (　　) on VHF channel 16.
>   VHF 채널16에서 대기하고 있어라.

① PAN-PAN/abandon/ Call
② PAN-PAN/abandon/Stand by
③ MAYDAY/ jettison /Standing by
④ MAYDAY/ abandon /Stand by

03 다음은 UNCLOS 상 Ports에 대한 설명이다. 빈칸에 순서대로 올 내용을 고르시오.

> Article 11 Ports
> For purpose of delimiting the territorial sea, the outer most permanent harbour works which form an (   ) part of the harbour system are regarded as forming part of the coast. Off-shore installations and artificial islands (   ) be considered as permanent harbour works.

① integral - shall not ② unessential - shall not
③ integral - shall ④ unessential - shall

04 다음 빈칸에 들어갈 말로 가장 적합한 것은?

> If shipowner registers his ship in a country other than his own to escape paying some home taxation, to employ labour cheaper than that at home, to benefit financially in any similar way, his ships are said to fly a (   ).

① flag of discrimination ② flag of convenience
③ flag of destination ④ courtesy flag

05 다음 SMCP 용어 중 틀린 것은?

① IMO class : Group of dangerous or hazardous goods, harmful substances or marine pollutants in sea transport as classified in the International Maritime Dangerous Good code (IMDG Code).
② Cable : One hundred fathoms or one tenth of a nautical mile.
③ Cardinal point : A seamark, ie a buoy, indicating the North, East, South or West, ie. the cardinal points from a fixed point such as a wreck, shallow water, banks, etc.
④ Ordnance exercise : Naval firing practice.

06 다음 보기는 SOLAS 상 훈련에 관한 규정이다. 밑줄 친 내용 중 옳지 않은 것은 모두 몇 개인가?

> - The drills of the crew shall take place within ㉠24h of the ship leaving a port if more than 25% of the crew ㉡have participated in abandon ship and fire drills on board that particular ship in the previous month.
> - When a ship enters service for the first time, after modification of a major character or when a new crew ㉢is engaged, these drills shall be held ㉣after sailing.

① 1개　② 2개　③ 3개　④ 4개

07 IAMSAR 상의 Sector Search에 대한 설명으로 가장 옳지 않은 것은?

① Most effective when the position of the search object is accurately known and the search area is small. Used to search a circular area centred on a datum point.
② Due to the small area involved, this procedure must not be used simultaneously by multiple aircraft at similar altitude or by multiple vessels.
③ Search legs are parallel to each other and to the long sides of the sub-area.
④ A suitable marker (for example, a smoke float or a radio beacon) may be dropped at the datum position and used as a reference or navigational aid marking the centre of the pattern.

08 다음 중 항해일지의 기사를 바르게 해석한 것은 모두 몇 개인가?

> ⓐ Secured all derrick booms & other fittings.
> 　　: 데릭 붐 및 기타 속구를 모두 점검함.
> ⓑ Singled up fore & aft, prepared for sea.
> 　　: 선수미에 계류삭을 하나씩만 남기고 거두어 들였으며 출항준비를 함.
> ⓒ Laboured heavily shipping seas on deck frequently.
> 　　: 선체가 심하게 흔들리고 해수가 갑판으로 자주 올라옴.
> ⓓ Last line to pier let go.
> 　　: 부두의 마지막 계류삭을 벗김.
> ⓔ Started to heave up port anchor.
> 　　: 좌현묘를 내리기 시작함.

① 2개　② 3개　③ 4개　④ 5개

09 다음 빈칸에 알맞은 단어를 고르시오.

> ( ) is brought about when the ship is supported fore and aft by two waves, so that the middle of the vessel is strained in the opposite direction.

① Rolling ② Stranding ③ Hogging ④ Sagging

10 다음 중 COLREG 내용 상 틀린 것의 개수는?

> Rule 9 Narrow Channels
> (a) A vessel proceeding along the course of a narrow channel or fairway shall keep as near to the ①outer limit of the channel or fairway which lies on her starboard side as is safe and practicable.
> (b) A vessel of less than ②12 metres in length or a sailing vessel shall not impede the passage of a vessel which can safely navigate only within a narrow channel or fairway.
> (c) A vessel ③engaged in fishing shall not impede the passage of any other vessel navigating within a narrow channel or fairway.
> (d) A vessel shall not cross a narrow channel or fairway if such crossing ④impedes the passage of a vessel which can safely navigate only within such channel or fairway. The latter vessel may use the sound signal prescribed in Rule 34(d) if in doubt as to the intention of the crossing vessel.

① 없음 ② 1개 ③ 2개 ④ 3개

11 다음은 SOLAS 협약 상 Line-throwing appliances에 관한 설명이다. 항목 중 옳지 않은 것은 몇 개인가?

> ⓐ be capable of throwing a line with unaccuracy.
> ⓑ include not less than 4 projectiles each capable of carrying the line at least 250m in calm weather.
> ⓒ include not less than 4 lines each having a breaking strength of not less than 2kN.
> ⓓ have brief instructions or diagrams clearly illustrating the use of the line- throwing appliance.

① 1개 ② 2개 ③ 3개 ④ 4개

12 다음 COLREG 상의 sailing vessel에 대한 등화 설명 중 틀린 것은?

> Rule 25 : Sailing Vessels underway and Vessels under Oars
> (a) A sailing vessel underway shall exhibit :
>   (i) sidelights;
>   (ii) a stern light.
> (b) In a sailing vessel of less than ①20meters in length the lights prescribed in paragraph (a) of this Rule may be combined in one lantern carried at or near the top of the mast where it can best be seen.
> (c) A sailing vessel underway may, in addition to the lights prescribed in paragraph (a) of this Rule, exhibit at or near the top of the mast, where they can best be seen, two all-round lights in a vertical line, the upper being ②red and the lower ③green, but these lights ④may be exhibited in conjunction with the combined lantern permitted by paragraph (b) of this Rule.

13 다음은 COLREG의 내용 중 정박선의 등화 표시에 관한 내용이다. 옳지 않은 것의 개수는?

> (a) A vessel at anchor shall exhibit where it can best be seen :
> (i) in the fore part, ⓐan white masthead light or one ball
> (ii) at or near the stern and at ⓑa higher level than the light prescribed in sub-paragraph(i), ⓒan all round white light.
> (b) A vessel of less than ⓓ100metres in length may exhibit an all-round white light where it can best be seen instead of the lights prescribed in paragraph (a) of this Rule.

① 1개   ② 2개   ③ 3개   ④ 4개

14 빈칸에 순서대로 들어갈 단어를 고르시오.

- ( ) are circles on a sphere whose planes pass through the center of the sphere.
- In case all efforts to save damaged vessel prove to be unsuccessful, she will be ( ).

① Great Circle, jettisoned
② Great Circle, abandoned
③ Meridian, abandoned
④ Meridian, jettisoned

15 다음은 SOLAS 내용 중 유아 및 어린이용 life-jacket 비치에 관한 내용이다. 틀린 것은?

(Chapter III / Regulation 7 Personal life-saving appliances)
2.1.1 for passenger ships on voyages less than 24h, a number of infant lifejackets equal to at least ①2.5% of the number of passengers on board shall be provided;
.2 for passenger ship on voyages 24h or greater, infant life-jackets shall be provided for ②each infant on board.
.3 a number of lifejackets suitable for children equal to at least ③10% of the number of passengers on board shall be provided or such ④smaller number as may be required to provide a lifejacket for each child;

16 UNCLOS 상 관할국이 다음 관할권을 지니게 되는 해역을 고르시오.

sovereign rights for the purpose of exploring and exploiting, conserving and managing the natural resources, whether living or non-living, of the waters superjacent to the seabed and of the seabed and its subsoil, and with regard to other activities for the economic exploitation and exploration of the zone, such as the production of energy from the water, currents and winds.

① continental shelf
② territorial sea
③ contiguous zone
④ exclusive economic zone

17 What is mean by the term "anchor aweigh?"
① Anchor is clear of the bottom.
② Anchor is up anchor with short stay.
③ brought up anchor with short stay.
④ the direction of anchor is right angled to the sea bottom.

18 다음 구조법 중 One turn에 대한 설명으로 옳은 것은 몇 개인가?

> ⓐ fastest recovery method.
> ⓑ very difficult for a single-screw vessel.
> ⓒ takes the ship farther away from the scene of the incident.
> ⓓ make good original track line.
> ⓔ good for ships with tight stability.
> ⓕ used most by ship with normal power.

① 1개　② 2개　③ 3개　④ 4개

19 다음은 SOLAS 내용 중 일부이다. 빈칸에 들어갈 알맞은 말은?

> (Chapter III / Regulation 19 Emergency training and drills)
> On a ship engaged on voyage, where passengers are scheduled to be on board for more than 24h, musters of newly-embarked passengers shall take place (　　　). Passengers shall be instructed in the use of the lifejackets and the action to take in an emergency.

① weekly
② within 24h after their embarkation
③ prior to or immediately upon departure
④ before sailing

20 다음 약어 설명 중 틀린 것은?
① GPS - Global Positioning System
② E.P - Estimated Position
③ ARPA - Automatic Radar Position Aids
④ MOB - Man Over Board

해사영어 모의고사

01 빈칸에 들어갈 말을 순서대로 고른 것은?

> ⓐ (　　　) : A winch which applies tension to mooring line to keep them tight.
> ⓑ (　　　) : Orders of the Master to the officer of watch which s/he must comply with.
> ⓒ (　　　) : A position a vessel has to pass or at which she has to alter course according to her voyage plan.

① Tension winch / Standing Order / Way point
② Tension winch / Night Order / Way point
③ Fairlead / Standing Order / Way point
④ Fairlead / Night Order/ Rhumb line

02 What is the underlined means?

> Our ship passed over eye of hurricane, and encountered a lull, rain stopped and wind became weak for a short time.

① trade wind　　　　　② calm interval
③ high pressure　　　　④ isobar

03 SMCP의 Message Marker에 예시 중 빈칸에 들어갈 말은?

> "(　　　), unknown vessel will overtake to the west of another unknown vessel."

① Instruction　② Intention　③ Information　④ Danger

04 다음 UNCLOS 상 규정 빈칸에 공통으로 들어갈 말은?

> Article 26
> Charges which may be (　) upon foreign ships
> 1. No charge may be (　) upon foreign ships by reason only of their passage through the territorial sea.
> 2. Charges may be (　) upon a foreign ship passing through the territorial sea as payment only for specific services rendered to the ship. These charges shall be (　) without discrimination.

① navigated　② gone　③ levied　④ called

05 UNCLOS Article 27 상의 내용 중 틀린 것의 개수는?

> Article 27(Criminal jurisdiction on board a foreign ship)
> 1. The criminal jurisdiction of the coastal State should not be exercised on board a foreign ship passing through the territorial sea to arrest any person or to conduct any investigation in connection with any crime committed ㉠on board the ship during its passage, save only in the following cases :
> (a) if the consequences of the crime extend to the ㉡flag State;
> (b) if the crime is of a kind to disturb the peace of ㉢the country or the good order of the territorial sea;
> (c) if the assistance of the local authorities has been requested by the master of the ship or by a diplomatic agent or consular officer of the ㉣coastal State; or
> (d) if such measures are necessary for the suppression of illicit traffic in narcotic drugs or psychotropic substances.

① 1개　② 2개　③ 3개　④ 4개

06 다음 IAMSAR의 용어 중 틀린 것은?

① Rescue Search Centre (RSC)
② On-Scene Coordinator (OSC)
③ Ship Reporting System (SRS)
④ Vessel Traffic Services (VTS)

07 다음은 UNCLOS 상 Contiguous zone 내에서 통제할 수 있는 사항에 관한 것이다. 빈칸에 들어가기에 적절하지 않은 것은?

> Prevent infringement of its (   ) or sanitary laws and regulations within its territory and territorial sea.

① customs ② passage ③ fiscal ④ immigration

08 COLREG 상 통항분리대, 통항분리선에 들어갈 수 있는 경우를 고르시오.

> A vessel other than a crossing vessel, or vessel joining or leaving a lane shall not normally enter a separation zone or cross a separation line except;
> ⓐ in cases of emergency to avoid immediate danger
> ⓑ vessels of less than 20meters in length
> ⓒ sailing vessel
> ⓓ to engage in fishing within a separation zone

① 1개 ② 2개 ③ 3개 ④ 4개

09 다음 빈칸에 들어갈 단어를 고르시오.

> (ⓐ) of the radar is discrimination between two object at the same range but on different bearings. It depends on the range at which targets are situated and the (ⓑ).

    ⓐ   ⓑ
① Bearing resolution – blind sector
② Bearing resolution – pencil beam width
③ Range resolution – pencil beam width
④ Range resolution – blind sector

10 다음 중 화재 소화방법으로 가장 옳지 않은 것은?

① Fuel removal
② Temperature reduction (under flash point)
③ Chemical Inhibition
④ Oxygen inclusion

11 다음은 SMCP에 의한 문장이다. 올바른 Message Marker는?

( ). Stand by on VHF channel 16.

① WARNING   ② INFORMATION   ③ INSTRUCTION   ④ ADVICE

12 다음 COLREG 상의 내용 중 틀린 것은?

Rule 10 : Traffic Separation Schemes
(a) This Rule Applies to traffic separation schemes adopted by the Organization and does not relieve any vessel of her ①obligation under any other rule.
(b) A vessel using a traffic separation scheme shall :
   (i) proceed in the appropriate traffic lane in the ②opposite direction of traffic flow for that lane;
   (ii) so far as practicable keep clear of a traffic separation line or separation zone;
   (iii) normally join or leave a traffic lane at the termination of the lane, but when joining or leaving from either side shall do so at as ③small an angle to the general direction of traffic flow as practicable.
(c) A vessel shall so far as practicable avoid crossing traffic lanes, but if obliged to do so shall cross on a heading as nearly as practicable ④at right angles to the general direction of traffic flow.

13 다음 SMCP 단어의 연결이 잘못된 것의 개수를 고르시오.

> ⓐ Station : Place or deck, in mess rooms, etc. assigned to crew and passengers where they have to meet according to the muster list when the corresponding alarm is released or announced.
> ⓑ Scene : The area or location where the event or an accident has happened.
> ⓒ Assembly station : The allotted place or the duties of each person on board.
> ⓓ Berth : The place assigned to a vessel when anchored or lying alongside a pier.
> ⓔ Muster station : Place assigned to crew and passengers to muster before being ordered into the lifeboat.

① 1개 ② 2개 ③ 3개 ④ 4개

14 빈칸에 들어갈 말로 가장 옳은 것은?

> (   ) means the condition under which the main propulsion plant, boilers and auxiliaries are not in operation due to the absence of power.

① Deadship condition
② Emergency condition
③ Distress
④ Abandon vesse

15 다음 중 아래에서 설명하고 있는 IAMSAR 매뉴얼 상 용어는?

> A survival craft transponder that, when activated, sends out a signal automatically when a pulse from a nearby radar reaches it. The signal appears on the interrogating radar screen and gives the bearing and distance of the transponder from the interrogating radar for search and rescue purposes.

① SART ② EPIRB ③ VHF-DSC ④ INMARSAT

16 다음 통신부호를 사용할 수 있는 대상의 개수를 고르시오.

> "INSTRUCTION, do not enter the fairway."
> 가. VTS-Station
> 나. fishing vessel
> 다. passenger ship
> 마. other fully authorized personnel
> 라. Naval vessel

① 1개 ② 2개 ③ 3개 ④ 4개

17 SOLAS 상 빈칸에 들어갈 말로 올바른 것은?

> Chapter III / Reg. 25 Muster stations
> Every passenger ship shall, in addition to complying with the requirements of regulation 11, have passenger muster stations which shall :
> .1 be in the vicinity of, and permit ready access for the passengers to, the embarkation stations unless in the same location; and
> .2 have ample room for marshalling and instruction of the passengers, but at least( )m² per passenger.

① 0.25 ② 0.35 ③ 0.45 ④ 0.50

18 SOLAS의 적용 제외 선박은 몇 개인가?

ⓐ Ships of war and troopships
ⓑ Passenger ships of less than 500 tons gross tonnage
ⓒ Ships not propelled by mechanical means
ⓓ Wooden ships of primitive build
ⓔ Pleasure yachts engaged in trade
ⓕ Fishing vessels

① 1개　　② 2개　　③ 3개　　④ 4개

19 다음 ships log book 기사 중 빈칸에 들어갈 말로 가장 적절한 것은?

Crossed the (　　) into west longitude at Lat. 43°N June 12 was (　　).

① Greenwich Meridian, repeated
② International Date Line, skipped
③ International Date Line, repeated
④ Greenwich Meridian, omitted

20 다음은 STCW의 당직 인수인계에 관한 내용이다. 빈칸에 순서대로 들어갈 수 있는 것은?

The relieving officer shall ensure that the members of the relieving watch are fully capable of performing their duties, particularly as regards their adjustment to (　　). Relieving officers shall not take over the watch until their (　　) is fully adjusted to the light conditions.

① night vision - vision
② the view of the sea - vision
③ stability - stability
④ watch keeping - watch

21회차 해사영어 모의고사

01 다음에서 설명하는 것은 무엇인가?

> Any system of one or more routes or routing measures aimed at reducing the risk of casualties.

① Routing system
② Traffic Separation Scheme
③ Roundabout
④ Traffic lane

02 다음 중 의미가 올바르게 연결되지 않은 것은 몇 개인가?

> ⓐ Height : Height of highest point of vessel's structure above waterline, e.g. radar, funnel, cranes, masthead.
> ⓑ Dredging anchor : anchor moving over the sea bottom involuntarily because it is no longer preventing the movement of the vessel.
> ⓒ Receiving point : A mark or place at which a vessel comes under obligatory entry, transit, or escort procedure(such as for port entry, canal transit or ice-breaker escort).
> ⓓ Spill : Escape of oil or liquid from a tank because of a two-fold condition as a result of overflowing, thermal expansion, change in vessel trim or vessel movement.
> ⓔ Flooding : Major uncontrolled flow of seawater into the vessel.

① 1개　　② 2개　　③ 3개　　④ 4개

03 다음 빈칸에 들어갈 말을 순서대로 고른 것은?

> ⓐ (   ) : Recommended route to be followed when proceeding between pre-determined positions.
> ⓑ (   ) : An area within definite limits inside which one-way traffic is established. Natural obstacles, including those forming separation zones, may constitute a boundary.
> ⓒ (   ) : When message is not properly heard, say like this.

① fairway - traffic line - repeat
② Track - traffic lane - say again
③ fairway - traffic lane - say again
④ Track - traffic line - no information

04 다음 중 표준해사통신용어의 일반 용어에 대한 의미가 옳지 않은 것은 몇 개인가?

> ⓐ Crew list : List of crew, passengers and all on board and their functions in a distress or drill.
> ⓑ Heading : The horizontal direction the vessel's bows at a given moment measured in degrees clockwise from north.
> ⓒ Embark(to) : To go from a vessel.
> ⓓ Casualty : Case of death in an accident or shipping disaster.
> ⓔ Leaking : Escape of liquids such as water, oil, etc., out of pipes, boilers, tanks, etc., or a minor inflow of seawater into the vessel due to damage to the hull.

① 1개   ② 2개   ③ 3개   ④ 4개

05 다음 중 표준해사통신영어 상 해석이 올바르지 않은 것은 무엇인가?

① What is the diameter of the turning circle?
　→ 선회권의 직경은 얼마인가?
② My anchor is clear of the bottom.
　→ 닻의 격납 작업이 완료되었음.
③ Is it safe to fire a rocket?
　→ 로켓 발사는 안전합니까?
④ What time can I enter the canal?
　→ 본선은 몇 시에 운하에 들어갈 수 있습니까?

06 다음 빈칸에 들어갈 말을 순서대로 고른 것은 무엇인가?

> ⓐ Dense fog (　　), S.B.E. proceeded at safe speed. :
> 　 짙은 안개가 꼈음, 기관준비, 안전속력으로 전진하라.
> ⓑ Fog (　　). : 안개가 걷혔음.
> ⓒ Sounded Fog signal and kept a (　　) lookout. :
> 　 : 무중신호를 울리고 견시를 철저히 하시오.

① set in – lifted – sharp　　　② set in – located – sharp
③ set up – got cleared – high　④ set up – fire – good

07 다음 중 문장과 그 해석이 올바르게 이루어지지 않은 것은 모두 몇 개인가?

> ⓐ No ship can move in this area.
> 　→ 이 해역에서 선박은 이동할 수 없다.
> ⓑ I am making way through the water.
> 　→ 본선은 대지속력이 있다.
> ⓒ Tide is setting in direction NE.
> 　→ 조류는 북동 방향에서 흘러오고 있다.
> ⓓ 풍속계가 작동하지 않는다.
> 　→ Barometer is not working.
> ⓔ Tanker Amoco, I am now making identification signal.
> 　→ 탱커 Amoco, 나는 지금 호출부호를 보내고 있다.

① 1개　② 2개　③ 3개　④ 4개

08 다음 중 SAR에 관한 용어의 약어로 올바르게 짝지어진 것은 모두 몇 개인가?

> ⓐ ACO – Air craft organization 항공기조정관
> ⓑ AMVER – Automated mutual assistance vessel rescue system 미국선위통보제도
> ⓒ ILO – International Labour organization 국제노동기구
> ⓓ MID – Maritime identification digits 해양 식별 숫자
> ⓔ VTS – Vessel Traffic Separation 선박 교통 분리

① 1개   ② 2개   ③ 3개   ④ 4개

09 To carry out parallel track search in a coordinated manner, all vessels should proceed at what speed?

① The maximum speed of the slowest ship present.
② The minimum speed of the fastest ship present.
③ At the speed each vessels will best accomplish an efficient search.
④ The maximum speed of each vessels.

10 다음은 UNCLOS의 원문이다. 옳지 않은 것의 개수는 몇 개인가?

> ⓐ Waters on the landward side of the baseline of the territorial sea are part of the contiguous zone of the State.
> ⓑ Every state has the right to establish the breadth of its territorial sea up to a limit not exceeding 12 nautical miles, measured from base lines determined in accordance with this Convention.
> ⓒ No state may validly purport to subject any part of the territorial seas to its sovereignty.
> ⓓ The normal baseline for measuring the breadth of the territorial sea is the high-water line along the coast as marked on large-scale charts officially recognized by the coastal State.

① 1개   ② 2개   ③ 3개   ④ 4개

11 다음 밑줄 친 빈칸에 포함되지 않는 해역을 고르시오.

The hot pursuit of a foreign ship may be undertaken when the competent authorities of the coastal State have good reason to believe that the ship has violated the laws and regulations of that State. Such pursuit must be commenced when the foreign ship or one of its boast is within (   ) of pursuing State.

가. the internal waters
나. the archipelagic waters
다. the territorial sea
라. the contiguous zone
마. the high seas
바. the exclusive economic zone

① 없다.   ② 1개   ③ 2개   ④ 3개

12 다음 빈칸에 들어갈 말을 순서대로 고른 것은?

ⓐ (   ) : A protective suit which reduces the body heat loss of a person wearing it in cold water.
ⓑ (   ) : A bag or suit made of waterproof material with low thermal conductivity.

① Thermal protective aid - life jacket
② Immersion Suit - Thermal protective aid
③ diver's suit - Immersion Suit
④ Immersion Suit - diver's suit

13 다음 빈칸에 들어갈 내용으로 옳은 것은?

> Chapter III / Regulation 7 personal life-saving appliances
> 2.1.4 a sufficient number of lifejackets shall be carried for person on watch and for use at remotely located survival craft station.
> The lifejackets carried for persons on watch should be stowed on the (ⓐ), in the (ⓑ) and any other manned watch station.

① toilet, shower room
② bridge, engine control room
③ messroom, recreation room
④ emergency steering room, cabin

14 다음 SOLAS 내용 중 옳지 않은 것은 몇 개인가?

> ⓐ The normal equipment of every lifeboat shall consist of five rocket parachute flares complying with the requirements of regulation.
> ⓑ The normal equipment of every lifeboat shall consist of two hand flares complying with the requirements of regulation.
> ⓒ The normal equipment of every lifeboat shall consist of four buoyant smoke signal complying with the requirements of regulation.

① 없음   ② 1개   ③ 2개   ④ 3개

15 다음 빈칸에 들어갈 말을 순서대로 고르시오.

> ⓐ (   ) : it is regulated with suspicion of crime in the territorial sea.
> ⓑ (   ) : It is regulated with the straits used for international navigation.
> ⓒ (   ) : It is regulated with suspicion of crime in the high seas.

① Criminal jurisdiction
　Right of transit passage
　Right of visit

② Right of visit
　Right of transit passage
　criminal jurisdiction

③ Right of visit
　Right of visit
　Right of hot pursuit

④ Criminal jurisdiction
　Right of passage
　Right of visit

16 STCW에 따라, 옳지 않은 것의 개수를 고르시오.

> ⓐ Radio operators are responsible for maintaining a continuous radio watch on appropriate frequencies during their periods of duty.
> ⓑ When master comes to the bridge, the duty of navigational watch officer is transferred to the master.
> ⓒ The duties of the look-out and helmsman are combined and helmsman shall be considered to be the look-out while steering.
> ⓓ Officers in charge of the navigational watch are responsible for navigating the ship safely during their periods of duty, when they shall be physically present on the navigating bridge or cabin.

① 없다. ② 1개 ③ 2개 ④ 3개

17 다음 중 아래에 열거된 표준 조타 명령으로 의미가 옳지 않은 것은 무엇인가?

① Steady : Steer a steady course on the compass heading indicated at the time of the order.
② Hard-a-starboard : Rudder to be held fully over to starboard.
③ Meet her : Check the swing of the vessel's head in turn.
④ Midships : Rudder to be held in the fore and aft position.

18 SMCP에 사용되는 용어에 대한 정의로 옳지 않은 것은 몇 개인가?

> ⓐ Not Under Command : A vessel restricted by her ability to manoeuvre by the nature of her work
> ⓑ Roll call : To assemble crew, passengers or both in a special place for purposes of checking
> ⓒ Muster : The act of checking who if the passengers and crew members are present, e.g. at assembly stations, by reading aloud a list of their names
> ⓓ Ordnance exercise : Naval firing practice

① 1개 ② 2개 ③ 3개 ④ 4개

19 다음은 COLREG의 내용 중 제한 시계 내 정박선의 음향신호에 관한 내용이다. 틀린 것의 개수는?

> A vessel at anchor shall at interval of not more than ⓐ2minutes ring the bell rapidly for about ⓑ5seconds. In vessel ⓒ100meters or more in length the bell shall be sounded in the fore part of the vessel and immediately after the ringing of the bell the ⓓblast shall be sounded rapidly for ⓔ5seconds in the after part of the vessel.

① 없다.   ② 1개   ③ 2개   ④ 3개

20 다음은 COLREG의 내용 중 제한 시계 내 정박선의 음향신호 중 기적신호에 관한 내용이다. 빈칸에 들어갈 내용을 고르시오.

> An area of restricted visibility, a vessel at anchor may in addition sound three blasts in succession, namely (   ), to give warning of her position and of the possibility of collision to an approaching vessel.

① two short, one prolonged blast
② three short blast
③ one short, two prolonged blast
④ one short, one prolonged and one short blast

22회차 해사영어 모의고사

01 다음 중 (   )에 들어갈 말로 옳은 것은 무엇인가?

> A mark or place, at which a vessel is required to report to the local VTS-Station to establish its position, is called (   ).

① way point
② reporting point
③ receiving point
④ manual call point

02 다음 중 단어와 의미가 올바르지 않게 연결된 것은 몇 개인가?

> ⓐ Recommended Track : A designated area between the landward boundary of a traffic separation scheme and adjacent coast intended for coastal traffic.
> ⓑ Two-way route : A route within definite limits inside which two-way traffic is established, aimed at providing safe passage of ships through waters where navigation is difficult or dangerous.
> ⓒ Roundabout : A circular traffic lane within definite limits in which traffic moves in a counter-clockwise direction around a specified point or zone.
> ⓓ Area to be avoided : A routing measure comprising an area within defined limits where ships must navigate with particular caution and within which the direction of traffic flow may be recommended.

① 1개   ② 2개   ③ 3개   ④ 4개

03 다음 영문 (   ) 안에 들어갈 적합한 것은?

> According to SOLAS, (   ) means the finding of ships, aircraft, units or persons in distress.

① researching   ② loading   ③ detection   ④ locating

04 다음 중 빈칸에 들어갈 말을 순서대로 고른 것은 무엇인가?

> ⓐ Tide is (　　) in direction NE.
> ⓑ I am making (　　) through the water.
> ⓒ Advise you keep clear of sea area Po-hang bay, search and rescue (　　) operation.

① setting – way – in
② blowing – wave – out
③ setting – wave – of
④ falling – course – in

05 다음 문장에서 빈칸에 올 수 있는 것은?

> A vessel is proceeding at 7knots against a strong current which equals the ship's speed. The vessel is (　　).

① not underway
② underway but not making way through the water
③ underway but not making way over the ground
④ at anchor

06 다음 중 약자와 원어가 잘못 짝지어진 것은?

> ⓐ L.H – Light House 등대
> ⓑ P/S – Pilot Station 도선사 승선 지점
> ⓒ A/C – Alter Course 변침
> ⓓ R/up eng. – Rung(Ring) up engine
> 　 출항 후 엔진을 항해계획 최대속력으로 하는 것
> ⓔ K.O. – Knock over 작업중지
> ⓕ S/Co – Stop compass 컴퍼스 중지

① 1개　　② 2개　　③ 3개　　④ 4개

07 SMCP에서 숫자 표현 방식 중 옳지 않은 것은 몇 개인가?

> ⓐ My draft is one-three decimal seven meters
> ⓑ My present speed is twelve knots
> ⓒ My present position is bearing one three five, distance three miles from a light house
> ⓓ Port one five (Rudder orders)
> ⓔ steer to two four five
> ⓕ Steady on one eight two

① 2개   ② 3개   ③ 4개   ④ 5개

08 표준해사통신용어 상 다음의 용어 중 바르게 설명하지 않은 것은 몇 개인가?

> ⓐ Hampered vessel : A vessel restricted by her ability to manoeuvre by the nature of her work
> ⓑ Retreat Signal : Sound, visual or other signal to a team ordering it to return to its base
> ⓒ Fire patrol : A crew member of the watch going around the vessel at certain intervals so that an outbreak of fire may be promptly detected
> ⓓ Embark : To go from a vessel
> ⓔ Destination : Port which a vessel is bound for
> ⓕ Cardinal buoy : The four main points of the compass, i.e. North, East, South and West

① 2개   ② 3개   ③ 4개   ④ 5개

09 다음은 IAMSAR의 Williamson turn에 대한 설명이다. 옳지 않은 것은 몇 개인가?

> ⓐ make good original track
> ⓑ good in reduced visibility but takes the ship farther away from the scene of the incident
> ⓒ slow procedure
> ⓓ very difficult for a single-screw vessel

① 없다.　② 1개　③ 2개　④ 3개

10 다음 중 COLREG에서 정의하는 "조종 제한선"에 속하지 않는 것은 몇 개인가?

> ⓐ a vessel engaged in dredging, surveying or underwater operations
> ⓑ a vessel engaged in the launching or recovery of aircraft
> ⓒ a vessel engaged in replenishment or transferring persons, provisions or cargo while underway
> ⓓ a vessel engaged in a towing operation such as renders her unable to deviate from her course
> ⓔ a vessel engaged in fishing
> ⓕ a vessel in damage to navigational equipment

① 2개　② 3개　③ 4개　④ 5개

11 다음 중 "Safe Speed"를 결정함에 있어 고려해야 할 사항이 아닌 것은 몇 개인가?

> ⓐ the manoeuvrability of the vessel with special reference to stopping distance and turning ability in the prevailing conditions
> ⓑ the state of wind, sea and current, and the proximity of navigational hazards
> ⓒ the state of density of seawater
> ⓓ the draught in relation to the available depth of water
> ⓔ the traffic density including concentrations of fishing vessels or any other vessels;
> ⓕ at night the presence of background light such as from shore lights or from back scatter of their own lights

① 없다.　② 1개　③ 2개　④ 3개

12 다음 빈칸에 들어갈 단어로 가장 옳은 것은?

> The term 'from the nearest land' means from the (　　) in accordance with international law except certain areas specified.

① coastline at high water
② coastline at low water
③ coastline at approximate highest high water
④ baseline from which the territorial seas is established

13 다음 중 UNCLOS에서 외국 선박이 영해에서 통항할 때 유해하다고 판단되는 행위로 옳은 것은?

> ⓐ any exercise or practice with weapons of any kind
> ⓑ any fishing activities
> ⓒ the carrying out of research or survey activities
> ⓓ the launching, landing or taking on board of any aircraft
> ⓔ calling at roadstead
> ⓕ proceeding to internal water

① 1개　② 2개　③ 3개　④ 4개

14 다음은 ISPS의 보안등급이다. 빈칸에 들어갈 말을 순서대로 표기한 것은?

> ⓐ Security level 1 : The level for which (　　　) protective security measures shall be maintained at all times.
> ⓑ Security level 2 : The level for which (　　　) protective security measures shall be maintained for a period of time as a result of heightened risk of a security incident.
> ⓒ Security level 3 : The level for which (　　　) protective security measures shall be maintained for a limited period of time when a security incident is probable or imminent, although it may not be possible to identify the specific target.

① minimum appropriate - further specific - appropriate additional
② minimum appropriate - appropriate additional - further specific
③ further specific - appropriate additional - minimum appropriate
④ appropriate additional - further specific - minimum appropriate

15 다음 중 올바르지 않은 것은 몇 개인가?

> ⓐ Recovery time : for rescue boat is the time required to raise the boat to position where persons on board can disembark to the deck of the ship
> ⓑ Anti-exposure suit : protective suit for use by rescue boat and marine evacuation system parties
> ⓒ Detection : determination of the location of survivors or survival crafts
> ⓓ Free-fall launching : method of launching a survival craft whereby the craft is automatically released from a sinking ship and is ready for use

① 없다.　　② 1개　　③ 2개　　④ 3개

16 다음은 STCW의 선원 자격에 대한 사항이다. 빈칸에 들어갈 숫자의 합은?

> Every officer in charge of a navigational watch serving on a seagoing ship of (　)gross tonnage or more shall hold an appropriate certificate. Every candidate for certification shall
> - be not less than (　)years of age
> - have approved seagoing service of not less than (　)months as part of an approved training programme which includes on-board training which meets the requirements of section A-11/1 of the STCW Code and is documented in an approved training record book, or otherwise have approved seagoing service of not less than (　)months

① 510　　② 536　　③ 566　　④ 593

17 아래 내용은 해양에 관한 국제법의 일부이다. 다음 중 빈칸에 들어갈 말로 가장 적절한 것은?

> The use of an international distress signal, except for the purpose of indicating that a ship, air craft or person is in distress, and the use of any signal which may be confused with an international distress signal, are (　).

① granted　　② prohibited　　③ recommended　　④ obeyed

18 다음 빈칸에 들어갈 말로 가장 옳은 것은?

> The X-band radar as compared to a S-band radar with similar specifications will (　).

① give better range performance in rain, hail etc.
② display small targets in a mass of dense sea clutter
③ display a more maplike presentation for inshore navigation
④ have less sea return in choppy rough seas

19 다음 중 빈칸에 들어갈 말을 순서대로 연결한 것은?

> The direction of the current is true, not (　), and is the direction (　) which the current is setting, while the wind given is in the direction (　) which it is blowing.

① magnetic – toward – from
② relative – from – toward
③ magnetic – from – toward
④ relative – toward – from

20 다음 빈칸에 들어갈 말로 가장 옳은 것은?

> (　) are tides that have lows lower than normal and highs higher than normal.

① Low tide　② High tide　③ Neap tide　④ Spring tide

23 해사영어 모의고사

01 다음 중 (   )에 들어갈 말을 순서대로 고른 것은 무엇인가?

> A recommended track is a route which has been specially examined to ensure so far as possible that is free of (   ) and along which ships are (   ) to navigate.

① rocks, advised
② shoal, required
③ dangers, advised
④ dangers, compelled

02 다음 중 알맞지 않은 것은 몇 개인가?

> ⓐ Meet her : Reduce the swing as rapidly as possible.
> ⓑ No information : When the information requested cannot be obtained, say like this.
> ⓒ Steerageway : The minimum speed at which a vessel will answer the helm.

① 없다.   ② 1개   ③ 2개   ④ 3개

03 다음은 TSS이용에 관련한 VTS의 통신 내용이다. 빈칸에 들어갈 말을 알맞게 고른 것은?

> "Advise you to cross the fairway on a heading as nearly as practicable at (   ) angles to the (   ) direction of traffic flow."

① small, opposite
② right, general
③ small, general
④ large, general

04 다음은 SOLAS 내용 중 일부이다. 해당 규정 상 틀린 것의 개수를 고르시오

> Auxiliary steering gear : Capable of putting the rudder over from ⓐ15° on side to 15° on the other side in not more than ⓑ28s with the ship at its deepest seagoing draught and running ahead at the ⓒmaximum ahead service speed or ⓓ6knots, whichever is the ⓔgreater.

① 1개 ② 2개 ③ 3개 ④ 4개

05 다음 중 옳지 않은 것은 몇 개인가?

> ⓐ Transit : The transfer of goods from one vessel to another outside harbours.
> ⓑ Jettison : To evacuate crew and passengers from a vessel following a distress.
> ⓒ Escort : Attending a vessel, to be available in case of need, e.g. ice-breaker, tug, etc.
> ⓓ Berth : A sea room to be kept for safety around a vessel, rock, flat form, etc.
> ⓔ Bob-cat : A mini-caterpillar with push-blade used for the careful distribution of loose goods in cargo holds of bulk carriers.

① 1개 ② 2개 ③ 3개 ④ 4개

06 다음 중 빈칸에 들어갈 말을 순서대로 연결한 것은 무엇인가?

> ⓐ The instruction to haul or pull on board all but essential lines mentioned, so that the ship is ready to leave the quay or berth is ( ).
> ⓑ In standard Marine Navigational Vocabulary, the height of a vessel is defined as the height of highest point of vessel's structure ( ).

① single up – above the waterline
② make fast – above the ship's bottom
③ let go – above the waterline
④ single up – above the sea bottom

07 다음 중 Hours propelling에 대한 설명으로 옳은 것은?

① Hours from 'R/UP Engine' to 'S.B.E' prior to entering port.
② Hours from 'Let go anchor' to 'Up & down anchor'.
③ Hours from 'Last line let go' to 'Frist line to pier'.
④ Hours from 'Up & down anchor' to 'Let go anchor'.

08 1979년 해상수색 및 구조에 관한 협약에 대한 용어 설명 중 옳지 않은 것은 몇 개인가?

> ⓐ "Search and rescue area" – An area of defined dimensions within which search and rescue services are provided
> ⓑ "Rescue Unit" – A unit composed of trained personnel and provided with equipment suitable for the expeditious conduct of search and rescuer operations
> ⓒ "Distress Phase" – A situation wherein apprehension exists as to the safety of a vessel and the persons on board
> ⓓ "To ditch" – in the case of an aircraft, to make a forced landing on water

① 1개   ② 2개   ③ 3개   ④ 4개

09 다음은 IAMSAR 매뉴얼에 나오는 수색방식 중 하나이다. 가장 적합한 수색 방식은?

> ⓐ Used to search a large area when survivor location is uncertain.
> ⓑ Usually used when a large search area must be divided into sub-areas for assignment to individual search facilities on-scene at the same time.
> ⓒ The commence search point is in one corner of the sub-area, one-half track space inside rectangle from each of the two sides forming the corner.

① Track Line search   ② Expanding Square Search
③ Parallel Sweep Search   ④ Sector Search

10 다음 COLREG내용 상 ㉠과 ㉡에 들어갈 단어가 순서대로 배열된 것은?

> When vessels in sight of one another are approaching each other and from any cause either vessel fails to understand the intentions or actions of the other, or is in (㉠) whether sufficient action is being taken by the other to avoid collision, the vessel in (㉠) shall immediately indicate such (㉠) by giving (㉡) and rapid blasts on the whistle.

	㉠	㉡
①	doubt	at least five short
②	danger	at least five short
③	doubt	less than five short
④	danger	at least six short

11 다음 빈칸에 들어갈 가장 적당한 것을 고르시오.

> In the exclusive economic zone, the Republic of Korea has sovereign rights for the purpose of exploring and exploiting, (   ) the natural resources, whether living or non-living, of the waters superjacent to the sea-bed and of the sea-bed and of the sea-bed and its subsoil.

① managing and controlling ② developing and utilizing
③ developing and cultivating ④ conserving and managing

12 다음 중 COLREG 상 용어의 정의에 대한 설명으로 가장 옳지 않은 것은 몇 개인가?

> ⓐ The word 'underway' means that a vessel is not at anchor, or made fast the shore, aground or not making way through the water
> ⓑ The word 'length of a vessel' means L.O.A.(Length Overall)
> ⓒ The term 'restricted visibility' means any condition in which visibility is restricted by fog, mist or any other similar causes
> ⓓ The term 'prolonged blast' means a blast of from four to six seconds duration

① 없다. ② 1개 ③ 2개 ④ 3개

13 다음 ISPS에 관한 설명 중 옳은 것의 개수는?

> ⓐ "ISPS Code" means the International Code for the Security of ships and of port Facilities consisting of part A(the provisions of which shall be treated as mandatory) and part B(the provisions of which shall be treated as recommendatory).
> ⓑ "Security Incident" means the qualification of the degree of risk that a security incident will be attempted or will occur.
> ⓒ "Security Level" means any act or circumstances that threatens the security of a ship, a mobile offshore drilling unit, a high speed craft, a port facility, a ship/port interface or any ship to ship activity.
> ⓓ "Port Facility" is a location, as determined by the Contracting Government or by the Designated Authority, where the ship/port interface takes place. This includes areas such as anchorages, waiting berths and approaches from seaward, as appropriate.

① 1개　② 2개　③ 3개　④ 4개

14 다음 중 좌초선의 주간 형상물에 대해 올바르게 설명한 것은?

① One black ball or similar shape in a vertical line where they can best be seen.
② three black balls or similar shapes in a vertical line where they can best be seen.
③ a cylinder shape in a vertical line where they can best be seen.
④ two black balls or similar shapes in a vertical line where they can best be seen.

15 다음 COLREG에 관한 설명 중. 빈칸에 들어갈 말로 알맞은 것을 순서대로 연결한 것은 무엇인가?

> – When vessels are (㉠), a power-driven vessel underway, when manoeuvring as authorized or required by these Rules, shall indicate that manoeuvre by signals on her whistle.
> – (㉡) short blast to mean "I am altering my course to starboard."
> – (㉢) short blasts to mean "I am altering my course to port."
> – (㉣) short blasts to mean "I am operating astern propulsion."

	㉠	㉡	㉢	㉣
①	in sight of one another	two	one	three
②	in restricted visibility	two	one	five
③	in sight of one another	one	two	three
④	in restricted visibility	one	two	three

16 다음 중 빈칸에 들어갈 단어로 옳은 것은?

> The vertical distance on a given day between water surface at high and that at low water is called (   ).

① high water　　② slack　　③ tidal range　　④ stand of tide

17 다음 빈칸에 들어갈 말로 가장 적절한 것은 무엇인가?

> The action of bringing your vessel alongside a jetty or dock is called (   ).

① berthing　　② unberthing　　③ make fast　　④ first line to pier

18 다음 중 옳지 않은 것은 몇 개인가?

> ⓐ According to SOLAS, a "Passenger ship" is a ship which carries more than twelve passengers.
> ⓑ According to SOLAS, a "Cargo ship" is any ship which is not a passenger ship.
> ⓒ According to SOLAS, a "New Ship" is a ship the keel of which is laid or which is at a similar stage of construction on or after 25 may 1980.
> ⓓ According to SOLAS, a "Existing ship" is a ship which is not a new ship.

① 없음　　② 1개　　③ 2개　　④ 3개

19 다음 중 빈칸에 들어갈 말로 알맞은 것은?

> According to SOLAS'83 a life jacket shall have buoyancy which is not reduced by more than (　　)% after 24h submersion in fresh water.

① 5　　② 30　　③ 10　　④ 20

20 다음 중 옳지 않은 것은 무엇인가?

> According to MARPOL 73/78, oil tanker can discharge oil or oily mixtures into the sea when the following conditions are satisfied except :

① the tanker is not within a special area.
② the tanker is more than 30 nautical miles from the nearest land.
③ the tanker is proceeding.
④ the instantaneous rate of discharge of oil content not exceed 30litres per nautical mile.

24 해사영어 모의고사

01 다음 빈칸에 들어갈 말로 가장 적합한 것은 무엇인가?

> Distress calls have absolute (　　　) over all other communication. When hearing them, all other transmissions should (　　　) and listen in.

① right – repeat　　　　② compulsority – be known
③ right – concentrate　　④ priority – cease

02 다음 빈칸에 옳은 숫자를 고르시오.

> The STCW code advice government to prescribe a maximum blood alcohol level of (　)% for ship's personnel during watchkeeping and to prohibit alcohol consumption within 4 hours prior to commencing a watch.

① 0.3　　② 0.03　　③ 0.5　　④ 0.05

03 다음 중 단어의 연결이 잘못된 것은 몇 개인가?

> ⓐ EPIRB : Emergency Position Indicating Radio Beacon
> ⓑ APRA : Automatic Radar Positioning Aids
> ⓒ GPS : Global Positioning System
> ⓓ VHF : Ultra Heigh Frequency
> ⓔ P/S : Port Side
> ⓕ E/R : Engine Room

① 2개　　② 3개　　③ 4개　　④ 5개

04 빈칸에 들어갈 말을 순서대로 연결한 것은?

> ⓐ (   ) is a stress which a ship's hull or keel experiences that the middle of the ship is pushed to bend upward.
> ⓑ When a ship's bow is pushed first to port and then to starboard, she is said to be (   ).

① Sagging - swaying
② Hogging - yawing
③ Surging - heaving
④ Rolling - pitching

05 아래 문장을 입항 시 시간에 따라 순서대로 배열한 것 중 옳은 것은?

> ⓐ first line to pier.
> ⓑ S/B eng. for entering harbour area.
> ⓒ made her fast on pier.
> ⓓ pilot on board.

① ⓓⓑⓐⓒ   ② ⓑⓐⓓⓒ   ③ ⓑⓓⓐⓒ   ④ ⓐⓑⓓⓒ

06 다음 중 문장의 해석이 잘못된 것은 몇 개인가?

> ⓐ Arrived at pier and started to make her fast.
>   -〉 안벽에 계류를 시작했다.
> ⓑ Made fast port side to pier. F.W.E.
>   -〉 좌현 안벽 접안을 완료했다. 기관사용 개시.
> ⓒ Made her stern fast to pier.
>   -〉 부두에 선수 계류함.
> ⓓ The ebb tide. It is one hour after low water.
>   -〉 조류가 올라가고 있다. 저조 한 시간 후이다.
> ⓔ How is the cable leading?
>   -〉 (투묘과정 작업 중) 닻줄의 방향은 어떠한가?

① 없다.   ② 1개   ③ 2개   ④ 3개

07 다음 빈칸에 들어갈 말로 가장 적합한 것은?

( ) is the angle that the center line of a vessel, or the vessel's keel makes with the meridian.

① Course   ② heading   ③ Deviation   ④ Variation

08 다음은 COLREG 상 등화에 관한 내용이다. 옳지 않은 것을 고르시오.

A vessel engaged in fishing, other than trawling shall exhibit :
i) two all-round light in a vertical line, the ①upper being red and the lower white, or a shape consisting of two cones with apexes together in a vertical line one above the other.
ii) when there is outlying gear extending more than ②150 metres horizontally from the vessel, an all-round ③red light or a ④cone apex upward in the direction of the gear.
iii) when making way through the water, in addition to the lights, prescribed in this paragraph, sidelights and a stern light.

09 다음 중 무해통항(Innocent Passage)조항에서 외국 선박이 연안국의 평화, 공공질서 또는 안전을 해치는 활동으로 규정한 것은 모두 몇 개인가?

ⓐ any exercise or practice with weapons of any kind
ⓑ the launching, landing or taking on board of any aircraft
ⓒ any fishing activities
ⓓ any act of propaganda aimed at affecting the defence or security of the coastal State
ⓔ the carrying out of research or survey activities

① 2개   ② 3개   ③ 4개   ④ 5개

10 79' 해상수색 및 구조에 관한 국제협약에서 말하는 영문 표기 설명 중 틀린 것은 모두 몇 개인가?

> ⓐ A/C : 변침 ⓔ SMC:현장지휘관
> ⓑ IMO:국제해사기구 ⓕ RB:구조정
> ⓒ MID:해양식별숫자 ⓖ RV:구조선박
> ⓓ WMO : 세계기상기구 ⓗ IALA:국제항로표지협회

① 없다. ② 1개 ③ 2개 ④ 3개

11 다음 중 아래의 상황에서 쓸 수 있는 로그북 기사는?

> Select the most appropriate one for the remark at sea. (at sea; not anchor, or made fast to the shore, or aground).

① Single up fore and aft and prepared for sea
② Cleared out of canal, R/up eng. and dismissed the station
③ F.W.E, pilot and tug away and dismissed the station
④ S.B.E and prepared unmooring

12 다음 중 옳지 않은 것은 몇 개인가?

> ⓐ "Thermal protective aid" means a protective suit which reduces the body heat loss of a person wearing it in cold water.
> ⓑ "Immersion Suit" means a bag or suit made of waterproof material with low thermal conductivity.
> ⓒ "Survival Craft" menas a craft capable of sustaining the lives of persons in distress from the time of abandoning the ship.
> ⓓ "Rescue Boat" means a boat designed to rescue persons in distress and to marshal survival craft.
> ⓔ "Search" is the safe recovery of survivors.

① 1개 ② 2개 ③ 3개 ④ 4개

13 다음은 UNCLOS 상 archipelagic baselines에 대한 규정이다. 옳지 않은 것의 개수를 고르시오.

> A. The length of archipelagic baselines shall not exceed ①100 nautical miles except that up to ②5% of the total number of baselines enclosing any archipelago may exceed that length up to a maximum length of ③125 nautical miles.
> B. The drawing of such baselines shall not depart to any appreciable extent from the ④general configuration of the archipelago.

① 없다.   ② 1개   ③ 2개   ④ 3개

14 다음 중 옳은 것은 무엇인가?

> On a ship engaged on a voyage where passengers are scheduled to be on board for more than 24h, musters of newly-embarked passengers shall take place (   ). Passengers shall be instructed in the use of the lifejackets and the action to take in an emergency.

① within 48h
② after departure
③ within 24h
④ prior to or immediately upon departure

15 다음 빈칸에 들어갈 적절한 것을 순서대로 고른 것은?

> ⓐ Every vessel (   ) any other shall keep out of the way the (   ) vessel.
> ⓑ Safe speed is that speed of a vessel allowing the (   ) possible time for effective action to be taken to avoid a collision and to be (   ) within an appropriate distance.

① overtaking – overtaken – minimum – left
② overtaken – overtaking – maximum – stopped
③ overtaken – overtaking – minimum – left
④ overtaking – overtaken – maximum – stopped

16 STCW에 따라 빈칸에 공통으로 들어갈 적절한 용어를 고르시오.

> Each administration shall, for the purpose of preventing fatigue require that watch systems are so arranged that the efficiency of all watchkeeping personnel is not impaired by fatigue and that duties are so organized that the first watch at the commencement of a voyage and subsequent relieving watches are (   ) and otherwise fit for duty.

① sufficiently concentrated ② sufficiently relieved
③ sufficiently rested ④ sufficiently arranged

17 SMCP의 일반용어 중 General emergency alarm에 대한 설명이다. 각각의 빈칸에 들어갈 말로 가장 옳은 것은?

> A sound signal of (   ) blast and (   ) blast given with the vessel's sound system.

① seven short, one prolonged ② seven prolonged, one short
③ one short, seven prolonged ④ one prolonged, seven short

18 다음은 SOLAS 상의 설명 중. 밑줄 친 부분 중 옳지 않은 것은?

> Muster stations shall be provided close to the embarkation stations. Each muster station shall have sufficient clear deck space to accommodate all persons assigned to muster at that station, but at least (   )m² per person.

① 2.5 ② 0.35 ③ 1 ④ 0.5

19 다음 중 빈칸에 들어갈 말로 알맞은 것은?

ⓐ (   ) is a great circle through the geographical poles of the earth.
ⓑ (   ) are tides that have low tide higher than normal and high tide lower than normal.

① Meridian, Neap tide
② Meridian, Spring tide
③ Great Circle, Neap tide
④ Great Circle, Spring tide

20 다음은 COLREG 상 'Action to avoid collision'에 대한 설명이다. 밑줄 친 단어 중 옳지 않은 것의 개수는?

Any alternation of course and/or speed to avoid collision, shall, if the circumstances of the case admit, be ⓐ<u>large</u> enough to be readily ⓑ<u>ambiguous</u> to another vessel observing ⓒ<u>visually</u> or by radar, a(an) succession of ⓓ<u>large</u> alternations of course and/or speed should be avoided.

① 1개   ② 2개   ③ 3개   ④ 4개

01 Rewrite the following sentence into Standard Marine Navigational Vocabulary.

> I will bring the vessel beam on to the wind and sea, to protect the vessel in distress from the wind.

① I will protect you from the wind.
② I am going to make a wind for you.
③ I am coming to rescue you in distress.
④ I will make a lee for you.

02 다음 빈칸에 들어갈 내용을 순서대로 고른 것은?

> ⓐ The (   ) order that a captain has to give his men in the perils of the sea is 'abandon ship!'.
> ⓑ The change-over from automatic to manual steering and vice versa shall be made by or under the supervision of a (   ).

① first, helmsperson
② first, responsible officer
③ last, helmsperson
④ last, responsible officer

03 다음 중 단어의 연결이 잘못된 것은 몇 개인가?

> ⓐ Wreck - A vessel which has been destroyed or sunk or abandoned at sea
> ⓑ Veering - Counter clockwise change in the direction of the wind
> ⓒ Transit speed - Speed of vessel required for the passage through a canal, fairway, etc.
> ⓓ Hull : The main body of a ship
> ⓔ Even keel : her draft is the same at bow and stern

① 1개
② 2개
③ 3개
④ 4개

04 다음은 COLREG 조종제한선중 수중작업 선박의 작업방향 지시등에 대한 설명이다. 빈칸으로 순서대로 오기에 옳은 것은?

> A vessel engaged in dredging or underwater operation, when restricted in her ability to manoeuvre, shall exhibit the lights and shapes prescribed in sub-paragraph in sub-paragraphs (b)(i),(ii) and (iii) of this rule and shall in addition, when an obstruction exists, exhibit :
> 1. Two all round (㉠) lights or two ball in vertical line to indicate the side on which the obstruction exists.
> 2. two all round (㉡) lights or two diamonds in a vertical line to indicate the side on which another vessel may pass.

	㉠	㉡
①	red	red
②	red	white
③	red	green
④	white	white

05 다음 중 옳은 것은 무엇인가?

> A stand-on vessel, in order to avoid collision,
> (A) : must take action when situation is in extremes.
> (B) : may change course when it is apparent that give-way vessel is not taking action in compliance with the rules.

① A only   ② B only   ③ both A and B   ④ neither A nor B

06 IAMSAR 상의 용어에 대한 설명으로 옳은 것은 모두 몇 개인가?

> ⓐ craft : any air or sea surface vehicle or submersible of any kind or size.
> ⓑ Datum : point, normally specified by the SMC, where a SAR facility is to begin its search pattern.
> ⓒ Hypothermia : Abnormal lowering of internal body temperature from exposure to cold air, wind, or water.
> ⓓ Rescue unit : An operation to retrieve persons in distress.
> ⓔ Fetch : The distance the wave have been driven by a wind blowing in a constant direction, without obstruction.

① 2개 ② 3개 ③ 4개 ④ 5개

07 다음 중 옳지 않은 것은 무엇인가?

> For determining a safe speed, all of the following factors are mentioned by the rules, except;

① the draft, in relation to the available depth of water
② the presence of background light at night
③ the competency of crew
④ constraints imposed by the radar range scale in use

08 다음 중 SMCP표현 문장과 해석이 옳지 않은 것은 무엇인가?

① Prepare an emergency muster list for drill.
　→ 훈련을 위해 비상배치표를 준비해라.
② There are enough LSA for everyone on board.
　→ 선상의 모든 사람에게 충분한 소화 설비가 있음.
③ I am maneuvering with difficulty.
　→ 본선은 조종에 어려움이 있음.
④ Ice-breaker service suspended until 1st October.
　→ 쇄빙선 서비스가 10월 1일까지 일시중단 되었다.

09 다음 용어 및 통신부호의 설명으로 옳지 않은 것은 몇 개인가?

> ⓐ Ship stability : The ability of the ship to return to the upright when slightly inclined.
> ⓑ Transfer : This is the distance travelled in the direction of the original course by midship point of a ship from the position at which the rudder order is given to the position at which the heading has changed 90 degree from the original course.
> ⓒ Walk back : To reverse the action of a windlass to lower the anchor until it is clear of the hawse pipe and ready for dropping.
> ⓓ REQUEST : This indicates that the following message if the reply to previous question.
> ⓔ WARNING : This indicates that the following message implies the intention of the sender to inform others about danger.

① 2개　② 3개　③ 4개　④ 5개

10 다음 문장의 밑줄 친 부분과 같은 뜻을 가진 것은?

> You are getting closer to the vessel ahead.

① approaching　② departing　③ overtaking　④ crossing

11 다음 중 urgency signal에 해당하지 않는 것은?

① The signal implies that the ship is in imminent danger or requires immediate assistance.
② The urgency signal may be addressed to all stations or to a specific station.
③ The urgency signal may be used when the master desires to issue a warning that circumstances may become necessary for him to send out a distress signal at a later stage.
④ The signal may be sent on the distress frequencies only on the authority of the person responsible for the vessel.

12 SMCP 상 빈칸에 들어갈 단어로 가장 옳은 것은?

> "How is the cable (   )?"
> "The cable is coming tight."

① weighing   ② growing   ③ moving   ④ leading

13 다음은 통항분리방식의 용어에 관한 설명이다. 옳은 것은 몇 개인가?

> ⓐ Area to be avoided : A route which has been specially examined to ensure so far as possible that it is free of dangers and along which ships are advised to navigate.
> ⓑ Roundabout : A routing measure comprising a separation point or circular traffic lane within defined limits.
> ⓒ Inshore Traffic Zone : A routing measure comprising a designated area between the seaward boundary of a traffic separation scheme and the adjacent coast, intended for local traffic.
> ⓓ Precautionary Area : A routing measure comprising an area within defined limits where ships must navigate with particular caution and within which the direction of traffic flow may be recommended.

① 1개   ② 2개   ③ 3개   ④ 4개

14 다음 빈칸에 들어갈 알맞은 말은 무엇인가?

> (   ) up No.2 ballast tank with fresh water.

① Finished   ② Filled   ③ Replaced   ④ Tested

15 빈칸에 들어갈 알맞은 말을 고르시오.

> The local name of the tropical storm in north pacific ocean is (   ).

① willy-willy ② typhoon ③ cyclone ④ hurricane

16 다음 중 빈칸에 들어갈 숫자를 합한 것은 몇인가?

> In or near an area of restricted visibility, a power-driven vessel making way through the water shall sound at intervals of not more than (   )minutes (   ) prolonged blast.

① 2 ② 3 ③ 4 ④ 5

17 To ensure the best route for a line, it passes through a (   ) at the vessel's side

① pipe ② winch ③ hole ④ fairlead

18 다음 중 옳은 것은 무엇인가?

> According to SOLAS'83, each member of the crew shall participate in at least one abandon ship drill and one fire drill (   ). The drills of the crew shall take place within (   ) ship leaving a port if more than (   ) of the crew have not been participated in abandon ship and fire drills on board in the previous month.

① every month, 24h, 25%
② every 2months, 12h, 50%
③ every month, 12h, 25%
④ every 3months, 24h, 25%

19 다음 중 STCW에 따라 옳지 않은 것을 고르시오.

> The officer in charge of the navigational watch shall :

① avoid leave the bridge until properly relieved except for calling Captain.
② continue to be responsible for the safe navigation of the ship, despite the presence of the master on the bridge.
③ notify the master when in any doubt as to what action to take in the interest of safety.
④ keep the watch on the bridge.

20 다음 중 빈칸에 들어갈 가장 알맞은 말은?

> You are in charge of a power driven vessel at night and you see the red green light in horizontal line and two white light in vertical line of another vessel right ahead. You should : (   ).

① alter course to port.
② alter course to starboard.
③ stop the engine.
④ put crash astern order.

26 해사영어 모의고사

01 다음 중 빈칸에 들어갈 내용으로 가장 옳은 것은?

> "The (   ) is the maximum distance at which a light may be seen clear weather (meteorological visibility of 10 miles) expressed in nautical miles".

① nominal range ② luminous range
③ visible range ④ geographical range

02 Choose best answer for below paragraph.

> This is a position acquired by measuring compass bearing and expected distance from the start position. Celestial body or any electronic navigational equipment is not used to get position, instead this position can be acquired using gyro encoder, speed log.

① actually recorded position ② dead reckoning position
③ expected position ④ reckoning position

03 다음 중 빈칸에 들어갈 단어와, 아래 문장을 올바르게 해석한 것은?

> ⓐ CAPT : I have rigged (   ) on my starboard side.
> ⓑ Pilot : Roger, Please make a lee for my boat.

① embarkation ladder - 귀선이 배를 돌려서 내 보트가 갈 수 있는 길을 만들어라.
② pilot ladder - 귀선이 내 보트의 풍하측이 되도록 하여라.
③ combination ladder - 내 보트가 귀선의 선미로 오게 만들어라.
④ pilot ladder - 내 보트가 귀선의 풍하측이 되도록 하여라.

04 다음 중 SMCP표현으로 올바르지 않은 것을 고르시오.

① Does the radar have any blind sectors?
   -〉 레이더에는 맹목 구간이 있습니까?
② Attention! Turn in cable.
   -〉 주의! 닻줄을 감아라.
③ 5 persons are missing.
   -〉 5명의 사람이 실종되었음.
④ Pilot boat is coming to you. You must heave up anchor right away.
   -〉 도선사 보트가 귀선을 향해 가고 있습니다. 지금 즉시 닻을 감아 들이시오.

05 다음 중 약어가 올바르게 연결되지 않은 것은 몇 개인가?

ⓐ VTS : Vessel Traffic Services
ⓑ ETA : Estimated Time of Approval
ⓒ RCC : Rescue co-ordination center
ⓓ F.W.T : Fresh Wing Tank
ⓔ B.W.E : Break Water Entrance
ⓕ S.B.E : Stand by Engine

① 1개   ② 2개   ③ 3개   ④ 4개

06 다음 괄호 안에 들어갈 단어가 적절하게 짝지어진 것은?

ⓐ I am in danger of (   ).
  본선은 침몰의 위험이 있습니다.
ⓑ What is your (   )?
  귀선의 호출부호는 무엇입니까?
ⓒ (   ) what direction are you approaching?
  귀선은 어느 방향에서 접근중입니까?
ⓓ What was your (   )?
  귀선의 최후 기항지는 어디입니까?

① capsizing - MMSI - To - last port of call
② sinking - MMSI - From - port of destination
③ sinking - Call sign - From - last port of call
④ capsizing - Call sign - To - port of destination

07 다음은 선박의 6자유 운동 중 3가지의 회전운동에 대한 내용이다. ⓐⓑⓒ에 알맞은 선박 운동의 이름을 고르시오.

> there are three special axes in any ship called vertical, lateral, and longitudinal axes. the movements around them are known as roll, pitch, and yaw.

> (ⓐ) is the tilting rotation of a vessel about its longitudinal axis. An offset or deviation from normal on this axis is referred to as "Stability".
> (ⓑ) is the up and down rotation of a vessel about its lateral axis. An offset or deviation from normal on this axis is referred to as "trim".
> (ⓒ) is the turning rotation of a vessel about its vertical axis. An offset or deviation from normal on this axis is referred to as "course keeping ability".

	㉠	㉡	㉢
①	Roll	Pitch	Yaw
②	Roll	Yaw	Pitch
③	Pitch	Roll	Yaw
④	Yaw	Pitch	Roll

08 COLREG에 의거하여 달 수 있는 등화나, 형상물로 틀린 것의 개수를 고르시오.

> A vessel aground shall exhibit the lights of where they can best be seen.
> ⓐ in fore part, an all round white light.
> ⓑ at or near the stern and at a lower level than the light prescribed in sub-paragraph ⓐ, an all-round white light.
> ⓒ three all-round red lights in vertical line.
> ⓓ three ball in vertical line.
> ⓔ one ball in vertical line.

① 1개　② 2개　③ 3개　④ 4개

09 Select the improper one to fill the blank.

> "A vessel using a TSS comply with all of the following, (   )."

① proceed in the appropriate traffic lane.
② join traffic lanes at as small an angle as practicable.
③ if anchoring is necessary, anchor in the separation zone.
④ so far as practicable, avoid crossing traffic lanes.

10 COLREG 상 TSS에서의 항법 중 틀린 것의 개수는 몇 개인가?

> ⓐ A vessel navigating in areas near the terminations of traffic separation schemes shall do so with particular caution.
> ⓑ A vessel shall so far as practicable avoid anchoring in a traffic separation scheme or in areas near its terminations.
> ⓒ A vessel not using a traffic separation scheme shall avoid it by as narrow a margin as is practicable.
> ⓓ A sailing vessel, vessel less than 20m in length and vessel engaged in fishing may enter into separation zone.

① 없다.   ② 1개   ③ 2개   ④ 3개

11 다음 중 UNCLOS의 원문 내용으로 옳지 않은 것은 무엇인가?

① Ships shall sail under the flag of one state only and, save in exceptional cases expressly provided for in international treaties or in this Convention, shall be subject to its exclusive jurisdiction on the high seas.
② A ship which sails under the flags of two or more States, using them according to convenience, may claim any of the nationalities in question with respect to any other State.
③ In the territorial sea, submarines and other underwater vehicles are required to navigate on the surface and to show their flag.
④ A ship may not change its flag during a voyage or while in a port of call, save in the case of a real transfer of ownership or change of registry.

12 다음 중 Sector Search(VS)에 대한 설명으로 옳지 않은 것은?

ⓐ Most effective when the position of the search object is accurately known and the search area is small.
ⓑ Used to search a circular area centered on a datum point.
ⓒ A suitable marker(for example, a smoke float or a radio beacon) may be dropped at the datum position and used as a reference or navigational aid marking the center of the pattern.
ⓓ An air craft and a vessel may not be used together to perform independent sector searches of the same area.
ⓔ Often appropriate for vessels or small boats to use when searching for persons in the water or other search objects with little or no leeway.

① 없다.   ② 1개   ③ 2개   ④ 3개

13 빈칸에 들어갈 알맞은 말은 무엇인가?

International NAVTEX Service means the coordinated broadcast and automatic reception on (   ) of (   ) by means of narrow-band direct-printing telegraphy using the english language.

① 518kHz - maritime safety information
② INMARSAT - maritime safety information
③ 518kHz - distress information
④ INMARSAT - global maritime distress and safety

14 "식별을 위해서 귀선의 위치를 다시 말하라"를 SMCP 상 바르게 표현하기 위해 괄호의 단어를 고르시오.

Say again your position for (   ).

① discrimination   ② detection
③ recognize   ④ identification

15 다음 중 shipowner가 flag of convenience 선박을 사용하는 이유가 아닌 것은?

① to escape paying some home taxations
② to employ labour cheaper than that at home
③ to bound for next port faster than normal
④ to benefit financially in any similar way

16 다음은 COLREG의 일부 내용이다. 빈칸에 들어갈 말로 가장 옳은 것은?

> Action taken to avoid collision with another vessel shall be such as to result in passing at (   ). The effectiveness of the action shall be carefully checked until the other vessel is finally past and clear.

① avoid collision   ② safe speed
③ a safe distance   ④ the port side

17 빈칸에 순서대로 들어갈 단어를 고르시오.

> ⓐ If a vessel goes from salt water to fresh water, her freeboard will be (   ).
> ⓑ When the vessel is trim by the head, discharge the ballast water from (   ) tank to make it to be even keel.

① increased - aftpeak   ② decreased - aftpeak
③ decreased - forepeak   ④ increased - forepeak

18 다음 중 빈칸에 들어갈 알맞은 말을 고르시오.

> Vessel must proceed in the usual way directly and without (   ) or unnecessary delay, from port of departure to port of destination.

① draft   ② cargo   ③ speed thorough water   ④ deviation

19 COLREG에 따라 점등해야하는 등화로 잘못된 내용의 개수는?

> A hampered vessel is making way through the water shall exhibit
> - Three all-round lights in a vertical line. The highest and lowest of these lights shall be ⓐwhite and the middle light shall be ⓑred.
> - ⓒA masthead light
> - ⓓSidelights
> - ⓔSternlight

① 없다. ② 1개 ③ 2개 ④ 3개

20 다음 중 빈칸에 들어갈 말을 순서대로 고른 것은?

> ⓐ (   ) : The ladder provided at survival craft embarkation stations to permit safe access to survival craft after launching.
> ⓑ (   ) : All equipments, such as pilot ladder, accommodation ladder, hoist, etc, necessary for a safe transfer of the pilot.

① embarkation ladder - boarding speed
② accommodation ladder - boarding arrangements
③ embarkation ladder - boarding arrangements
④ accommodation ladder - pilot arrangements

01 다음 중 빈칸에 들어갈 말을 순서대로 고른 것은 무엇인가?

> ⓐ Traffic lane : An area within defined limits in which (　　　) is established. Natural obstacles, including those forming separation zones, may constitute a boundary.
> ⓑ Inshore Traffic Zone : A routing measure comprising a designated area between the (　　　) boundary of a traffic separation scheme and the adjacent coast, where local special rules may apply, and normally not to be used by through traffic.
> ⓒ Deep water route : A route within limits which defined limits which has been accurately surveyed for (　　　) of sea bottom and (　　　) as indicated on the chart.

① separate traffic – seaward – clearance – submerged obstacles
② separate traffic – landward – berth – wreck and derelict
③ one way traffic – seaward – berth – wreck and derelict
④ one way traffic – landward – clearance – submerged obstacles

02 SMCP 상 빈칸에 들어갈 말로 가장 옳은 것은?

> (　　), two outward vessels are in the entrance of the breakwater.

① Intention　② Instruction　③ Information　④ Warning

03 Select the correct one for the blank.

> (　　) is the angle the ship's keel, or center line, makes with the wake of the vessel, or track through the water.

① Heading　② Leeway　③ Course　④ Set and drift

04 다음 중 단어와 그 의미가 잘못 연결된 것은 몇 개인가?

> ⓐ Spill control gear : Anti-pollution equipment for combating accidental spills of oils or chemicals.
> ⓑ Compatibility(of goods) : State whether different goods can be safely stowed together in one cargo space.
> ⓒ Fire monitor : Fixed foam/powder/water cannon shooting fire extinguishing agents on tank, deck, manifold, etc.
> ⓓ Briefing : Concise explanatory information to crew and/or passengers.
> ⓔ Oil clearance : Oil skimming from the surface of the water.

① 없음 ② 1개 ③ 2개 ④ 3개

05 다음 중 ISPS의 SSAS(The Ship Security Alert system)의 작동원칙에 대한 설명으로 잘못된 것의 개수를 고르시오.

> The SSAS, when activated, shall :
> ⓐ initiate and transmit a ship-to-ship security alert identifying the ship, its location and indicating that the security of the ship is under threat or it has been compromised.
> ⓑ Send the ship security alert to any other ship.
> ⓒ Raise any alarm on-board the ship.
> ⓓ Continue the ship security alert until deactivated and/or reset.
> ⓔ the ship security alert system shall be capable of being activated only from the navigation bridge.

① 1개 ② 2개 ③ 3개 ④ 4개

06 보기가 설명하는 것이 무엇인지 고르시오.

> A method to obtain ship's position is by crossing-bearing of landmark, aids to navigation etc. This can be useless when the weather gets poor.

① meteorologic navigation ② celestial navigation
③ electronic navigation ④ geo-navigation

07 다음 중 의미가 다른 하나를 고르시오.
① Pilot on board
② Pilot left her
③ Dropped pilot
④ Disembark pilot

08 다음 중 항해일지의 기사를 바르게 해석한 것은 모두 몇 개인가?

> ⓐ Secured all derrick booms & other fittings.
> → 데릭 붐 및 기타 속구를 모두 고박하였다.
> ⓑ Singled up fore and aft, prepared for sea.
> → 선수미에 계류삭을 하나씩만 남기고 거두어 들였으며 출항준비를 함.
> ⓒ Laboured heavily, shipping seas on deck frequently.
> → 선체가 심하게 흔들리고 해수가 갑판으로 자주 올라옴.
> ⓓ Last line to pier let go.
> → 부두의 마지막 계류삭을 벗김.
> ⓔ Started to heave up port anchor.
> → 좌현묘를 내리기 시작함.

① 2개　② 3개　③ 4개　④ 5개

09 다음 중 항해일지 작성 시 오기가 발생한 경우에 수정하는 방법으로 가장 옳은 것은?
① Remove this page of the log book and rewrite all entries on a clean page.
② Blot out the error completely and rewrite the entry correctly.
③ Cross out the error with a single line and rewrite the entries correctly.
④ Carefully and neatly erase the entry and rewrite it correctly.

10 ISPS에 따라, 선박이나 항만에 공격위험이 식별됐을 경우 연안국이 실시할 수 있는 항만 통제로 옳지 않은 것은?
① Inspection of the ship
② Delaying the ship
③ Detention of the ship
④ imposing charges

11 MARPOL에 따라, 빈칸에 들어갈 적절한 것을 고르시오.

> According to MARPOL Annex 1,
> (   ) means a sea area where for recognized technical reasons in relation to its oceanographical and ecological condition and to the particular character of its traffic the adoption of special mandatory methods for the prevention of sea pollution by oil is required.

① Special Area ② Coastal Area
③ Prohibited Area ④ Nearest land

12 IAMSAR 매뉴얼 상 Williamson turn의 절차에 맞지 않는 것의 개수는?

> - ⓐNot to be used in an "immediate action situation".
> (1) ⓑRudder hard over.
> (2) After deviation from the original course by ⓒ240 degree, rudder hard over to the opposite side.
> (3) When heading ⓓ20 degree short of opposite course, rudder to ⓔmidship position so that ship will turn to opposite course.

① 2개 ② 3개 ③ 4개 ④ 5개

13 다음은 UNCLOS 상 high sea에 대한 규정이다. 옳지 않은 것의 개수는 몇 개인가?

> The high seas are open to all state, weather coastal or land locked. Freedom of the high seas is exercised under the conditions laid down by this Convention and by other rules of international law, it comprises, inter alia, both for coastal and land locked states.
> ⓐ freedom of navigation.
> ⓑ freedom of overflight.
> ⓒ freedom of lay submarine cables and pipelines, subject to part Ⅵ;
> ⓓ freedom of slave trade.
> ⓔ freedom of fishing, subject to the conditions laid down in section 2.
> ⓕ freedom of scientific research, subject to Part Ⅳ and Ⅷ.

① 없다. ② 1개 ③ 2개 ④ 3개

14 다음 중 빈칸에 들어갈 단어로 가장 옳은 것은?

> The position which is determined by only true course and distance without any other effect is (　　　　).

① Doubtful position
② Estimated position
③ Actual position
④ Dead reckoning position

15 What will below A and B do?

> A : Where is the rendez-vous position?
> B : 150 degree and 2' off from breakwater.
> A : OK, please prepare fender your side, I don't have it.

① pilotage
② berthing to pier
③ reporting to VTS
④ ship to ship activity

16 다음 중 SMCP 표현으로 올바른 것의 개수를 고르시오.

> ⓐ What kind of assistance is required?
>   어떤 원조가 필요한가?
> ⓑ Search all cabins for missing persons.
>   실종자를 찾기 위해 모든 객실을 수색하라.
> ⓒ I will make a lee for your vessel.
>   본선을 귀선의 풍하측으로 오게 하라.
> ⓓ Can you jettison cargo to stop listing?
>   선박전복을 막기 위해 화물을 투하할 수 있는가?

① 1개　　② 2개　　③ 3개　　④ 4개

17 다음 중 빈칸에 들어갈 내용으로 가장 옳은 것은?

> "Change of trim is caused either by shifting weight forward or aft, or by adding or removing weight before or abaft the ship's (   )".

① center of buoyancy ② center of gravity
③ metacenter ④ center of floatation

18 빈칸에 들어갈 말로 가장 옳은 것은?

> A vessel using traffic separation scheme shall join or leave from the side (   ).

① as nearly as practicable at right angles to the general direction of traffic flow.
② at as small an angle to the opposite direction of traffic flow as practicable.
③ as nearly as wide a margin as is practicable.
④ at as small an angle to the general direction of traffic flow as practicable.

19 MARPOL에 따라 산적 유해액체물질(noxious liquid substances in bulk)의 배출에 관련된 사항으로 옳지 않은 것을 고르시오.

① Discharging is made at a distance of not less than 12 nautical miles from the nearest land.
② The ship is proceeding an route at a speed of at least 7 knots in the case of self-propelled.
③ Discharging is made in a place of which depth of water is not less than 25 meters.
④ Discharge is made above the waterline through the underwater discharge outlet.

20 아래는 IAMSAR 협약에 대한 용어이다. 다음 중 틀린 것의 개수를 고르시오.

> ⓐ ELT – Aeronautical radio distress beacon for alerting and transmitting homing signal.
> ⓑ Distress Alert – Distress alert initiated for other than an appropriate test, by communications equipment intended for alerting, when no distress situation actually exists.
> ⓒ False Alarm – Notification by any means that a distress situation exists and assistance is needed.
> ⓓ Search – An operation to retrieve persons in distress, provide for their initial medical or other needs, and deliver them to a place of safety.

① 1개   ② 2개   ③ 3개   ④ 4개

해사영어 모의고사

01 빈칸에 들어갈 알맞은 말을 고르시오.

> The coastal State shall not hamper (   ) of foreign ships through the territorial sea except in accordance with UNCLOS.

① the innocent passage
② the transit passage
③ the rapid passage
④ the restricted passage

02 다음 빈칸에 들어갈 단어로 가장 적절한 것은?

> On the mercator chart the rhumb line appears (   ).

① curved line   ② circle   ③ straight line   ④ true course

03 다음은 군도 기선(Archipelagic baseline)에 대한 설명이다. 가장 옳지 않은 것은 무엇인가?

① An archipelagic State may draw straight archipelagic baselines joining the outer most points of the outermost islands and drying reefs of the archipelago provided that within such baselines are included the main islands.
② The length of such baselines shall not exceed 100 nautical miles except that up to 3 percent of the total number of baselines enclosing any archipelago may exceed that length, up to maximum length of 125 nautical miles.
③ The drawing of such baselines shall depart to any appreciable extent from the general configuration of the archipelago.
④ The system of such baselines shall not applied by an archipelagic State in such a manner as to cut off from the high seas or the exclusive economic zone the territorial sea of another State.

04 다음 빈칸의 해역에 들어갈 수 있는 용어와 가장 거리가 먼 것은?

> UNCLOS Article 110 - Right of visit.
> Except where acts of interference derive from powers conferred by treaty, a warship which encounters on the (   )(s) a foreign ship, other accordance with articles 95 and 96, is not justified in boarding it unless there is reasonable ground for suspecting that.

① open sea   ② high sea   ③ international water   ④ marine sea

05 빈칸에 들어갈 용어를 순서대로 나타낸 것은 무엇인가?

> ⓐ All vessels are advised to keep wide (   ).
>   모든 선박은 안전공간을 확보하는 것을 권고 받는다.
> ⓑ The SMCP is divided into (   ) communication phrases and (   ) communication phrases.

① range, external, internal
② range, external, distress
③ berth, external, on board
④ berth, internal, distress

06 다음 중 SMCP 표현으로 문장이 옳지 않은 것은 무엇인가?

① Change the radar to three miles range scale.
   -> 레이더를 3마일 레인지 스케일로 바꾸시오.
② My anchors are clear of water.
   -> 본선 앵커가 물에서 나왔다.
③ Transmit the distress alert.
   -> 조난 경보를 송신하시오.
④ Fill the tank with 30 tons of ballast water to refloat.
   -> 선박을 이초시키기 위해 평형수 30톤을 배출하시오.

07 다음 SMCP 상, 양묘 작업 시 아래의 문장을 영어로 표현할 수 없는 것 몇 개인가?

> 묘쇄를 얼마나 더 감아 들여야 하는가?
> ⓐ How many shackles are to come in?
> ⓑ How much shackles are to go?
> ⓒ How many shackles are in water?
> ⓓ How many shackles left?

① 없음 ② 1개 ③ 2개 ④ 3개

08 다음은 UNCLOS의 원문이다. 옳지 않은 것의 개수를 고르시오.

> ⓐ Waters on the landward side of the outer limit of the territorial sea form the internal water of the state.
> ⓑ Every State has the right to establish the breadth of its territorial sea up to a limit not exceeding 24 nautical miles, measured from baselines determined in accordance with this Convention.
> ⓒ Every State may validly purport to subject any part of the high seas to its sovereignty.
> ⓓ Except where otherwise provided in this Convention, the straight baseline for measuring the breadth of the territorial sea is the low-water line along the coast as marked on large-scale charts officially recognized by the coastal state.

① 1개 ② 2개 ③ 3개 ④ 4개

09 다음은 SOLAS규정 내용이다. 빈칸에 들어갈 내용을 고르시오.

> Muster lists and emergency instructions shall be exhibited in conspicuous places throughout the ship including the navigation bridge, engine-room and ( ).

① crew accommodation spaces
② steering gear room
③ launching station
④ pilot station

10 다음 밑줄 친 This가 설명하는 것으로 가장 옳은 것은?

> This is used for the exchange of data in ship to ship communications and also in communication with shore-based facilities. The purpose of this is to help identify vessels; assist in target tracking; simplify information exchange (eg. reduce verbal reporting); and provide additional information to assist situation awareness. This may be used together with VHF voice communications.

① Maritime Safety Information (MSI)
② Digital Selective Calling (DSC)
③ Enhanced Group Calling (EGC)
④ Automatic Identification System (AIS)

11 UNCLOS 상, 공해에서 외국 선박이 Right of visit을 시행할 수 있는 경우로 옳은 것의 개수를 고르시오.

> ⓐ the ship is engaged in fishing operation.
> ⓑ the ship is engaged in piracy.
> ⓒ the ship is constructing an artificial islands.
> ⓓ the ship is engaged unauthorized broadcasting and the flag state of the warship has jurisdiction under article 109;
> ⓔ the ship is carrying out scientific survey.
> ⓕ though flying a foreign flag or refusing to show its flag, the ship is, in reality, of the same nationality as the warship.

① 1개   ② 2개   ③ 3개   ④ 4개

12 다음 항행통보에 대한 설명을 보고 빈칸에 들어갈 말로 적합한 것을 고르시오.

> (   ) should be checked to see that they have been corrected through the latest (   ).

① log book and light list, sailing direction.
② chart and light list, notice to mariners.
③ chart and log book, sailing direction.
④ chart and log book, notice to mariners.

13 다음 VTS 통신 중 빈칸에 들어갈 말을 순서대로 고르면?

> VTS : M/V MCM, Your present course is too close to port limit of the fairway.
> M/V MCM : Copy that.
> VTS : (   ), alter course to (   ).

① INSTRUCTION - starboard
② ADVICE - port
③ ADVICE - starboard
④ INSTRUCTION - port

14 다음은 UNCLOS이다. 빈칸에 들어가기에 가장 옳지 않은 것을 고르시오.

> In the exclusive economic zone, the Republic of Korea has sovereign rights the purpose of (   ) the natural resources, whether living or non-living, of the waters superjacent to the sea-bed and of the sea-bed and its subsoil, and with regard to other activities for the economic exploitation and exploration of the zone, such as the production of energy from the water, currents and winds.

① exploring   ② charging   ③ managing   ④ conserving

15 다음 빈칸에 들어갈 말을 순서대로 고른 것은?

> ⓐ (   ) means any substances which, if introduces into the sea, is liable to create hazards to human health, to harm living resources and marine life, to damage amenities or to interfere with other legitimate uses of the sea, and includes any substances subject to control by the present Convention.
> ⓑ Any ship of 10,000 tons gross tonnage and above shall be provided with oil filtering equipment, and with arrangements for an alarm and for automatically stopping any discharge of oily mixture when the oil content in the effluent exceed (   ) parts per million.

① harmful substance - 15
② harmful substance - 30
③ sewage - 15
④ sewage - 30

16 밑줄 친 단어가 의미하는 것을 고르시오.

> Crew and passengers can stay <u>this place</u> of vessel and rest and eat, some vessel equipped with swimming pool or basket ball station.

① Accommodation space ② Recreation space
③ Seaman's club ④ Crew's messroom

17 다음 설명 중 옳지 않은 것의 개수를 고르시오.

> ⓐ The basic principle of "gyro compass" pointing to the north is the combined effects of the force of gravity and the daily rotation of the earth.
> ⓑ All distances given on the charts for the visibility of lights are calculated for a "height of an observer's eye" of 5 meters.
> ⓒ "deviation" means angle caused between the magnetic meridian and true meridian.
> ⓓ The action of bringing your vessel alongside a jetty or dock is called "unberthing".
> ⓔ "Way point" is an imaginary line on which a ship at sea must lie to satisfy certain data obtained by the observation of terrestrial or celestial object.

① 없다.   ② 1개   ③ 2개   ④ 3개

18 다음은 STCW 상 승무원의 자격에 대한 요건이다. 빈칸에 들어갈 숫자를 모두 합한 것은?

> Every officer in charge of a engineering watch in a manned engine-room or designated duty engineer officer in a periodically unmanned engine-room on a seagoing ship powered by main propulsion machinery of (   )KW propulsion power or more shall hold an appropriate certificate. Every candidate for certification shall
> - be not less than (   ) years of age
> - have completed not less than (   ) months seagoing service in the engine department in accordance with section A-II/1 of the STCW code

① 774   ② 780   ③ 524   ④ 519

19 다음은 STCW의 Watch System의 원문 일부를 발췌한 것이다. 빈칸에 들어갈 말을 순서대로 고른 것은?

> ⓐ The master of every ship is bound to ensure that (   ) are adequate for maintaining a safe navigational watch.
> ⓑ Under the master's general direction, the officers of the navigational watch are responsible for navigating the ship safely during their periods of duty, when they will particularly concerned with avoiding (   ).
> ⓒ The duties of the look-out and helmsperson are (   ).

① watchkeeping arrangements/ collision and stranding/ separate
② bridge watch level/ collision and stranding / combined
③ watchkeeping arrangements/ restricted visibility / combined
④ bridge watch level/ restricted visibility / separate

20 다음이 설명하는 것은 무엇인가?

> It means all kinds of food wastes, domestic and operational waste excluding fresh fish and parts thereof, generated during the normal operation of the ship and liable to be disposed of continuously or periodically except those substances which are defined or listed in other Annexes to the present MARPOL Convention.

① Sewage ② Bilge ③ Sludge ④ Garbage

29회차 해사영어 모의고사

01 다음 설명 중 틀린 것은 모두 몇 개인가?

> ⓐ Walk out(of anchor) : To reverse the action of a windlass to lower the anchor until it is clear of the hawse pipe and ready for dropping.
> ⓑ Dredging : A movement of an anchor over sea bottom to control the movement of the vessel.
> ⓒ Backing : When the wind direction moves clockwise.
> ⓓ Hogging : A stress which a ship's hull or keel experiences that the middle of the ship is pushed to bend downward.
> ⓔ A warm front : Where a cold air mass moves under warmer air mass.

① 1개 ② 2개 ③ 3개 ④ 4개

02 표준해사통신영어(SMCP)의 통신문으로 가장 옳은 표현은?

① I read you six.
② I am bound to next port.
③ May enter the fairway?
④ Stand-by the look out.

03 다음 용어 설명 중 옳은 것의 개수를 고르시오.

> ⓐ Correction : to plus the corrected part of the message when a mistake is made in message.
> ⓑ Receiving point : a mark or place at which a vessel is required to report to the local VTS-Station to establish its position is defined.
> ⓒ veering : the wind direction moves clockwise.
> ⓓ Even keel : her draft is the same at bow and stern.
> ⓔ Leeway : Vessels sideways drift leeward of the desired course.
> ⓕ Capsize : Inclination of the vessel to port side or starboard side.

① 3개 ② 4개 ③ 5개 ④ 6개

04 SMCP 표현 중 가장 옳지 않은 것은?

① 귀선의 위치에서의 기상상태는 어떠한가? :
   what is the weather situation in your position?
② 귀선은 항해중인가? : Are you underway?
③ 닻이 끌리고 있는가? : Are you dredging anchor?
④ 기관사용이 선교 조작으로 되어있습니까? : Is the engine on bridge control?

05 다음 빈칸에 들어갈 수 없는 단어를 고르시오.

㉠ Damage control team : A group of crew members trained for fighting (　　).
㉡ Refloat : To pull a vessel off after (　　); to afloat again.
㉢ Beach : To run a vessel up on a beach to prevent its (　　) in deep water.

① sinking　② grounding　③ capsizing　④ flooding

06 빈칸에 공통적으로 들어갈 말을 고르시오.

가. I picked (　) in position ...
   본선은 ... 위치에서 사람을 인양하였음.
나. Person picked (　) is crew member of MT ...
   인양된 사람은 유조선 ...호의 승무원임.
다. Picked (　) two river pilot at 1230LT.
   지방시 12시30분에 두 명의 강 파일럿을 태웠음.

① in　② up　③ out　④ on

07 다음 보기 중 IALA 해상 부표식에 따른 표지의 영문표기가 옳지 않은 것은 무엇인가?

① Lateral mark (측방위표지)
② Cardinal mark (방위표지)
③ Isolated danger mark (침선표지)
④ Safe water mark (안전수역표지)

08 다음 SMCP 예문과 해석이 올바르게 연결된 것을 고르시오.

① How many shackles are to come in?
(묘쇄 얼마나 더 감아 들여야 하는가?)
② How is the cable growing?
(앵커는 파주력이 있는가?)
③ There is turn in cables.
(묘쇄의 방향이 바뀌고 있다.)
④ Fairway speed is 6kts.
(항로 내 평균속력은 6노트이다.)

09 다음 설명 중 옳은 것의 개수를 고르시오.

> ⓐ 'Position line' is an imaginary line on which a ship at sea must lie to satisfy certain data obtained by the observations of terrestrial or celestial object.
> ⓑ 'Great circles' are circles on a sphere whose planes pass through the center of the sphere.
> ⓒ 'Equator' is a great circle through the geographical poles of the earth.
> ⓓ All the distances given on the charts for the visibility of lights are calculated for a height of an observer's eye of 5 meters.

① 1개   ② 2개   ③ 3개   ④ 4개

10 다음 중 UNCLOS에 따라, Right of visit에 대한 설명으로 옳지 않은 것을 고르시오.

① a warship of the country may send a boat under the command of an officer to the suspected ship.
② Although suspicion remains after the documents have been checked, it shall be stopped.
③ If the suspicions prove to be unfounded, and provided that the ship boarded has not committed any act justifying them, it shall be compensated for any loss or damage that may have been sustained.
④ These provisions also apply to any other duly authorized ships or aircraft clearly marked and identifiable as being on government service.

11 표준해사통신영어(SMCP)의 표현으로 빈칸에 적합한 것을 순서대로 고르시오.

> 가. "(   ). Arrange two tug boats for me."
> 나. A steering order to reduce swing as rapidly as possible is (   ).

① REQUIRE - Steady   ② REQUEST - Steady
③ REQUEST - Meet her   ④ REQUIRE - Meet her

12 "What is your heading?"의 질문에 대한 조타수의 응답으로 옳은 것을 고르시오.

① one-eight-zero degrees
② one hundreds eighty degrees
③ Nothing to port
④ Port ten

13 다음은 COLREG규정의 일부이다. 빈칸에 들어갈 숫자를 순서대로 고른 것을 고르시오.

> ⓐ "Side lights" means a green light on the starboard side and a red light on the port side each showing an unbroken light over an arc of the horizon of (   ) degrees and so fixed as to show the light from right ahead to (   ) degrees abaft the beam on its respective side.
> ⓑ "Flashing light" means a light flashing at regular intervals at a frequency of (   ) flashes or more per minute.

① 112.5-22.5-160   ② 112.5-67.5-160
③ 135-67.5-120   ④ 112.5-22.5-120

14 "Which of the following would not come under the Rule of Good seamanship?

① moderate speed in crowded waters.
② hand steering in restricted visibility.
③ ordering sea speed in harbour area.
④ safe speed in fog.

15 표준해사통신영어(SMCP)의 표현으로 빈칸에 적합한 것은?

> To reduce the oxygen in a tank by (   ) gas to avoid an explosion atmosphere.

① inert   ② fumigation   ③ flooding   ④ extinguish

16 다음은 SOLAS 상 안전증서, 비상대피장소의 규정이다. 빈칸의 숫자를 합한 값은?

> - A passenger ship safety certificate shall be issued for a period not exceeding (   ) months. A Cargo Ship Safety Construction Certificate, Cargo Ship Safety Equipment Certificate and Cargo Ship Safety Radio Certificate shall be issued for a period specified by the Administration which shall not exceed (   ) years.
> - A life jacket shall have buoyancy which is not reduced by more than (   )% after 24h submersion in fresh water

① 25   ② 34   ③ 22   ④ 36

17 밑줄 친 것이 설명하는 것을 고르시오.

> Before a vessel arrives this position, she should check all crew's health condition and sanitary condition all over the ship to get free pratique.

① Quarantine anchorage   ② Outer anchorage
③ Inner anchorage   ④ Special anchorage

18 When you are navigating vessel in fog, you heard two short blast on the whistle your starboard. what this means?

① Unknown vessel is changing course to port.
② Unknown vessel is changing course to starboard.
③ Unknown vessel is using engine now.
④ Unknown vessel is stopping now.

19 다음 빈칸에 들어갈 단어를 고르시오.

> Distances shall be expressed in (   ) or (   ), and the (   ) always to be stated.

① meters – cables – number ② nautical miles – cables – unit
③ meters – cable – number   ④ nautical miles – meters – unit

20 다음 영어 약자와 그 설명이 잘못 짝지어진 것의 개수를 고르시오.

> ⓐ Ah'd – 정횡 방향
> ⓑ M/V – 동력선
> ⓒ RB– 구조보트
> ⓓ RV– 구조선
> ⓔ NUC – 조종제한선
> ⓕ BWE – 방파제 입구
> ⓖ CPA – 최근접점
> ⓗ LMT – 지방평균시

① 1개   ② 2개   ③ 3개   ④ 4개

해사영어 모의고사

01 다음 SMCP의 문장 중 어색한 것의 개수를 고르시오.

> 가. I can not locate you on my radar.
> 나. Say again your position to assist identification.
> 다. Your present course is too close to outbound vessel. Keep your course.
> 라. Please make a leeway for my boat.

① 1개　② 2개　③ 3개　④ 4개

02 다음 SMCP 표현 중 해석과 문장이 올바르게 연결된 것이 아닌 것을 고르시오.

① Secure the heavy goods immediately.
　(중량 화물을 즉시 고박하시오.)
② Replace the damaged ladder.
　(손상된 사다리를 교체하시오.)
③ I will transfer bunkers to stop list.
　(본선은 횡경사를 멈추도록 연료유를 이송하겠음.)
④ Fog is set in.
　(안개가 걷힘.)

03 다음 SMCP 용어 중 설명이 옳지 않은 것의 개수를 고르시오.

> 가. Beach – To run a vessel up on a beach to prevent its sinking in deep water
> 나. Drifting – Being driven along by the wind, tide or current
> 다. Flooding – Major uncontrolled flow of seawater into the vessel
> 라. Leeway – On or towards the sheltered side of a ship
> 마. Hampered vessel – A vessel restricted by her ability to manoeuvre by the nature of her work
> 바. Crash stop – An emergency reversal operation of the main engine to avoid a collision
> 사. Transit speed – Speed of a vessel required for the passage through a canal, fairway, etc.
> 아. Muster – List of crew, passengers and others on board and their functions in a distress or drill

① 2개   ② 3개   ③ 4개   ④ 5개

04 다음 빈칸에 들어갈 가장 알맞은 말을 순서대로 고르시오.

> 가. (   ) up with 4 shackles of port cable in 10 meters of water at Busan Anchorage.
> 나. Take immediate action to (   ) injured persons.

① Picked, recover
② Picked, provide
③ Brought, recover
④ Brought, provide

05 다음 중 해사영어의 약어의 설명으로 옳은 것은 모두 몇 개인가?

ⓐ M/V : Motor Vessel
ⓑ W/H : Wheel House
ⓒ C.O.W : Crude Oil Washing
ⓓ Q.M : Quarantine Master
ⓔ O/B : On Board
ⓕ D.W.T : Dead Weight Tonnage
ⓖ G.T : Great Tonnage
ⓗ L.S.T : Local Separate Time
ⓘ D.R. : Dead Reckoning
ⓙ F/H : Full Ahead

① 5개 ② 6개 ③ 7개 ④ 8개

06 다음 빈칸에 들어갈 가장 알맞은 말을 순서대로 고르시오.

가. (　　) chart available should always be used when coasting since errors are reduced to a minimum and detail is shown.
나. Weather report received at 1235LT and indicated better weather ahead, and wind and swell had (　　). So pilot who had remained aboard agreed to try and dock. Tug was obtained and vessel proceeded to berth 17. Docking at 1430.

① The largest-scale, become rough   ② The largest-scale, eased
③ The smallest-scale, become rough ④ The smallest-scale, eased

07 밑줄 친 부분과 바꾸어 쓸 수 있는 것을 고르시오.

No.3 Anchorage has been <u>allocated</u> to you.

① changed   ② obstructed   ③ closed   ④ alloted

08 SOLAS규정에 맞게 다음의 빈칸을 채우시오.

> Inspection of the life-saving appliances, including lifeboat equipment, shall be carried out (   ) using <u>checklist required by regulation.</u>

① weekly   ② monthly   ③ daily   ④ annually

09 다음 중 단어와 설명이 옳게 연결되지 않은 것을 고르시오.

① Magnetic course : The angle between the ship's track and the true meridian.
② Cold front : Where a cold air mass moves under warmer air mass.
③ Track : The recommended route to be followed when proceeding between pre-determined positions.
④ Recommended direction of traffic flow : A traffic flow pattern indicating a recommended movement of traffic where it is impractical or unnecessary to adopt an established direction of traffic flow.

10 다음 빈칸에 들어갈 가장 적절한 단어를 고르시오.

> A drill will be held to (   ) passengers with their assembly stations, with their life-saving equipments and with emergency procedures.

① familiarize   ② master   ③ instruct   ④ educate

11 표준해사통신영어(SMCP)의 표현으로 빈칸에 적합한 것을 고르시오.

> My present position is, bearing, two five zero degrees, distance, (   ) from breakwater light-house.

① two zero one degree   ② latitude three two degree North
③ one decimal six miles   ④ no position

12 다음은 COLREG(International Regulations for Preventing Collisions at Sea)중 일부를 발췌한 것이다. ㉠의 선박을 고르고, 빈칸 ㉡에 들어갈 말을 고르시오.

> (a) (1) Where by any of these Rules one of two vessels is to keep out of the way the other shall keep her course and speed.
> (2) (㉠) may however take action to avoid collision by her manoeuvre alone, as soon as it becomes apparent to her that the vessel required to keep out of the way is not taking appropriate action in compliance with these Rules.
> (b) A power-driven vessel which takes action in a crossing situation in accordance with subparagraph (a)(ii) of this Rule to avoid collision with another power-driven vessel shall, if the circumstances of the case admit, not alter course to (㉡) for a vessel on her own port side.

	㉠	㉡
①	stand-on vessel	starboard
②	stand-on vessel	port
③	give-way vessel	starboard
④	give-way vessel	port

13 표준해사통신영어(SMCP)의 표현으로 빈칸에 적합한 것을 고르시오.

> You must stop immediately where you are. (   ), stop where you are.

① Say Again   ② Correction   ③ Mistake   ④ Repeat

14 빈칸에 들어갈 적절한 것을 고르시오.

> According to SOLAS convention, (   ) shall provide automatically to appropriately equipped shore stations, other ships and aircraft information, including the ship's identity, type, position, course, speed, navigational status and other safety-related information.

① AIS   ② VDR   ③ ECDIS   ④ RADAR

15 SMCP에 따라, 다음 메시지에 들어갈 수 없는 것의 개수를 고르시오.

> Upon receipt of the DSC Distress Alert acknowledgement, the vessel in distress should commence the distress traffic on one of the international distress traffic frequencies for telephony (VHF Channel 16 or 2,182kH).

> 가. The 9-digit MMSI code plus name
> 나. call sign
> 다. The position of the vessel
> 라. nature of distress
> 마. other information which might facilitate rescue
> 바. Location of the rescue vessel
> 사. Assistance required

① 없음　② 1개　③ 2개　④ 3개

16 다음 설명 중 옳은 것의 개수를 고르시오.

> 가. The action of bringing your vessel alongside a jetty or dock is called "berthing".
> 나. Crossed the meridian of 180° into west longitude at Lat. 43° N, Thursday July 12 was "repeated".
> 다. An instrument for measuring wind force or speed is a "thermometer".
> 라. A light line sent ashore or elsewhere to enable a heavier line to be hauled out is "messenger line".
> 마. The vertical distance on a given day between water surface at high and that at low water is called "tidal range".

① 2개　② 3개　③ 4개　④ 5개

17 다음 중 밑줄친 부분에 들어갈 수 있는 내용의 개수를 고르시오.

> VTS : What is your present position?
> My present "position" is (＿＿＿＿＿＿).

> 가. Lat. 23°-15`N, Long. 035°-25`E.
> 나. way point NO.5
> 다. in Indian ocean
> 라. bearing 135, distance 2 mile from C light house

① 1개 ② 2개 ③ 3개 ④ 4개

18 다음은 MARPOL에서 정의하는 단어들의 개념이다. 옳지 않은 것의 개수를 고르시오.

> 가. Centre tank : any tank adjacent to the side shell plating
> 나. Discharge : in relation to harmful substances or effluents containing such substances, means any release howsoever caused from a ship and includes any escape, disposal, spilling, leaking, pumping, emitting or emptying
> 다. Oily mixture : petroleum in any form including crude oil, fuel oil, sludge, oil refuse and refined products
> 라. Oil fuel : any oil used as fuel in connection with the propulsion and auxiliary machinery of the ship in which such oil is carried
> 마. Tank : an enclosed space which is formed by the permanent structure of a ship and which is designed for the carriage of liquid in bulk

① 1개 ② 2개 ③ 3개 ④ 4개

19 다음 빈칸에 들어갈 단어를 고르시오.

> In a tropical cyclone, a veering wind one changing direction to the right in the Northern Hemisphere and one changing direction to left in the Southern Hemisphere would mean that you were in the (＿＿＿).

① dangerous semicircle ② navigational semicircle
③ normal semicircle   ④ changeable semicircle

20 What is the below paragraph explain?

> This is caused that water or oil is not fully loaded at cargo hold or other tanks and moves randomly according to ship's movement like rolling and pitching. This make a negative effect to stability, and cause ship's capsize down.

① free surface reaction
② half liquid effect
③ random liquid effect
④ free surface effect

해사영어 모의고사

정답 및 해설

1회 | 모의고사

1	2	3	4	5	6	7	8	9	10
④	①	③	④	①	②	②	②	①	②
11	12	13	14	15	16	17	18	19	20
③	①	③	③	④	③	①	④	③	②

01 파일럿 보트는 파일럿 승선을 위해 본선으로 다가올 수밖에 없다. 이때 본선에서는 선속을 낮춰 파일럿 승하선을 위한 안전한 속력을 유지해 주어야하는데, 이때의 속력을 Boarding speed라고 한다.

02 SSO는 Ship Security Officer의 약자로 선박보안 담당관을 의미한다. 보기의 내용은 SSO가 보안 훈련을 1630UTC에 실시한다는 내용이다.

03 Vessel does not answer the wheel은 타를 써도 선박의 선회가 되지 않는 것을 의미한다. Vessel has no steerage way는 최소 타효속력이 없어 선박 선회가 되지 않는다는 말이므로, 밑줄친 문장에 대체되기에 가장 적합하다.

04 Fair leader는 갑판 상 설치되는 설비로 계류삭을 계류 중 선체로부터 통과하게 해주는 역할을 한다.

05 다가오는 선박의 Compass bearing(컴퍼스 방위)가 변하지 않는다면 이는 충돌의 위험이 있는 것이다.

06 가. Air draft는 수선에서부터 선박 상부구조물의 가장 높은 지점까지의 높이를 말하는데, highest point of the keel은 용골의 가장 높은 지점을 의미한다. 굳이 해석을 한다면 용골 상면부터 수면까지의 흘수인 형흘수(moulded draft)가 된다.
다. leeward(풍하측)에 대한 설명이다.
라. windward(풍상측)에 대한 설명이다.

07 safety(안전) 메시지에 관련한 정보를 전달할 때에는 SECURITE 부호를 3회 반복한다.

08 carry out = perform = 수행하다

09 선회권의 직경은 diameter of turning circle이다.

10 "How is the cable growing?" 은 닻줄의 장력 정도에 대해 묻는 질문이다. 총 세 가지가 질문에 대한 대답이 될 수 있다. tight 는 "팽팽함", slack은 "느슨함", coming tight는 "팽팽해지는 중" 으로 해석할 수 있다.

11 ① clearing은 문제 등을 해결하다란 의미로 사용 될 수 있다.
② towing은 예인하다를 의미한다.
④ picking up은 끌어 올리다, 인양하다 등을 의미한다.
③ lowering은 내리다, 하강시키다 등을 의미하므로 적합하

지 않다.

12 연안국의 sovereignty(주권)은 영토, 내수, 군도수역(군도국가의 경우), 그리고 영해까지 확장 될 수 있다.

13 IAMSAR에서 규정한 구명 용품 용기의 색상 중 yellow(노란색)은 blankets and protective clothing(담요, 보호복)을 담는 용기의 색상이다.

14 한 방향의 교통이 한계 내에 설정 된 해역은 Traffic lane(통항로)을 의미한다.

15 좁은 수로 내 만곡부(굴곡진 수로)에서 만곡부 반대쪽 선박이 가려져 보이지 않을 수 있는 경우 one prolonged blast(1회 장음)을 울려야 한다. 만일 만곡부 반대쪽에 장애물에 가려진 선박이 있다면 해당 선박은 마찬가지로 one prolonged blast(1회 장음)을 울려 줘야한다.

16 ㉠ 상단에 홍색 전주등, 하단에 백색 전주등을 점등하고, 꼭지 점이 모이는 두 개의 원추형 주간형상물을 설치하는 선박은 a vessel engaged in fishing, other than trawling(트롤링 어선을 제외한 어로종사선)을 의미한다.
㉡ 두 개의 홍색 전주등을 수직선상에 점등하는 선박은 a vessel not under command(조종불능 선박이다.)
㉢ 상부에 백색 전주등, 하부에 홍색 전주등을 수직선상에 점등한 선박은 a vessel engaged on pilotage duty (도선 업무에 종사중인 선박)이다.

17 A vessel restricted in her ability to manoeuvre(조종제한 선박)은 수직선상에 세 개의 전주등을 점등한다. 상부와 하부에 홍색, 중간에 백색의 전주등을 점등한다.

18 Sector search(부채꼴 수색)에 대한 설명이다.

19 Slop tank는 탱크 배수, 세정수 그리고 유성혼합물 등을 MARPOL 규정에 따라 특별히 따로 모아두는 탱크를 의미한다.

20 ㉡ COLREG 상 hampered vessel(조종제한선), vessel NUC(조종불능선)을 제외한 모든 선박은 vessel constrained by her draught(흘수제약선)에게 길을 비켜 줘야 한다. 때문에 Hampered vessel이 vessel constrained by her draught에게 길을 비켜 줘야한다는 설명은 잘못된 설명이다.

2회 | 모의고사

1	2	3	4	5	6	7	8	9	10
③	③	②	④	④	②	④	①	③	②
11	12	13	14	15	16	17	18	19	20
③	④	③	②	②	④	③	④	①	①

01 Ⓐ 선박이 전타를 쓰고 선수방위가 90도까지 바꾸었을 때 원침로 상에서 수직의(perpendicular) 방향으로 이동한 거리는 Transfer(횡거)이다.
Ⓑ 투묘를 위해 닻이 묘쇄공에서 빠져나올 때까지 양묘기를 역전시켜 닻을 내리는 동작을 walk out이라고 한다.

02 가. beach(좌안)에 대한 설명이다.
나. blind sector(맹목구간)은 레이더가 구조물 등에 가려 스캔되지 않는 구간으로 An area which can not be scanned 가 되어야한다.
라. 유령선처럼 버려진 채 떠다니는 선박인 derelict(유기선)에 대한 설명이다.

03 나. port officials는 항만관리인을 의미하며 하역인부는 shore man 혹은 stevedore라고 한다.
라. crash stop은 엔진을 full ahead 상태에서 full astern 상태로 역전시키는 기관명령을 나타냄으로 기관 정지라는 해석은 옳지 않다.

04 가. steady as she goes에 대한 설명으로 해당 명령이 내려졌을 때의 선수방위로 조타하라는 명령어다.

05 선저와 해저, 혹은 선저와 해저의 물체사이의 간격이 측되어진 항로를 뜻하는 Deep water route(심수심 항로)에 대한 설명이다.

06 다. Z - Zulu
라. M - Mike
마. R - Romeo

07 center line 선박의 중심을 가로지르는 선수미선에 대한 설명이다.

08 두 개 이상의 전파가 레이더에 동시에 수신되는 경우 radar interference(레이더 간섭)가 발생할 수 있다.

09 육지의 자연적 연장(natural prolongation)인 Continental shelf(대륙붕)에 대한 설명이다.

10 가. 선박이나 인명의 안전에 대하여 apprehension(의심)이 존재하는 경우 Alert phase(경계단계)가 된다.
나. 선박이나 인명이 중대하고 위태로운 위험에 위협받고 있거나 즉각적인 원조가 필요로 하는 상황에 대해 certainty(확실성)이 있다면 Distress phase(조난단계)가 된다.
다. 선박이나 인명의 안전에 대하여 uncertainty(불확실성)이 존재하는 경우 Uncertainty phase(불확실단계)가 된다.

11 다. 예인선단(예인선의 선미부 부터 예인선단의 끝까지)의 길이가 200미터를 초과하는 경우 three mast head lights (세 개의 마스트라이트)를 수직선상에 점등해야한다.
라. 예인등(towing light)를 선미등(stern light)의 위에 (above) 점등한다. 해당 항목에서는 ~~아래에(under)~~ 이라고 되어있다.

12 특수한 상황(exceptional circumstance)에 놓인 선박은 기관고장 등과 같은 상태에 있는 vessel not under command(조종 불능 선박)을 의미한다.

13 Ⓒ 선박의 길이가 100m이상인 경우 기적, 호종신호에 추가하여 징(동라)를 추가하여야 한다.
Ⓔ COLREG상 prolonged blast(장음)은 약 four to six seconds(4초에서 6초간)의 음향신호를 기적신호를 의미한다.

14 Line-throwing appliances는 구명줄 발사기로 조난자나 조난선박을 향해 줄을 발사시킬 수 있는 장비이다. SOLAS에서는 ⓐ상당한 정확도(resonable accuracy)를 요구한다 (ambiguous : 모호한). 또한 4개의 발사체를 요구하며-이는 줄을 ⓒ230m 이상 이동시킬 수 있는 것이어야 하고 , ⓓ2kN 이상의 파단력을 갖는 4개의 줄 또한 갖출 것을 설비규정으로 요구한다.

15 ⓐ 추적권은 권한 당국이 해당 선박이 법률을 위반했다는 좋은 이유가 있을 때에 행사 될 수 있다. 때문에 no reason 은 good reason으로 고쳐져야만 한다.
ⓒ 추적권은 피추적 선박이 자국이나 제3국의 territorial sea(영해)에 들어가는 경우 중단된다.

16 Until an OSC has been designated, the first facility arriving at the scene should assume the duties of an OSC.
현장조정관이 임명되기 전까지는 최초로 현장에 도착한 구조시설이 해당 임무를 담당한다.

17 An international Oil Pollution Prevention Certificate(국제기름오염방지증서는 총톤수 150t 이상의 oil tanker(유조선), 그리고 총톤수 400t 이상의 그 외의 선박에서 구비해야만 한다.

18 어떤 해상상태에서도 해수가 선내로 침투하지 못하는 상태를 weathertight(풍우밀)이라 한다.

19 MARPOL의 기름 배출 규제에 따라, 총톤수 400t 이상의 선박으로 부터의 oil(유류)혹은 oily mixtures(유성혼합물)의 배출시 유출액의 유분이 회석 없이 15ppm을 초과해서는 아니된다.

20 Pilot : 닻을 양묘할 준비가 되었습니까?

Captain : 네, 양묘기의 사용이 준비되었습니다.(양묘기에 기어를 넣어 사용 준비를 함).

3회 | 모의고사

1	2	3	4	5	6	7	8	9	10
①	④	④	①	①	①	③	③	②	②
11	12	13	14	15	16	17	18	19	20
③	②	②	③	②	②	③	①	④	③

01 충돌하다는 collide with, 인양하다는 pick up 이다.

02 keep clear(거리를 두다)는 stand clear로 대체될 수 있고, start again(다시 시작하다)는 resume와 대체될 수 있다.

03 화재가 발생된 것을 발견하였고, 화재의 확산을 방지하기 위하여 선속을 줄였다는 내용이므로 빈칸에는 발생을 의미하는 outbreak이 들어갈 수 있다.

04 high seas(공해)상에서는 어떠한 국가도 자국의 주권(sovereignty)을 행사할 수 없다.

05 가. VHF 통신 시 lowest transmitter power(가장 낮은 송신출력) 이 사용된다.
나. 인천 VTS와 선박간의 통신 중, 선박 측에서 Ebb(낙조)시 좌초가 우려됨으로 사용가능한 depth of water(수심)에 대해서 질문하는 내용이다.

06 '일시 중단되다' 는 suspend이다. suspect는 '의심하다' 이다.

07 Underway는 '항해 중' 상태를 말하는 것으로 투묘하지 않고, 접안하지 않고, 좌초하지 않은 선박의 상태를 의미한다. 때문에 부두 접안 중 쓰이는 기사인 '가, 나, 라' 는 항해중이 아닌 상태이고 묘박 중 양묘를 준비하려는 사, 또한 항해중이 아닌 상태이다.
다. 는 조종속력으로 전진중 이라는 기사이므로 underway로 볼 수 있다.
마. 는 운하 통과 후 Rung up engine을 하여 항해속력으로 전환한 기사이므로
바. anchor aweigh. 즉 닻이 해저에서 뜬 상태를 말하므로 항해중이 시작되는 기점인 anchor up &down(양묘 중 묘쇄공에서 닻줄이 해저로 수직이 됨) 이후의 단계이므로 항해중인 상태이다.

08 나. Fairway speed : Mandatory speed in a fairway.
라. Receiving point에 대한 설명이다.
마. Manoeuvring speed : A vessel's reduced speed in restricted waters such as fairway or harbours.

09 SMCP에서는 선미부에 설치된 Rudder(타)의 각도에 대한 명령 시 사용되는 숫자를 제외한 모든 숫자는 분리하여 말한다.
가. 200도로 침로 정침하라는 명령이므로 숫자를 분리하여 two-zero-zero 가 되어야한다.
나. 타각을 우현으로 10° 만큼 주라는 명령이므로 ten이 되어야한다.

10 가. Ship stability(복원성)에 대한 설명이다.
라. 통신부호 WARNING(경고)에 대한 설명이다.

11 ⓐ Scharnov turn은 immediate action(즉각적 동작)이 필요한 상황에서는 사용되지 않는 구조법이다.
ⓒ 240°

12 나. SMC - Search and Rescue Mission Coordinator(수색구조임무조정관)
마. ACO - Aircraft Coordinator(항공기조정관)

13 무중신호 상 2분을 넘지 않는 신호간격으로 1회 장음 이후 2회 단음을 울려야 하는 선박에 대한 내용이다.
나. 대수 속력이 없고 정지한 항해중인 선박은 2분을 넘지 않는 간격으로 two prolonged blast(2회 장음)을 울린다.
바. 피예인선은 one prolonged blast(1회 장음) 이후 three short blast(3회 단음)을 울린다.

14 가. stern light(선미등)는 백색의 등화로 선미에서 수평의 호 135도 만큼을 비춘다. 즉 정 선미에서부터 67.5도까지를 양측으로 비춰 주는 것이다.
나. mast headlight(전부마스트등)는 백색의 등화로 선수에서 수평의 호 225도 만큼을 비추어준다. 즉 정횡 후방 22.5도에서부터 정선수까지 양측으로 비춰 주는 것이다.

15 익수자 발생 시 당직자가 즉각 취해야할 동작은
다.익수자가 발생한 현쪽으로 전타 midship
가.기관정지
라.자기점화등이 부착된 구명부이 방출 로 이루어지며
나.긴급신호를 주변에 송출한다. 는 그 이후에 필요에 따라 사용될 수 도 있으나 IAMSAR MANUAL에서 명시하는 조치로는 적절하지 않다.

16 야간의 head-on situation(마주 오는 상황)에서는 상대선박의 양 현등을 볼 수 있으며 상대선 masthead lights(전부마스트등)또한 수직선상에서 볼 수 있다.
다. 야간의 overtaking situation(추월 상황)에 피추월선에게서 볼 수 있는 등화이다.
라. 야간의 crossing situation(횡단 상황)에서 자선 우측에 있는 유지선에게서 볼 수 있는 등화이다.

17 SMCP 상 선박 간 통신 시 go ahead는 전진의 의미가 아니라 "통신을 계속 이어가시오" 의 의미를 갖는다.

18 최신의 Notice To Mariners(항행통보)를 통하여 해도나 등대표 등을 확인하고 수정해야 한다.

19 preferably, notify the master when you are in doubts. 항해 당직 중 의심스러운 점이 있다면 즉각 선장에게 보고 해야한다.

20 가. 보안위험에 대해 등급을 매기는 것으로 Security level (보안 등급)을 의미한다.
나. 보안 상 최소한의 적절한 조치를 유지하는 단계는 Security level1이다.

4회 | 모의고사

1	2	3	4	5	6	7	8	9	10
②	②	④	①	②	①	②	③	②	③
11	12	13	14	15	16	17	18	19	20
③	③	④	③	②	②	②	①	②	①

01 take tug's line through the center fairlead. 예인선의 줄을 센터 페어레더 쪽으로 잡아라.

02 ㉠ 주권이 미치는 구역중 하나로 internal water(내수)가 있다.
㉢ 주권은 Air space(상공)에 미친다.
㉣ 영해에 미치는 주권은 본 규정과 그 외의 international (국제법) 아래에서 행사된다.

03 인접한 TSS내의 적절한 통항로를 안전하게 사용할 수 있는 선박은 inshore traffic zone(연안통항대)를 사용할 수 없다.

04 Where a risk of attack has been identified, the Contracting Government concerned shall advise the ships concerned and their Administrations of:
공격의 위험이 식별된 경우, 관련 권한 당국은 관련 선박과 그 선박의 기관들에게 다음의 사안을 권고하여야 한다.
the mandatory speed of the vessel(의무 선속)은 이에 해당하지 않는다.

05 나. Cargo ships of less than 500 tons gross tonnage이 되어야한다.
다. Pleasure yachts not engaged in trade이 되어야한다.

06 ㉠Derelict(유기선) ㉡Disabled(파손선박) ㉢Adrift(표류) ㉣Wreck(난파선)

07 The officer of the watch shall keep a proper look out(견시). Do not hand over(인계 하다) the duty to the relieving officer who is not good condition. 당직중인 항해사는 항상 적절한 견시를 유지하여야 하고, 좋지 않은 상태에 있는 사관에게는 당직의 인계를 해서는 안 된다.

08 ㉠ Parallel Sweep Search (PS)은 평행항적수색법이다.
㉣ 확대 사각 수색법은 little or no leeway(최소한의 풍압차)일 때 실시된다.

09 Your draft is more than the available depth of water. Your vessel is aground(좌초).

10 ⓐ two
ⓒ two
ⓔ sidelights, a stern light and masthead light.

11 ⓐA Passenger Ship Safety Certificate(여객선의 안전증서)는 유효기간은 12개월이다.
ⓒA Cargo Ship Safety Construction Certificate, Cargo Ship Equipment Certificate, Cargo ship Safety Radio Certificate(화물선안전구조증서, 화물선장비증서, 화물선안전통신증서)의 유효기간은 5년이다.

12 ⓑ Romeo, ⓒ Foxtrot, ⓔ Juliet

13 Precautionary area(경계해역)에 대한 설명이다.

14 VHF 채널 앞에 사용되는 전치사는 change channel(채널변경) 시 사용되는 전치사 to를 제외하곤 on이 사용된다.

15 라. Sea plane(수상항공기)에 대한 설명이다.

16 (1) 24시간미만 항해를 하는 여객선의 infant life jackets(유아용 구명조끼)의 숫자는 전체 승객의 2.5% 만큼 제공 되어야한다.
(3) life jackets suitable for children(어린이용 구명조끼)의 개수는 전체 승객수의 최소 10%만큼, 혹은 각 어린이의 수중 큰 높은 쪽의 개수로 제공되어야 한다.

17 Passage is innocent so long as it is not prejudicial(유해한) to the peace, good order or security of the coastal State.
통항은 연안국의 평화, 공공질서, 혹은 보안에 유해하지만 않다면 무해하다.

18 If a shipowner registers his ships in a country other than his own to escape paying some home taxations, to employ labour cheaper than that at home, or to benefit financially in any similar way, his ships are said to fly a flag of convenience(편의치적).

19 action to avoid collision(충돌을 피하기위한 동작)시 succession of small alterations(소각도 편침의 연속된 동작)은 피한다.

20 가. 엔진을 정지하라 : Stop engine.
나. 본선이 귀선의 풍하측이 되게 해 달라 : Pleas, make a lee for my boat

다. 선박의 횡경사를 수정하라 : Correct the list of the vessel

라. 하선이 불가능하다. : Disembarkation is not possible.

5회 | 모의고사

1	2	3	4	5	6	7	8	9	10
③	②	④	③	④	②	②	②	②	④
11	12	13	14	15	16	17	18	19	20
③	④	①	②	②	①	②	③	①	②

01 선박이 meridian of 180° 을 넘어 동경으로 넘어간다면 24시간이 전진하게 되므로 하루가 skip(생략)됐다고 할 수 있다. 항해 중 GMT-9시간대 지역에서 GMT-8시간대 지역으로(서→동) 이동하게 되었다면 1시간이 빨라지기 때문에 선내시계의 시각도 1시간을 <u>전진(Advance)</u> 해주어야한다.

02 다. Right of innocent passage - 무해통항권
라. Archipelagic State - 군도국가

03 좁은 수로나 좁은 항로를 항해하는 선박은 자선의 우측에 있는 <u>outer limit(바깥 경계)</u>에 가까이 붙어 항해해야 한다.

04 선미흘수(aft draft)가 선수흘수(fore draft)보다 높은 상태를 선미트림(trim by the stern)이라 한다.

05 vessel constrained by her draught(흘수제약선)의 주간 형상물은 <u>a cylinder(원통형상물 하나)</u>이다.

06 나. 채널에서의 통신이 불만족스러울 경우 채널의 변경을 지시하고 confirmation(확인)을 기다려야한다. → not wait confirmation

07 <u>ETA(Estimated Time of Arrival)</u>은 도착 예정시각으로 전치사 'at + 장소'가 사용된다.
ETD(Estimated Time of Departure)은 출항예정시각으로 전치사 'from + 장소'가 사용된다.

08 MV CAMBUS호가 좁은수로를 따라 항해하다 선수에 가깝게 붙어서 횡단하는 어선을 탐지했다. CAMBUS호가 충돌을 피하기 위해 닻을 투묘했다. 충돌을 피하기 위하여 투묘를 하여 닻을 끄는 것은 <u>Dredging</u>이다.

09 가. Rescue에 대한 설명이다.
나. SART에 대한 설명이다.
다. EPIRB에 대한 설명이다.

10 The state of a tidal current when it's speed is near zero, especially the moment when a current changes direction and its speed is zero : <u>Slack</u>
조류의 속도가 0일 때의 조류의 상태로, 특별히 조류의 방향이 바뀌고 속력도 0이 될 때의 순간을 말한다. : <u>계류</u>

11 SMCP는 <u>External communication(선외통신)</u>과 <u>On bard communication(선내통신)</u> 으로 나뉜다.

12 <u>shall not</u> assigned or undertake any duties which would interfere with the safe navigation of the ship.
선박의 안전 항해에 방해가 되는 업무는 맡아서는 안 된다.

13 VTS service중 <u>Navigational assistance service(항해원조 업무)</u>에 대한 설명이다.
항해 상 혹은 날씨 상황에 어려움이 있는 경우, 그리고 어떤 고장이나 결함이 선박에 있는 경우 매우 중요하다.

14 조난 통신 통제 국에서는 통신에 방해를 하는 선박국 등에 <u>silence(침묵)</u>을 부과할 수 있다. 이때 통신 용어 Seelonce Mayday를 사용한다.

15 충돌을 피하기 위한 동작은 (상황이 허락하는 한) 적극적(positive)이어야 하고, 적절한 시간에 이루어져야하고 (made in ample time), <u>적절한 선박운용술 준수를 염두(observance of good seamanship)</u>하여 이루어져야 한다.

16 –Two-way route(상호통항로)는 항행이 곤란하거나 위험한 해역을 통항하는 선박에게 <u>안전한 통로를 제공하는 것(providing safe passage)</u>을 목적으로 서로 방향이 다른 통항이 실시되고 있는 한정된 범위의 항로이다.
–Recommended track(추천항로)에 대한 설명이다.

17 – Traffic lane(통항로)는 그 내측에서는 <u>one-way(일방 통항)</u>이 정해진 한정된 해역으로, 자연 장애물(분리대를 형성하고 있는 것을 포함함)이 경계를 구성할 수 있다.
– Precautionary area(경계해역)은 선박이 특별한 <u>주의를 하면서(with particular caution)</u> 항행해야 하고, 그 해역 내에서 교통의 흐름의 방향을 권고 받을 수 있는 한정된 범위의 해역이다.

18 If the ship is to discharge at more than one port, the cargo for the first port of discharge is stowed in the upper part of the hold. In other words, cargo to be discharged at the first discharging port should be <u>loaded last(마지막에 적재)</u>
만약 선박이 한 개 이상의 항구에서 양하를 한다면, 가장 첫 항구에서 양하 될 화물은 화물창의 위쪽에 적재 돼야 할 것이다. 즉, 첫 항구에서 하역 될 화물은 <u>마지막에 적재해야한다.</u>

19 territorial sea(영해), contiguous zone(접속수역), exclusive economic zone(배타적 경제수역)의 경계를 정할 때 기준이 되는 선은 <u>base line(기선)</u>이다.

20 다. 이유 없이 정선하는 행위는 무해통항에 위배되는 점이나, 충돌을 피하기 위해 정선하는 것은 비상시에 포함되므로 유해하다고 보지 않는다.

라. 선내 훈련은 유해하다고 판단하지 않는다. 단 무기를 사용한 훈련(with weapon)은 유해하다고 판단한다.

6회 | 모의고사

1	2	3	4	5	6	7	8	9	10
③	①	④	②	④	④	②	②	②	④
11	12	13	14	15	16	17	18	19	20
②	②	③	①	④	②	④	①	④	③

01 walk back-VTS-check-Drop Back 순으로 연결된다.

02 ⓑ L - Lima

03 ㉠ Accommodation ladder(승선사다리)에 대한 설명이다.
㉡ Veering(순전)에 대한 설명이다.
㉢ General emergency alarm(일반비상경보)는 seven short blast(7회의 단음), one prolonged blast(1회의 장음)으로 이루어진다.
㉣ Jettison은 선박 안정성 등을 확보하기 위하여 의도적으로 화물을 투하하는 것을 의미한다. 그러나 accidently는 '사고로', '우연히'를 의미한다.

04 ㉠ Flooding(침수)에 대한 설명이다.
㉡ Make water(누수)에 대한 설명이다.

05 영해에 ①접한(contiguous) 수역을 접속수역이라고 한다.
②연안국(coastal)은 필요에 따라 통제를 할 수 있는데 다음을 위해서이다.
④영해(territorial sea) 내에서 일어난 관세, 재정, 출입국, 위생 법률이나 규정의
③위반(infringement)을 방지하기 위해.
접속수역은 영해에서 일어난 위의 4가지 법률적 위반에 대해 통제나 처벌할 수 있는 구역을 말한다.

06 선박은 협약에서 예외사항으로 두는 경우를 제외하고 오직 한 개 국가의 기(one State only)만을 달 수 있다. 또한 공해(high seas)에서는 배타적 관할권(exclusive jurisdiction)을 행사할 수 있다.

07 해사안전정보(Maritime Safety Information) 송신용 무선전신으로, 항해, 기상 경보, 그리고 긴급 정보 등을 MF/HF주파수를 통해서 송신 할 수 있는 장비는 NAVTEX이다.

08 ㉢ 타수가 집중하지 못하는 경우(inattentive) 타수는 선수 방위가 어떻게 되는가?(what is your heading)이라는 질문을 받아야한다. attentive는 '집중하는'를 의미한다
㉣ 조타 명령 중 특정 침로로의 정침을 하라는 명령이 내려지는 경우 그 숫자는 분리(separately)하여 복명복창해야 한다. 오직 타각을 통한 명령에서 나오는 타각만 붙여서 읽는

숫자이다. *combined : 합쳐진*
㉤ 화재가 진압되다. : fire is under control.
㉥ 파일럿 사다리를 설치하다. : Rig the pilot ladder.

09 turn in cable : 닻줄이 꼬이다.

10

11 ㉠ DSC : Digital Selective Calling (디지털선택호출)
㉡ E.P : Estimated Position (추정위치)
㉣ K.O : Knocked off (작업종료)
ELT는 항공기전용 EPIRB라고 생각하면 된다. Aeronautical(항공) distress beacon이다.

12 ㉠ Damage control team : A group of crew members trained for fighting (flooding) in vessel
㉡ Beach : to run a vessel up on a beach to prevent its (sinking) in deep water
㉢ Refloat : to pull a vessel off after (grounding); to set afloat

13 ㉠ 모든 선원들은 매달 한 번의 퇴선훈련과 한 번의 화재훈련을 받는다. 그러나 탑승 선원의 25%를 넘는 인원이 전달 선내 훈련에 참여하지 못하는 경우 출항 후 24시간 이내에 해당 훈련이 이루어져야 한다.
㉡ 상호시계내에 선박들이 있는 경우
(1) two short blast(2회 단음)은 좌현 변침을 의미한다.
(2) three short blast(3회 단음)은 후진 중을 의미한다.
㉢ 제한 시계 내에서 범선은 2분을 넘지 않는 간격으로 1회 장음에 이은 2회 단음을 울린다.
24+2+3+2= 31

14 선박 입항 시 무거운 계류(hawser)를 보내기 전에 가벼운 줄을 보내게 되는데 이를 Heaving line이라고 한다.

15 (d) 항내 접근 시 선박의 속력을 조종속력으로 전환했다. 이 때의 기준이 SBE이다.
(a) 파일럿이 승선하고 터그선이 붙었다.
(c) 부두에 첫줄을 연결했다. (입항기준)
(e) 모든 계류줄을 부두에 묶었다.
(b) 기관 종료를 하고. 모든 부서 해제했다.

16 사람이 물에 빠진 경우 사람이 빠진 현 쪽으로 전타를 해주어야한다. 본문에서 좌현에서 익수자가 발생했으므로 선박을 좌현으로 전타하여(turn the wheel hard left) kick현상으로부터 익수자를 보호한다.
*kick현상 : 선박의 선회 초기 선미가 회두방향의 반대로 빠져나가는 현상

17 Right of innocent passage(무해통항권)에서 passage(통항)이란 ①continuous and expeditious(지속적이고 신속)해야 한다.

18 ② 부채꼴 수색법(Sector Search)는 좁은(small) 수색구역에서 이루어진다.
    ④ 선박의 경우 2NM~5NM사이의 수색 직경에서 본 수색이 이루어진다.
    ⑤ 부채꼴은 우현(starboard)으로 120씩 전타하며 만들어진다.

19 ㉠ Scharnov turn은 사고 발생부터 수색을 시작한 시점까지 흐른 시간을 모르는 경우 효과적으로 이루어질 수 없다.(cannot be carried out.)
    ㉢ 240
    ㉣ midships(타 중립)

20 ㉠ 구조정(rescue boat)는 구명정 중 구조용 선박으로, 해당 선박의 진수설비는 본선으로의 회수와 진수가 가능한 한 가장 빠른 것이어야 한다.
    ㉡ 모든 구조정은 전진 속력이 잔잔한 바다에서 5노트까지인 경우에도 진수 가능한 것이어야 한다.
    ㉢ 구조정의 회수시간은 적당한 해상 조건에서 모든 인원과 장비를 실은 상태에서도 5분 이내여야 한다.
    5+5=10

7회 | 모의고사

1	2	3	4	5	6	7	8	9	10
④	④	③	①	②	③	①	①	④	①
11	12	13	14	15	16	17	18	19	20
②	②	③	①	②	③	④	③	②	②

01 ICS(국제해운회의소) : International Chamber of Shipping

02 Inshore Traffic Zone(연안통항대)에 대한 설명이다. TSS의 육지 쪽(landward)경계와 인접한 연안(adjacent coast)사이의 공간을 말한다.

03 ㉡ receiving point에 대한 설명이다.
    ㉣ position line or line of position(위치선)에 대한 설명이다.

04 만곡부(bend) 주변에 있는 선박은 1회의 장음(one prolonged)을 울림으로써 장애물 반대편에 있을 수 있는 선박에게 경고를 해주어야한다.

05 ㉠ 추적권은 오직 시각적 그리고 청각적인(visual and auditory) 정선 신호를 타선박이 듣거나 볼 수 있는 거리에서 준 이후에 시작될 수 있다.
    ㉡ 체포된 선박을 풀어주는 행위는 단지 해당 선박이 체포 후 호송되는 과정에서 배타적 경제 수역이나, 공해상을 통과

했다는 이유만으로는 주장될 수가 없다.(may not be claimed)

06 비상소집장소(Muster station)는 한 사람당 $0.35m^2$에 해당하는 갑판공간을 갖춰야한다.

07 피항동작(action to avoid collision)에 대한 설명으로 조기에 충분히(early and substantial) 이루어져야한다.

08 Free board(건현)은 선박 중심부상 수선에서부터 상갑판상까지의 높이를 말한다.

09 ㉡ Parallel track search(평행항적수색법)에 대한 설명이다.
    ㉢ Parallel track search(평행항적수색법)의 경우 생존자의 위치가 불명확 할 때에 사용되므로 certain 대신 uncertain이 들어가야 한다.
    ㉣ 알려진 항적을 따라 가던 흔적 없이 선박이나 항공기가 사라졌을 때에 사용 되는 수색법으로는 Track Line Search(TS)(항적선수색법)이 있다.
    ㉤ 가파른 고도 변화 때문에 일반적인 수색이 어려울 때, 산이나 계곡 등에서 사용되는 수색법은 Contour Search가 있다.

10 ② A/Co – Alter Course
    ③ TMAS – Medical Assistance
    ④ R/UP – Rung(Ring) up

11 방위 분해능을 결정짓는 성능은 같은 거리, 다른 방위에 있는 반사체(echo)를 구분하는 성능이며 수평 빔폭(horizontal beam width)에 영향을 받는다.

12 ㉡ 트롤링에 종사하지 않는 어선(Fishing vessel other than trawling)의 경우 상부 홍색(red) 하부 백색(white)의 전주등을 켠다.
    ㉣ 도선 업무에 종사하는 도선선의 경우 상부 백색(white) 하부에 홍색의(red) 전주등을 점등하지만 본문의 Pilot vessels not engaged on pilotage duty의 경우 도선 업무에 종사하지 않는 경우를 의미하기에 해당 등화를 점등하지 않는다.

13 선박의 승무원은 매달 화재훈련과 퇴선훈련을 받는다. 그러나 전체 인원의 25%를 넘는 인원이 전달의 훈련을 받지 않은 경우 선박 출항 24시간(24h)이내에 해당 훈련을 실시한다.

14 The officer in charge of the navigational watch shall *not* hand over the watch to the relieving officer if there is reason to believe that the latter is not capable of carrying out the watchkeeping duties effectively, in which case the master shall be notified
    (인수자가 효과적인 당직수행이 불가능하다고 판단되는 경우 당직 사관은 인수사관에게 당직인계를 해서는 안 된다.)

15 ㉡ D : Delta ㉣ V : Victor

16 Wing tank menas any thank adjacent to the side shell plating.
    (Wing tank는 현측 외판에 있는 탱크를 의미한다.)

17 Sailing vessel(범선)은 추진 기관이 설치되어 있다고 하여도 이를 <u>사용하지 않고</u> 돛을 달고 항해하는 모든 선박을 의미 한다:
    Any vessel under sail provided that propelling machinery, if fitted, is not being used.

18 ③은 area to be avoided(피항해역)에 대한 설명이다.

19 통상기선 : Normal base line

20 선박이 가장 가까운 육지로부터 ②3해리를 넘는 거리에서 ①주관청(Administration)이 승인한 시스템을 사용하여 분쇄하고 소독한 하수를 배출하는 경우, 또는 가장 가까운 육지로부터 ③12해리를 넘는 거리에서 분쇄하지 아니하거나 소독하지 아니한 하수를 배출하는 경우, 다만, 어떠한 경우에도 홀딩탱크에 저장한 하수는 동시에 배출하여서는 아니 되며 선박이 ④4노트 이상의 속력으로 항해 중에 적당한 비율로 배출하여야 한다. 이 배출율은 기구가 정하는 기준에 따라 주관청이 승인한 것이어야 한다.

8회 | 모의고사

1	2	3	4	5	6	7	8	9	10
③	①	①	④	②	③	①	④	④	④
11	12	13	14	15	16	17	18	19	20
②	②	①	③	④	①	②	①	②	②

01 선박이 위험한 침선을 발견했다는 내용이다. 발견을 했으나 해당 침선과 충돌을 했다거나 선박이 손상을 입었다거나 하는 내용의 언급은 없으므로, Safety message 신호인 SECURITE를 세 번 반복하고 해당 침선의 위치를 주변 선박에 알리는 것이 적절한 상황이다.

02 *지구에는 북(North)이 총 세 가지가 있다. 진북(True North)와 자북(Magnetic North)사이의 오차는 지구 자성으로 인한 편차(Variation)라 하고 자북(Magnetic North)과 나북(Compass North)사이 의 오차는 선박 자체의 철재에 의한 자차(Deviation)이라 한다. 편차와 자차를 모두 포함한 오차를 컴퍼스 오차 (Compass error)라 한다.*
    해당 지문 상 나북과 (   )북사이에서 컴퍼스오차(Compass error)가 발생했다. 컴퍼스 오차는 <u>진북(True North)</u>과 나북(Compass North) 사이에 발생한다.

03 When you hearing Distress calls/messages all other transmissions should cease and a listening watch should be kept.
    조난신호나 메시지를 들은 경우 모든 송신을 중단하고 청수당직을 <u>유지</u>해야한다.

04 임검권(right of visit)은 군함과 군용항공기뿐만 아니라 권한을 부여받고, 정부업무(on government service) 에 종사중이라는 식별이 가능한 선박들도 실시할 수 있다.

05 ⓒ 선박 속도는 knots로 표현되고 추가적인 언급이 없다면 이는 <u>대수속력(Speed Through the Water)</u>를 의미한다. Speed Over the Ground는 대지 속력이다.
    ⓒ 거리는 가급적 nautical miles이나 cables로 표현되고 이런 단위들은 상호 이해가 된 상황이라도 항상 언급해야 한다. ; the unit <u>always to be stated</u>

06 총톤수 <u>10,000톤</u> 이상의 선박에는 기름 필터링 장치를 설치하여야 하며 유출 액 중 유분이 15ppm을 초과할 경우 유성혼합물의 배출을 자동으로 중단시키기 위한 장치 및 경보장치를 설치하여야 한다.

07 순서는 투묘 작업 시간 순서로 옳은 것은 <u>라, 다, 나, 가</u> 이다.
    라. 좌현 닻 투묘를 위해 배치를 함.
    다. walk out(투묘를 위해 양묘기를 사용해 수면 상까지 닻을 내리는 동작)을 좌현 닻으로 실시
    나. 투묘
    가. brought up 은 닻이 해저에 완전히 박혔다는 의미이다.

08 <u>collision bulkhead(충돌격벽)</u> is the first water tight bulkhead in the ship.
    *격벽은 선박 침수 시 해수침투가 확장되지 못하도록 해주는 수밀 벽이다. 그중에서도 선수부에 위치한 격벽은 선박 충돌들과 같은 충격에 보다 강하게 버텨줘야 하기 때문에 보다 높은 강도를 지닌다. 이를 <u>충돌격벽(collision bulkhead)</u>라고 한다.

09 선박 갑판에 H로 페인트칠이 되어 헬기가 안전하게 착륙하게 해주는 지점을 <u>Landing point</u>라 한다.

10 간접반사(indirect reflection) 는 선박 구조물 등에 의해 전파가 반사되어 수신되는 것을 말한다. 해당 내용은 전파가 수면이나 창문, 건물 등에 반사되는 <u>경면반사(Specular reflection)</u>에 대한 설명이다.

11 When the information requested cannot be obtained, say <u>No information</u>
    요청된 정보를 확보하지 못한 경우 <u>No information</u>이라고 설명해야한다.

12 대한민국의 <u>배타적 경제수역(exclusive economic zone)</u>은 기선으로부터 200해리 까지 확장할 수 있는 바다의 해역을 말한다.

13 마.도끼(axes)

바. 요리도구(cooking utensils)

14 당직 항해사는 인수자(relieving officer)가 당직업무를 효과적으로 할 수 없다고 판단한 경우 당직을 인계(hand over)하여서는 아니 되며, 이 경우 선장에게 보고해야한다.

relieve는 경감시켜주다 라는 의미를 갖는다. 때문에 relieving officer라는 말은 당직 업무를 대신 경감시켜주는 사관이라는 뜻이 되므로 인수자로 해석하며 officer relieved는 그 경감을 당하는 사관이므로 인계자로 해석한다.

15 SMCP는 더 나은 항해의 안전과 선박 운항을 보조하기 위해 편집됐다.

16 The master of every ship is bound to ensure that watchkeeping arrangements(당직 배치) are adequate for maintaining a safe navigational watch.
모든 선박의 선장은 당직의 배치가 안전한 항해 당직을 유지하기 위해 적절히 이루어졌는지 확인할 의무가 있다.

17 COLREG 상 모든 선박은 항상(at all times) 안전한 속력(Safe speed)으로 항해해야한다.

18 MARPOL에서 정의하는 기름(Oil)은 기름 이외의 물질이 섞이지 않은 액체들을 의미한다. 그러나 oily mixture는 유성 혼합물로 기름과 그 외에 다른 물질이 섞여있는 액체를 의미한다.

19 ⓒ SRR - Search and rescue region(수색구조 지역)

20 Traffic lane은 한 방향으로의 진행 흐름을 갖는다. 때문에 two way 대신 one-way가 오는 것이 적절하다.

9회 | 모의고사

1	2	3	4	5	6	7	8	9	10
②	③	①	②	④	④	①	②	③	③
11	12	13	14	15	16	17	18	19	20
③	②	①	④	②	①	③	②	①	③

01 ① ~과 충돌하다 : collide with~
③ 항로내제한속력 : Fairway speed
④ 좌현 선미 : port quarter

02 ⓒ PPM : part(s) per million
ⓔ MSI : Maritime Safety Information
ⓑ MMSI : Maritime Mobile Service Identity number
ⓐ VTS : Vessel Traffic Service

03 안전속력(Safe Speed)는 선박이 충돌을 피하고, 적절한 거리 내에서 정지 할 수 있게끔 최대한(maximum)의 시간을 별개 해주는 속도이다.
minimum→maximum

04 충돌을 피하기 위한 동작은(Action to avoid collision)
첫 번째, 적극적이어야 한다.(positive)
두 번째, 충분한 시간에 이루어져야한다.(ample time)
세 번째, 적절한 항해 운용술을 준수한다.
또한 피항시 최대한 크게 변침한다.(large)

05 좌초된 선박(a vessel aground)에는 정박등에 부가하여 홍등 2개(two all-round red lights)를 점등하고 혹은 흑구 3개(three black balls)를 수직선상에 설치한다.

06 ㉠ TSS로 진입시는 되도록 종점부근으로 들어가는 것이 좋으나 양측에서 진입 시에는 최대한 소각도(small an angle)로 진입 한다 as right angle은 직각방향이므로 적절하지 않다.
ⓒ 되도록 TSS를 횡단해서는 안 되나 그렇게 할 의무가 있는 경우 그렇게 하되 직각(right angle)으로 횡단 한다. at as small angle은 소각도 이므로 적절하지 않다.
ⓓ 안전하게 TSS의 통항로를 항해할 수 있는 선박은 연안통항대(ITZ)로 진입해서는 안 되나, 길이 20m미만의 선박(vessels of less than 20m in length), 범선(sailing vessel), 어로에 종사중인 선박(vessels engaged in fishing)의 경우 연안통항대(ITZ)로의 진입이 가능하다.

07 ㉠ 기항하다 : call at
ⓒ ~를 따라 항해하다 : proceed by
ⓔ ~을 향해 가다 : bound for~

08 ㉠ 타각을 0도, 즉 선수미선에 맞추는 midships 명령이다.
ⓒ 선수가 돌아가는 움직임을 억제(check)하라는 meet her 명령이다.
ⓓ 명령이 내려진 순간에 선수방위가 향하던 침로로 정침하라는 명령 steady as she goes이다.
ⓔ 가능한 신속하게 선수 회두를 줄이라는 steady 명령이다.

09 12미터 미만의 선박(vessel of less than 12m in length)는 COLREG에서 지정한 음향 신호를 갖출 필요가 없다. 다만 기타 유효한 음향신호를 사용하고 신호간의 간격은 2분을 초과해서는 안 된다.

10 ① On passenger ships, an abandon ship drill and fire drill shall take place weekly
② Every passenger ship shall carry additional life jackets for not less than 5% of the total number of persons on board.
④ Different groups of life boats should not be used in turn at successive boat drills and every lifeboat shall be swung out and, if practicable and reasonable, lowered

at least once every 3months. (free fall type은 6개월에 1번)

11 International Maritime Dangerous Goods(IMDG)CODE는 SOLAS에 의거한다.

12 ⓒ if the crime is of a kind to disturb(훼방하다) the peace of the country or the good order of the territorial sea.

ⓔ 기국의 외교관(Diplomatic of the *Flag state*)뿐만 아니라, 기국의 영사관(Consular officer of the *Flag state*), 선박의 선장(Master of the ship)이 요청을 하는 경우도 형사적 관할권이 행사될 수 있다. 또한, Coastal state는 연안국을 의미한다.

13 점장도(mercator chart)의 장점은 해도 상에 침로(course)가 직선(straight line)으로 표시된다는 점이다.

14 총톤수 400톤 이상의 선박은 oil filtering equipment를 설비해야 하며, 총톤수 10,000톤 이상의 선박부터는 추가적으로 유출액의 유분이 15ppm을 넘을 시 알람을 울리고 정지를 시키는(automatically stopped) 설비를 갖추어야한다.

15 ⓒ 항해 중(underway)은 묘박하지 않고, 계류하지 않고, 좌초(aground) 되지 않은 상태를 의미한다.

16 선박이 기관속력인 대수속력(speed through the water)으로 8노트로 항해 중이었는데, 외력의 영향을 포함하여 측정되는 대지속력(speed over the ground)은 4노트로 측정되었다. 선박 진행 반대방향으로 4노트에 해당하는 외력이 작용하고 있다는 것을 알 수 있다. 보기 중 순조(with current)가 아닌 역조(counter current)가 적합하다. 또한 VTS 등에서 현재속력이 얼마냐는 질문을 할 시 추가적인 언급이 없는 경우 대수속력(speed through the water)으로 대답한다.

17 ⓒ REQUEST에 대한 설명이다.
ⓒ INFORMATION에 대한 설명이다.
ⓔ ANSWER(대답)통신 부호를 사용한 경우 응답에 질문이 포함이 되면 안 된다.

18 OSC에게 얼마나 많은 권한을 위임 할지에 대해 결정할 때에, SMC는 개인 역량(personnel capabilities)을 고려할 수 있다.

19 ⓒ SASS 경보는 주변에 포진했을 수 있는 해적선 등의 문제 때문에 선박들에게 전송하지 않는다.
ⓒ 선내에 해적 등을 자극 할 수 있기 때문에 선내 SASS경보가 울려서는 안 된다.
ⓔ SASS는 선교(Bridge)뿐만 아니라 그 외 1개 이상의 장소에도 설치 되어야한다.

20 ⓒ 가장 깊은 만재 흘수(deepest seagoing draught)
ⓔ 7노트

ⓔ 높은 쪽(greater)

10회 | 모의고사

1	2	3	4	5	6	7	8	9	10
③	③	①	④	④	③	①	①	③	②
11	12	13	14	15	16	17	18	19	20
②	③	③	④	①	①	④	②	①	③

01 ⓒ the 360 degrees notation from north (true north unless otherwise stated)
ⓔ to be expressed in nautical miles or cables, the unit always to be stated

02 ① "Routing System" means any system of one or more routes or routing measures aimed at reducing the risk of casualties.
② "Roundabout" means a routing measure comprising a separation point or circular traffic lane within defined limits.
④ "Area to be avoided" means a routing measure comprising an area within defined limits which either navigation is particularly hazardous or it is exceptionally important to avoid casualties.

03 ① Stand well clear of the spring line.
→스프링 라인에서 떨어져라.

04 ⓒ 타효를 갖는 속력은 최소타효속력(Steerageway)이라 한다.
ⓒ 선수가 우현으로 가지 않게 하라는 표준조타명령은 Nothing to starboard 이다.

05 ⓒ 범선(sailing vessel)은 어로 종사중인 선박(vessel not engaged in fishing)에게 길을 비켜줘야 한다.
ⓒ 어로종사중인 선박(vessel engaged in fishing)은 범선(sailing vessel)에게 길을 비켜줄 필요가 없다.
ⓒ COLREG 상 조종불능선(vessel not under command), 조종제한선(vessel restricted in her ability to manoeuvre)을 제외한 선박이 흘수제약선(vessel constrained by her draught)에게 길을 비켜준다.

06 두 선박간의 VHF통신 상 대화문이다.
송신상태가 어떠한지를 의미하는 SMCP는 how do you read me 이며, VHF채널 변경은 change to ch.08 이라 한다. 통신 중 주요한 정보를 강조하고 싶을 때에는 repeat을 사용하고 해당 내용을 한 번 더 언급한다.
*INSTRUCTION 통신부호의 경우 VTS, 해군 등의 권한이 주

어진 국에서 사용된다*

07 ISPS는 선박과 항만 시설의 보안(Security)에 관련된 국제 코드이다.

08 ㉠ : Hours underway는 항해 중 시간을 말하며 앵커가 해저로부터 직각이 되는 Up&down anchor부터 다음 투묘인 let go anchor까지의 시간도 항해중 시간에 속한다.
㉡ : Pitch는 한 번의 프로펠러 회전으로 선박이 전진하는 거리를 말한다.
㉢ : Range Resolution은 거리분해능으로 같은 방위에 위치한 다른 거리의 두 물표를 구분해내는 능력이다.

09 (Cock bill) : This is the situation standing by anchor and about to let go anchor.
(Yawing) : this is turning rotation when ship's bow is pushed first to port and than to starboard.

10 Tested steering gear, whistle, means of communications All in good order.
synchronized bridge & E/R clocks
조타기, 기적신호, 통신기기를 점검 하였고 이상무. 선교와 기관실의 시계를 일치시켰음.

11 ㉠ urgency 통신문은 긴급 통신문이기 때문에 Mayday 대신 Pan-Pan이 와야 한다.
㉡ MMSI는 해사이동업무식별번호로 9자리 숫자로 이루어진다.

12 총톤수 500톤 이상의 선박에 승선하는 항해사의 자격을 위해서는 규정에 맞게 구성된 1년 이상의 승무경력(seagoing service)을 갖춰야 한다.

13 ③ Often appropriate for vessels or small boats to use when searching for persons in the water or other search objects with little or no leeway.

14 선박이 담수(fresh water)에서 해수(salt water)로 이동하면 비중 증가로 선체가 물에 더욱 뜨게 된다. 자동적으로 건현(freeboard)는 증가(increase)하고 흘수(draft)는 감소(decrease)하게 된다.

15 Bulkheads는 수직의 칸막이로 벽으로, 모든 선박들이 길이에 따라 특정 숫자를 가지고 있다. 수밀 격벽으로 선박을 나눔으로써 구획에 파공이 생겨도 선박이 침몰하지 않게 해준다.

16 SMCP는 단순하고(simple), 정확하고(precise), 모호하지 않기(unambiguous) 위해 표준화 시킨 항해 안전 통신영어 이다. continuous는 지속적인 이라는 의미를 갖는다.

17 항해 선교(navigation bridge)에는 로켓낙하산화염신호(rocket parachute flares) 12개 이상이 비치 되어야한다.

18 COLREG 상 타 선박을 우측에 둔 선박이 피항선이므로 보기에 언급된 타 선박을 좌측에 둔 선박은 자연스럽게 유지선(stand on vessel)이 된다. 이 때 유지선은 침로와 선속을 유지한다.(keep course and speed). 또한 피항선은 피항시 타선의 선수로(ahead) 통과하지 않는다.

19 ③ Where a ship has been stopped or arrested outside the territorial sea in circumstances which do not justify the exercise of the right of hot pursuit, it shall not be compensated for any loss or damage that may have been thereby sustained.

20 50미터이상 정박선의 등화는 전부에 ㉠백색 전주등(all round white light) 혹은 ㉡흑구 하나(one ball) 그리고 후부에 전부보다 높이가 ㉢낮은(lower) ㉣백색 전주등(all round white light)이다.

11회 | 모의고사

1	2	3	4	5	6	7	8	9	10
②	③	①	③	②	④	③	①	①	②
11	12	13	14	15	16	17	18	19	20
①	③	②	③	②	③	②	④	①	③

01 REPORTED : in navigational warning ; position of object unconfirmed
LOCATED : in navigational warning ; position of object confirmed

02 이초(refloat)이란 좌초된 선체를 띄우는 것을 말한다.
① 고조가 될 때에 이초작업을 실시하는 것이 좋다.
② 날씨가 좋아질 때의 이초작업은 적절하다.
③ 흘수가 증가(draft increases)한다는 것은 선체가 더욱 가라앉는다는 뜻이므로 이초에 부적합하다.
④ 이초작업을 0900UTC에 실시한다는 의미로 어색할 것이 없다.

03 대축척 지도(The largest-scale)는 지도상에 작은 범위를 표시하는 지도로 확대가 많이 된 지도라고 할 수 있고, 소축척 지도(The smallest-scale)는 지도상에 넓은 범위를 표시는 지도로 대표적으로 세계지도, 총도가 있다. 연안항해(coastal navigation)는 연안에서 하는 항해 이므로 연안의 자세한 부분을 볼 수 있어 오류를 최소화 해주는 대축척 해도(The largest-scale)를 사용한다.

04 선박들은 서로 다른 선회권을 갖는다. 그러나 선회권을 그리는 선박의 회전은 전심(Pivoting Point)을 중심으로 이루어지며, 이는 선미에서부터 선박길이 1/3만큼 전방에 위치해 있다.

05 ② If the correspondences of the crime extend to the coastal State(연안국).

06 ⓒ **communications related to safety and navigation on port operation channels**은 안전과 항해에 관련된 항만작업 채널에서의 통신이므로 피해야하는 행위로는 적합하지 않다. **not related** 로 고쳐야 한다.

07 일반적인 침수가 있는 경우 선박이 완전 침몰(foundering)할 때까지 배를 포기하지 않아야 한다는 점을 기억해야한다. *foundering = sinking*

08 I. 두 선박이 마주 오는 상황(head-on situation)인 경우 <u>우현(starboard)</u> 변침하여 좌현 대 좌현으로 통과한다.
II. 나) 횡단상황(crossing situation)에서는 타선박을 <u>우현(starboard)</u>에 둔 선박이 피항선이 된다.
III. 다) 피항선은 가능한 한 <u>조기(early)</u>에, 그리고 충분한(substantial) 동작으로 피항 해야 한다.

09 ① 기뢰제거선(vessel engaged in minesweeping operations)은 녹색 등화 <u>세 개</u>를 단다.

10 (가) 선박의 상대방위(relative bearings)는 <u>선수(vessel's bow)</u>를 기준으로 한다.
(나) 선박에서 나는 기적 신호를 <u>blast</u>라고 한다.

11 <u>접속수역(contiguous zone)</u>내에서 연안국(coastal state)은 관세(customs), 재정(fiscal), 출입국(immigration), 위생(sanitary)에 관련된 <u>법률위반(infringement)</u>을 방지하기 위해 통제를 할 수 있다.

12 ⓒ Slop tank의 유성혼합물 배수
ⓔ Bilge tank의 배수

13 충돌(collision)의 위험이 있으므로 항로(fairway)를 통과하지 말라는 지시문이다. 통신부호 **Instruction**이 적합하다.

14 무선 통신 중 **Out**은 통신 전체를 종료한다는 의미이다. 반면 **over**는 통신대화 전체 중 자신의 송신을 끝낸 후 사용한다. 그러므로 ②의 '송신을 끝냄'은 over이고, ③의 '대화 전체를 종료함' 이 out이다.

15 I. 제한시계내에서는 정횡 전방(forward of the beam)방향의 선박에 대하여서 피추월상황을 제외하고는 <u>좌현(port)</u> 변침을 해서는 안 된다.

16 선박용골(keel) 혹은 선박중심선(centre line)이 선박의 항적(wake, track)과 만드는 각도를 <u>풍압차(leeway)</u>이다.

17 ① **Fetch** : The distance the waves have been driven by a wind blowing in a constant direction, without obstruction.
ⓒ CES : Coast Earth **Station**

18 너무 <u>가까워서(close)</u> 피항선(give-way vessel)의 동작만

으로는 충돌을 피할 수 없다고 판단되는 경우, 유지선(stand on vessel)도 충돌을 피하기 위해 최선의 동작을 취해야 한다.

19 두 선박 사이의 추후 침로변경이 추월선(overtaking vessel)을 횡단선(crossing vessel)으로 만들어 주지는 않으며, 이것이 <u>유지선(stand-on vessel)</u>에게 길을 비켜줘야 한다는 의무를 면제해주는 것도 아니다.

20 1. (Combination carrier) means a ship designated to carry either oil or solid cargoes in bulk
2. (Segregated ballast) means the ballast water introduced into tank which is completely separated from the cargo oil and oil fuel system.

12회 | 모의고사

1	2	3	4	5	6	7	8	9	10
④	④	②	④	②	②	④	①	②	④
11	12	13	14	15	16	17	18	19	20
③	③	④	③	②	③	③	③	③	②

01 ④ 정박, 계류 중에도 선박의 안전을 위해 당직이 필요하다 an appropriate and effective watch or watches do ~~not~~ need to be maintained for the purpose of safety at all times, while the ship is at anchor or moored

02 ⓒ UKC : **Under** Keel Clearance
ⓔ LMT : Local **Mean Time**
ⓕ ISM : International **Safety** Management Code
ⓗ Lat. : Latitude(위도)

03 ㉠ (Ship stability) can be defined as the ability of the ship to return to the upright when slightly inclined.
ⓒ When heading on a course, you put your rudder hard over. The distance traveled in the right angle direction of the original course from when you put your rudder over until your heading differs by 90 is known as : (Transfer)
ⓒ (Freeboard) is vertical distance from the uppermost deck to the center of the disc which is marked on the vessel's sides and which indicates the position of the load water line in summer.

04 ㉠ **walk out** : To reverse the action of a windlass to lower the anchor until it is clear of the hawse pipe and ready for dropping.
ⓒ **A cock bill state** : The situation standing by anchor

and about to let go anchor.

ⓒ **Veer out** : To let out a greater length of cable

ⓓ Dragging : Moving of an anchor over the sea bottom **involuntarily** because it is no longer preventing the movement of the vessel.

05 조류, 조석, 바람의 영향으로 바다에서 통제되지 않으며 움직이는 것을 **표류(adrift)**라고 한다.

06 ② 일반적으로 Pilot boat측에서 본선 측에 파일럿 사다리(pilot ladder)를 풍하측(lee-side)에 설치해달라고 요청한다.

옳지 않은 것:
① 풍하측을 만들어주는 쪽은 주로 본선측이다.
③ 파일럿 사다리를 어느 쪽 현에 설치하는지 질문하는 쪽은 주로 본선측이다.
④ 자선의 도선사 승선지점(P/STN)으로의 도착 예정시각(ETA)은 본선측에서 나올 수 있는 정보이다.

07 군도기선은 가장 바깥 섬(island), 산호초(drying reef), 군도(archipelago)를 이어서 만든다. 간조노출지(low-tide elevation)는 고조시 해수면 아래에 잠기고 저조시 수면 밖으로 드러나는 지형이기 때문에 해역의 경계를 정하는 기준선으로는 부적합하다.

08 ⓐ 피항선(vessel required to keep out of the way)이 적절한 동작을 취하고 있지 않다는 것이 명백해 지면 ⓑ**유지선은(stand-on vessel)** 피항동작을 취할 수 있다.

ⓑ 횡단상황(crossing situation)중이면서 위와 같은 상황을 적용해야 하는 선박이라면 자신의 좌현에 있는 선박과의 충돌을 피하기 위해 ⓒ**좌현(port)**으로 변침하는 일은 피해야 한다.

09 ② A vessel of less than **20 meters** in length or a sailing vessel shall not impede the passage of a vessel which can safely navigate only within a narrow channel or fairway.

10 -**(Give)** 2 short blasts (on the whistle) :
2 회의 단음을 울려라
-**(put)** 2 shackles in the water :
닻줄을 2사클 만큼 수면까지 풀어주시오.
-**(put)** the windlass in gear : 양묘기 사용 준비

11 ① Warning
② Question
④ Information

12 구명부환(life-buoy)은 전체의 개수의 ⓐ**절반(one half)** 이상 ⓑ**자기점화등(self-igniting light)**을 달고 있어야 하고 그 중 ⓒ**두 개(two)** 이상은 ⓓ자기발연부신호

(self-activating smoke signals)를 달고 있어야 하고 ⓔ**선교(bridge)**에서 빠르게 방출 할 수 있어야 한다.

13 표준구명정 일반장비 개수는,
로켓낙하산화염신호(rocket parachute flares) : **4개**
신호홍염(hand flares) : **6개**
발연부신호(buoyant smoke signal) : **2개**
로 구성된다.

14 본 협약에 반하는 **고의적이고, 심각한(wilful and serious)** 오염 행위, 그리고 **어로(fishing)**행위는 무해통항권(right of innocent passage)에 위배되는 행위 중 하나이다.

15 형사적 관할권을 행사할 수 있는 경우로는,
범죄가 국가의 ⓐ**영해(territorial sea)**의 ⓑ**평화(peace)**나 공공질서에 해가 되는 경우, 마약 혹은 향정신성 물질의 ⓒ**불법(illicit)** 운송 체포를 위해 필요한 경우.

16 ③ It is **not** necessary that, at the time when the foreign ship within the territorial sea or the contiguous zone receives the order to stop, the ship giving the order should likewise be within the territorial sea or the contiguous zone.

17 ⓒ **Commenced Search Point, CSP**
ⓓ **Rescue**

18 ⓐ Used to search a large area when survivor location is **uncertain**.
ⓑ 평행 항적 수색법은 **산(mountain)**에서는 부적합한 수색법이다.
ⓓ Search legs are **parallel(평행)** to each other and to long sides of the sub-area.

19 IAMSAR Manual 상 조난을 알리는 시각신호:
- A red parachute flare(적색 낙하산 화염신호)
- Flames(불꽃신호)
- Red flare(적색 화염신호)
- Yellow smoke(오랜지색 발연신호)
- The flags "N.C."(국제기류신호 "NC"기)
- A square flag having above or below it a ball (상부 또는 하부에 구 모양을 붙인 사각기)
- Slowly and repeatedly rising and lowering the arms-outstretched(천천히 그리고 반복적으로 팔을 올렸다 내렸다 하는 것.)
- S.O.S by light or sound(빛 또는 소리에 의한 SOS신호)

20 수동화재경보기(Manually operated call point)는 **20미터** 보다 멀지 않은 간격의 복도에 설치된다.

13회 | 모의고사

1	2	3	4	5	6	7	8	9	10
①	②	③	②	④	②	①	①	③	①
11	12	13	14	15	16	17	18	19	20
②	③	③	④	②	③	③	③	②	①

01 ① I will jettison cargo to stop **capsizing**
→ 본선은 <u>전복</u>을 막기 위해 화물을 투하할 것이다.

02 drop back은 본선의 후방(astern)이 아닌 전방(ahead)에 있는 선박에 대해서 선속을 줄여 거리를 늘리는 동작을 의미한다.

03 선박이 회두중 타를 중립으로 놓았다는 사실이 선박 회두가 정지했다는 것을 의미하지는 않는다. 일반적으로 선박은 타력 때문에 midships후 회두가 멈추는 데에 일정 시간이 필요하다. 때문에 "즉시 회두를 줄여라" 는 의미를 갖는 (A)Steady 명령은 더욱 빨리 회두를 멈추고 싶을 때에 사용될 수 있다. 타가 중립 상태이므로 우현 전타인 (B)Hard a starboard와 좌현으로 10도 명령인 (D)Port ten이 사용되지 못할 이유도 없다.

반면, 타가 중립상태에서 줄일 타각이 더 이상 없을 땐 "타각을 10도로 줄이시오" 의 의미를 갖는 (C)Ease to ten은 사용할 수 없다.

04 ⓒ **Datum** : The most probable position of a search target at a given time.
ⓔ **Destination** : port which a vessel is bound for.
ⓐ **PA-system** : Loudspeaker in the vessel's cabins, mess room, etc. and on deck through which important information can be broadcast from a central point.

05 ① 도선사(pilot)의 업무와 의무에 불구하고 도선사의 승선이 선장(master)과 당직항해사(officer in charge of the watch)를 당직의 의무로부터 면제시켜주지는 않는다.
② 선장(master)과 도선사(pilot)는 항해 절차, 지역의 상태 그리고 선박 성능에 관한 정보를 교환하여야 한다.
③ 선장(master)과 당직항해사(officer in charge of the watch)는 도선사(pilot)와 긴밀히 협업하여야 하고 선위와 선박 움직임을 정확히 유지 해주야 한다.
④ 만일 파일럿의 동작이나 의도에 의심구심이 드는 경우, 당직항해사는 파일럿으로부터 그에 대한 해명을 <u>요구할 수 있다.</u>
)If in any doubt as to the pilot's action or intentions, the officer in charge of the navigational watch shall ~~not~~ seek clarification from the pilot

06 ⓒ I will make a lee for your boat.
→ 귀선을 본선의 풍하측에 오게 하겠다.

07 SMCP 상 화재시 취해야할 행동으로는
(**Call out**) "Fire" : "불이야" 라고 외친다.
(**Operate**) the nearest fire alarm : 가장 가까운 화재경보기를 작동시킨다.
(**Inform**) a member of the crew : 승무원에게 알린다.
(**Telephone**) the navigation bridge : 선교에 전화한다.

08 가) Attention! the cargo operation (**turn to**).
(주목, 화물 <u>작업이 시작</u> 됩니다.)
나) Vessel (**idle**), frequent rounds (**made**) for lines.
(선박 <u>대기 중</u>, 계류 줄 순찰이 수시로 <u>진행됨</u>)

09 ⓐ One turn – difficult because approach to person is <u>not</u> straight
ⓑ Scharnove turn – will ~~not~~ take vessel back into her wake.
ⓒ Williamson turn – <u>slow</u> procedure.

10 SafetyNET은 EGC(고기능집단호출)시스템의 서비스로 GMDSS의 해사안전정보(MSI)를 공포하는 용으로 만들어졌다.

11 ㉠ 인공섬(artificial), 설치물(installations) 그리고 구조물(structures)의 사용과 설치에 관한 관할권
㉢ 해양과학조사에 관한 관할권
㉣ 해양 환경의 보전과 보호에 관한 관할권
옳지 않은 것 : ㉡, ㉣은 접속수역(Contiguous Zone)에서의 권한이다.

12 공해(high seas)나 배타적경제수역(exclusive economic zone)의 일부 사이의 <u>해협(strait)</u>를 통과하는 권리는 <u>통과통항권(Right of transit passage)</u>이다.

13 (1) 두 범선이 서로 다른 현(different side)로 바람을 받는 경우 ㉠<u>좌현(port)</u>에서 바람을 받는 선박이 피항선이 된다.
(2) 서로 다른 현으로 바람을 받고 있다면 ㉡<u>풍상측(windward)</u>에 있는 선박이 피항선이 되고 ㉢<u>풍하측(leeward)</u>에 있는 선박이 유지선이 된다.
(3) 바람을 ㉣<u>좌현(port side)</u>에서 받는 선박이 풍상측에 위치한 선박이 어느현으로 바람을 받는지 알 수 없을 때에는 바람을 좌현으로 받던 그 선박이 길을 비켜준다.

14 ④ How many persons are <u>on board</u>? : 몇 명의 선내 인원이 승선중입니까?
당직 중은 on watch

15 ㉠,ⓒ는 잘못된 설명이다. "steady"는 선수 회두를 줄여 정침만 하면 되지만 "Steady as she goes" 는 정침 후 명령이 내려진 순간에 선수가 가리키던 방위로 다시 정침하여야

하기 때문에 침로의 결과는 같을 수 없고, 두 명령어는 엄연히 다른 명령어다.

16 ① "Relative bearing" can be expressed in degrees relative to the vessel's head or head bow. More frequently this is in relation to the port or starboard bow. ② The angle caused between the axis of the compass and magnetic meridian is called "deviation".
④ "bulkhead" are vertical partitions of walls. All ships must have a specified number of compartments depending on their length.

collision bulkhead는 bulkhead중 선수 쪽에 설치되는 충돌격벽을 의미한다.

17 ㉠55m 미만선박의 조종구역에서의 시야는 선박길이 2배, 혹은 ㉡500m길이 중 ㉢짧은 값보다 가려져서는 안 된다. 이것은 흘수, 트림, 갑판화물의 모든 조건에서 정선수로부터 양측으로 ㉣10° 씩 만큼만 적용한다.

18 타선박의 동작을 이해하지 못하거나 의심이 있는 선박은 급속한 단음을 최소 5회(at least 5 short and rapid) 울려준다.

19 Every oil tanker of 150 tons gross tonnage and above and every ship 400 tons gross tonnage and above other than oil tanker shall be provided with an Oil Record Book whether as part of this ship's ㉢official log book or otherwise in the form specified in appendix 3 to this Annex.

The Oil Record Book shall be kept in such place as to be readily available for inspection at all reasonable times and except in the case of unmanned ships under tow, shall be kept on board the ship, it shall be preserved for a period of ㉣three years after the last entry has been made.

20 모든 여객선(passenger ship)은 전체 승선 인원의 5%에 달하는 추가 구명조끼(life jackets)를 갖춰야 한다.

14회 | 모의고사

1	2	3	4	5	6	7	8	9	10
③	④	④	③	③	④	①	①	③	③
11	12	13	14	15	16	17	18	19	20
③	①	③	④	②	④	②	②	③	③

01 ① SMCP 무선통신 감도신호는 1부터 5까지 있다.
② I am on fire : 본선에 화재 발생
④ Which side must I rig the pilot ladder? : 어느 현에 도선사 사다리를 설치하는가?

02 ETA는 Estimated Time of Arrival(도착예정시간)의 약자이다. 때문에 ~로 부터를 의미하는 전치사 from은 부적합하다. *출항예정시간인 ETD의 경우 from 전치사사용*

03 ㉠ Wreck – A vessel which has been destroyed or sunk or abandoned at sea.
㉡ Refloat – To pull a vessel off after grounding to set afloat again.
㉢ Recover – To pick up shipwrecked persons
㉣ heading – The horizontal direction of the vessel's bows at a given moment measured in degrees clockwise from the north.

04 Fairway speed는 항로내제한속력으로 지켜야만 하는 의무속력이다.

05 조난무선통신 청수 당직자가 SECURITE라는 메시지가 세 번 반복 되는 것을 듣는다면 해당 메시지는 항해의 안전과, 중요한 기상경보 메시지(safety of navigation or important meteorological warnings) 라는 것을 예상할 수 있다.

06 ㉠ 조난 무선 메시지(wireless distress signal)를 수신한 선장은 조난에 빠진 사람에게 원조(assistance)를 하기 위해 전속력으로 항진할 의무가 있다.
㉡ 항해 당직자는 누구든지 안전 항해를 방해하는(interfere with) 업무를 할당받아선 안 된다.

07 ㉡ The right of hot pursuit ceases although the ship pursued enters the territorial sea of its own State or of a third State.
㉢ Where a ship has been stopped or arrested outside the territorial sea in circumstances which do not justify the exercise of the right of hot pursuit, it shall ~~not~~ be compensated for any loss or damage that may have been thereby sustained.
㉣ The release of a ship arrested within the jurisdiction of a State and escorted to a port of that State for the purposes of an inquiry before the competent authorities may **not** be claimed solely on the ground that the ship, in the course of its voyage, was escorted across a portion of the exclusive economic zone or the high seas, if the circumstances rendered this necessary.

08 화물 적재, 묘박 등에 사용되는 정박지(Roadsteads)가 영해 경계의 바깥으로 일부분 혹은 전체가 벗어나 있는 경우 이것은 영해 안에 포함되어 있는 것이다.

09 상호 시계 내에서 우현 추월은 ㉠장음 2회(two prolonged blasts)에 이은 ㉡단음 1회(one short blast)이다.
좌현 추월은 ㉢장음 2회(two prolonged blasts)에 이은

ⓔ단음2회(two short blasts)이다.
해당 동작에 동의하는 경우 ⓓ1회 장음, 1회 단음, 1회 장음, 1회 단음(one prolonged, one short, one prolonged, one short blast)을 울려준다.

10 ⓒ 선전활동(propaganda), ⓐ 오염행위(pollution) 이 두 가지는 공해의 자유에 해당하지 않는다.

11 제한 시계 내에서 한 대 혹은 그이상의 선박이 예인되고 있는 경우 예인의 ⓐ마지막(last vessel)에 있는 선박이 (만약 사람이 타고 있다면) ⓒ2분(two minutes)을 넘지 않는 간격으로 ⓒ1회의 장음(one prolonged)에 이은 ⓔ3회의 단음(three short)을 울려줘야 한다. 가능하다면 이 신호는 예인선이 신호를 낸 ⓓ다음(after) 바로 이루어져야 한다.

12 모두 옳음

13 ⓙ RCC에 부수적인 RSC(Rescue Sub-Centre)에 대한 설명이다.
ⓒ 수색 구조의 효과적 조직화의 촉진(promoting efficient organization of SAR services)에 책임이 있고, 수색구조 수행 조정(co-ordinating the conduct of SAR operations)에 책임이 있는 기관, RCC(Rescue Coordination Centre)에 대한 설명이다.

14 야간에 A선박이 B선박의 정횡 후방 2점(22.5°)보다 더욱 후방의 위치에서부터 접근하고 있는 경우, A선박이 B선박의 존재를 확인할 수 있는 유일한 시각적 표시는 후자선박(B선박)의 선미등 일 것이다.

15 ⓔ 임검권의 행사는 공해상에서 이루어진다. 어로 활동(fishing)은 공해의 자유에 해당한다.
ⓓ 조사활동(research operation) 또한 공해상 자유에 속한다.

16 ① Give way에 대한 설명이다.
② Turn to 에 대한 설명이다. *Knock off : 작업 중단*
③ Inert(불활성화)에 대한 설명이다.

17 ⓙ QUESTION에 대한 설명이다.
ⓒ WARNING에 대한 설명이다.

18 ⓒ When two power-driven vessels are crossing, the vessel which has the other on the starboard side must give way.

19 MARPOL에는 선박 평형수 배출 오염(pollution control by discharge of ships ballast water)에 대한 부속서(Annex)는 없다.
Annex1 : Prevention of pollution by oil & oily water
Annex2 : Control of pollution by noxious liquid substances in bulk
Annex3 : Prevention of pollution by harmful substances carried by sea in   packaged form
Annex4 : Prevention of pollution by sewage from ships
Annex5 : Prevention of pollution by garbage from ship
Annex6 : Prevention of air pollution from ship

20 선박이 가장 가까운 육지로부터 (3)해리를 넘는 거리에서 주관청이 승인한 시스템을 사용하여 분쇄하고 소독한 하수를 배출하는 경우 또는 가장 가까운 육지로부터 (12)해리를 넘는 거리에서 분쇄하지 아니하거나 소독하지 아니한 하수를 배출하는 경우, (단 어떠한 경우에도 홀딩탱크에 저장한 하수는 동시에 배출하여서는 아니 되며) 선박이 (4)노트 이상의 속력으로 항행 중에 적당한 비율로 배출하여야 한다. 이 배출율은 기구가 정하는 기준에 따라 주관청이 승인한 것이어야 한다.
3+12+4=19

15회 | 모의고사

1	2	3	4	5	6	7	8	9	10
④	②	①	①	④	④	②	②	④	②
11	12	13	14	15	16	17	18	19	20
②	②	②	①	①	④	③	①	②	②

01 길이 12m 미만의 선박(vessel of less than 12 metres in length)은 마스트등(masthead light) 2해리, 현등(sidelight) 1해리, 선미등(stern light) 2해리, 예인등(towing light) 2해리의 등화 가시거리를 가져야한다.

02 ⓔ TSS(Traffic Separation Scheme), 통항분리방식에 대한 설명이다.

03 ⓒ leeward(풍하측)에 대한 설명이다.

04 선박 작업의 성질(nature of her work) 상 조종이 제한 받는(restricted in her ability) 선박은 조종제한선(Vessel restricted in her ability to manoeuvre)이다.

05 Emergency Phase : A generic term meaning, as the case may be, uncertainty phase, alert phase or distress phase.

06 채널에서의 통신이 원활하지 못한 경우, 채널의 변경을 지시한 이후 그에 대한 확인도 기다려야 한다.(await confirmation.)

07 일반 선박 A와 Pilot station B 사이의 통신문이다.
ⓒPilot station으로의 도착 예정시각을 일반적으로 선박의 입항예정시각 ⓙETA(Estimated Time of Arrival)로 잡는다.
'도선사 사다리 설치' 는 SMCP 상 ⓒrig pilot ladder라고 표현한다.
해석

A : 여기는 사라호. 감도 좋습니까?

B : 감도 좋습니다. 좋은 아침입니다. 사라호. 여기는 울산 파일럿입니다. 귀선의 ETA가 어떻게 됩니까?

A : ETA는 UTC 0900입니다.

B : 알겠습니다. Pilot station으로 극미속 전진으로 접근하십시오.

A : 알겠습니다. 어느 현에 사다리를 설치(rig) 합니까?

B : 풍하측(Lee-side)에 부탁합니다.

08 간조 노출지(low tide elevation)는 저조시(low tide)엔 물위로 올라오고, 고조시(high tide)에는 물에 잠기는 자연적으로 형성되는 지형이다.

09 생존정(Survival craft)에 대한 설명이다. 생존정은 조난에 빠진 사람의 생명을 연장하는 탈것이다.

10 ⓐVery High Frequency : VHF
ⓑUltra High Frequency : UHF
ⓒMedium Frequency : MF
ⓓHigh Frequency : HF

11 연안 항해 시, 해도에 표시돼 있는 물 위나 물 아래의 암초, 사주 혹은 장애물을 피하기 위해서, 항해사들은 **측심(sounding)**이라 알려진 것을 통해 이런 것들과 원하는 거리를 두고 통과 할 수 있다.

12 Security Level means the qualification of the degree of risk that a security incident will be attempted or will occur.

13 해도 상 모든 빛의 시정에 거리는 관측자의 **안고높이(a height of observer's eye)** 5m로 계산된다.

14 공기량과 습기가 일정한 곳에서 온도가 감소하는 경우, 특정 온도 점에서 습도는 상대적으로 증가하고 공기 중의 수증기는 액화되기 시작한다. 이 온도를 **이슬점온도(dew point)**라 부른다.

15 ⓐ If two more radio waves arrive simultaneously at the same point in space, result in radar interference (간섭효과)

ⓑ Multiple reflection (다중반사) can be created by reflection between own ship and an object before the scanner finally collects its energy. we will see a line of targets on the same bearing and with equal distance between them.

ⓒ Specular reflection(경면반사) may be caused by radio-waves reflected by water surface or windows, buildings.

16 항해사의 적절한 항해 운용술(the officer's good seamanship)은 안전속력(Safe speed)을 정하는 요소로 적합하지 않다.

안전속력 결정 요소로는 주변 환경, 선박의 성능 등이 있으며 레이더를 운용하는 경우 해당 레이더의 성질, 한계 등을 고려한다.

17 Retreat Signal : a kind of signal with sound, visual or other methods to a team ordering it to return to its base in the search ad rescue operation.

18 ⓐ 등대(Light house)는 해상의 위험한 바위 위에 설치된다. 등대의 랜턴은 항해사들이 위험물로부터 거리를 두도록 (keep their ships from being wrecked) 어두운 바다에 빛을 비춰준다.

* 수심이 얼마나 깊은지(judge how deep the sea is)는 등대의 빛으로는 알 수 없다.*

ⓑ 조류의 방향은 자북이 아닌 진북으로 부터의 방향이며 조류가 **흘러가는(toward which the current is setting)** 방향을 말한다. 반면 바람은 **불어오는 (from which it is blowing)**방향을 말한다.

19 ⓐ 수면 아래로 가라앉는 선박으로부터 자동 방출되는 Float-Free launching에 대한 설명이다.

ⓑ 장비나 사람의 조작을 통해 선외로 낙하하는 Free-fall launching에 대한 설명이다.

20 선박은 주의하여 항해하라 : vessel must navigate with caution

16회 | 모의고사

1	2	3	4	5	6	7	8	9	10
③	①	③	①	③	②	④	①	③	③
11	12	13	14	15	16	17	18	19	20
④	④	①	②	③	②	②	③	④	①

01 ⓐ 풍우밀(weathertight)에 대한 설명이다.

ⓑ 수밀(watertight)에 대한 설명이다. 수밀은 치수(Scantlings)와 설비(arrangements)가 수두(head of water) 상태에서 어떤 방향으로도 물이 통과하지 못하게 해주는 것을 의미한다.

02 You must (heave) up anchor.

The tide is (with) you.

The tide is (against) you.

You are (running) into danger.

03 등화에 관련된 COLREG규정은 일몰(sunset)시부터 일출(sunrise)시까지이다.

04 만약 기적이 선박에 100터를 초과한 거리에 설치되어 있다면 오직 하나의 기적신호만이 조종이나 경고 신호에 사용되어만 한다.

05 중력(gravity)과 부력(buoyance)사이의 선박균형이 깨지면, 선박은 복원성(stability)을 잃게 되고 그 결과(result)로 전복(capsized)된다.

06 ⓑ Cospas-sarsat에 대한 설명이다.
   ⓓ Inmarsat에 대한 설명이다.

07 조난(distress), 긴급(urgent) 안전(safety) 메시지가 아닌 사용가능한 공용의 통신은 일반통신(General Communication)이다.

08 (a) Security level 1 : 최소한의(minimum) 적절한 보호 보안 조치가 유지되는 단계이다.
   (b) Security level 3 : 보다 구체화된(further specific) 보호 보안 조치가 유지되는 단계이다.
   (c) Security level 2 : 적절한 추가적인(additional) 보호 보안 조치가 유지되는 단계이다.

09 이 규정의 어떤 조항도 규정준수의 태만, 적절한 항해사의 능력과 특수 상황에서 요구하는 주의에 대한 태만으로부터의 결과로부터 선박의 선장(master), 선원(crew), 선주(owner of the ship)를 면제해주지 않는다. port control officer는 항만 통제관이므로 선박의 책임과는 무관하다.

10 ⓒ 안전속력을 정하는 요소로는 side direction light 아니라 배경광(background light)이 있다.

11 COLREG에서 규정하는 어로종사선(vessel engaged in fishing)은 그물, 낚싯줄, 트롤어망 등을 사용하되 그 장비들이 선박의 조종을 제한할 때의 선박을 말한다.
   vessel engaged in fishing : any vessel fishing with nets, lines, trawls or other fishing apparatus which do not restrict maneuverability

12 구조정(rescue boat)과 해양탈출시스템(marine evacuation system)의 인원이 착용하는 것은 Anti-exposure suit이다.

13 충돌의 위험을 판단할 때에는 접근하는 선박의 Compass bearing을 확인하는 것이 중요하다.

14 당직 선원은 임의의 24시간 기간 내에 최소한 (10)시간의 휴식시간을 가져야 하며 이 휴식시간은 2회 이내로 나눌 수 있으며, 그 기간 중 하나는 적어도 (6)시간이어야 한다. 그리고 연속된 휴식시간 사이의 간격은 (14)시간을 초과할 수 없다.
   10+6+14=30

15 오수(Seawage)를 담아두기 위해 사용되는 탱크의 이름은 Holding tank이다.

16 겸용선(Combination carrier)에 대한 설명이다.

17 분리 평형수(Segregated ballast)는 오일과 연료 시스템으로부터 완전히 분리된 탱크(tank)에 주입되었던 평형수를 말한다. 그리고 평형수(ballast water) 운반을 위해 영구적으로 지정된 탱크를 말한다.

18 주 조타장치(main steering gear)는 한쪽 현 35도에서 반대쪽 30도 까지 타가 들어오는데 28초를 초과해서는 안 되며, 이때 선박은 최대흘수상태 그리고 최대(maximum)진진 속력으로 항주 중이어야 한다.

19 익수자가 싱가폴 해협에 발생했다. 수색구조 원조(with search and rescue assistance)를 요청한다.

20 The duties of the look-out and helmsperson are separate and helmsperson shall not be considered to be the look-out while steering.

17회 | 모의고사

1	2	3	4	5	6	7	8	9	10
②	③	①	①	②	①	②	③	④	②
11	12	13	14	15	16	17	18	19	20
④	②	①	④	①	①	②	③	③	③

01 berth -> accommodation ladder -> berth

02 (QUESTION). Do I have permission to enter the fairway?
   (INTENTION). I will alter my course to 225° (자선의 행동)
   (WARNING). You are running into danger. (위험에 대한 경고)

03 ACO : Aircraft Co-ordinator.

04 (Part2. Section3. Article18 - Meaning of passage)
   1. Passage means navigation through the territorial sea for the purpose of:
   -traversing that sea without entering ⓐinternal(내) waters or calling at a roadstead or port facility outside internal waters: or
   -proceeding to or from ⓑinternal waters or a call at such roadstead or port facility.
   2.Passage shall be ⓒcontinuous and expeditious. However, passage includes stopping and anchoring, but only in so far as the same are incidental to ordinary navigation or are rendered necessary by ⓓforce majeure or distress or for the purpose of rendering assistance to persons, ships or aircraft in danger or distress.

05 l. A succession of small alternations of course

and/or speed should be ⓒavoided.

II. if there is ⓒsufficient sea room, ⓓalteration of course alone may be the most effective action to avoid a close-quarters situation provided that it is made in good time, is substantial and does not result in another close-quarters situations.

III. if necessary to avoid collision or allow more time to assess the situation, a vessel shall ⓔslacken her speed or take way off by stopping or reversing her means of propulsion.

IV. A vessel the passage of which is not to be impeded remains fully ⓓobliged to comply with the rules of this part when the two vessels are approaching one another so as to involve risk of collision.

06 ⓑ L : Lima

07 put on은 "걸치다, (옷 등을) 입다"의 의미를 갖는다. 나머지는 연기, 지연의 의미를 갖는다.

08 군함(Warship), 해군보조함(Naval auxiliaries), 혹은 정부에 의해서 소유(owned)되거나 운영(operated)되는 선박

09 밑줄 친 부분은 선박을 재부양 하기 위해 화물을 투하한다는 내용이다. lighten(가볍게 하다)이 대체될 수 있다.

10 Assumptions ②shall not be made on the basis of scanty information, especially scanty radar information. (빈약한 정보를 기초로 가정을 하여서는 안 되며 특히 빈약한 레이더정보를 기반 해서 가정해서는 안 된다.)

11 Seaplane : includes any aircraft designed to manoeuvre on the water.

12 -Send (out) the 00 spring(s) forward/aft :
선수 선미의 스프링 라인을 00줄 내어주시오.
-Heave (on) the fore breast line :
줄을 계속 감으시오.
-pick (up) the slack on the bow line :
줄의 늘어짐을 팽팽하게 하시오.

13 A1구역은 VHF통신 장비 범위내의 구역이다.
A2구역은 MF통신 장비 범위내의 구역이다.
A3 : INMARSAT위성 범위내, A4 : A3,2,1을 제외한 구역, 극지방

14 음식물 쓰레기를 분쇄(comminuter), 연마(grinder)한 경우 그 크기가 25mm보다 크지 않은 개구(opening)를 가진 스크린을 통과하는 정도여야 한다.

15 유해물질(harmful substances)에 대한 설명이다.

16 Seawage가 분쇄되고 소독된(comminuted and) 경우 가장 가까운 육지로부터 ①3해리 이내에서 배출해서는 안 된다.

17 Holding tank의 용량은 ⓐ승선한 인원의 숫자(number of person)에 관련이 있다. 그리고 이 탱크는 ⓑ시각적(visually)으로 용량을 표시할 수 있어야한다.

18 군도기선이 둘러싼 해역의 비율(ratio of the area)은 물의 비율과 땅의 비율이 1:1에서 9:1 사이어야한다.

19 keep clear of는 피하다, 거리를 두다의 의미를 갖는다. 피하다의 의미를 갖는 avoid와 같은 의미로 사용될 수 있다.

20 일반비상경보(general emergency alarm)가 울린 경우 승객들은 비상소집장소(muster station)로 가야한다.

18회 | 모의고사

1	2	3	4	5	6	7	8	9	10
④	④	②	①	①	②	②	③	③	②
11	12	13	14	15	16	17	18	19	20
①	②	②	③	①	①	③	①	②	②

01 ⓐ blast
ⓑ blind sectors
ⓒ capsizing

02 -I am (under) attack by pirates.
본선은 해적에게 공격받고 있다.
-I am (aground).
본선은 좌초되었다.
-I (require) tug assistance.
본선은 예인원조를 요청한다.
-I am (not under command).
본선은 조종불능상태이다.

03 선박이 함부르크 항에서 출항하는 시간이 21시30분인 경우 21시30분은 출항예정시각(ETD)이다.

04 -EEZ는 기선으로부터 200해리까지 지정할 수 있다.
-길이 20m 미만의 선박, 범선, 어로종사 선박은 ITZ를 사용할 수 있다.
-기름기록부는(oil record book) 150t 이상 유조선(oil tanker), 400t 이상의 일반선에서 갖춰야 한다.

05 Emergency Position Indicating Radio Beacon

06 위치를 가장 정확히 알고 있을 때 사용하는 수색법은 부채꼴수색법이다(sector search)
ⓒ 항적선수색법(Track line search)에 대한 설명이다.

ⓓ 평행항적수색법(parallel track search)에 대한 설명이다.
ⓔ 항정선 수색 법 중 TSN(Track line Search Non-return)에 대한 설명이다.

07 옳지 않은 것 :
나. 기국(flag state)의 외교관(diplomatic agent) 요청할 수 있다.
라. 기국(flag state)의 영사(consular office)가 요청할 수 있다.

08 모든 선박이 안전속력(safe speed)을 항상 유지해야 하는 이유는 충돌을 피하기위한 적절한 효과적인 동작을 취하기 위해서(you can take proper and effective action to avoid collision.) 이다.

09 —Every vessel shall at all times maintain a proper (look out) by sight and hearing as well as by all available means appropriate in the prevailing circumstances and condition so as to make a full appraisal of the situation and of (the risk of collision).

—(passage) shall be continuous and expeditious. However, (passage) includes stopping and anchoring, but only in so far as the same are incidental to ordinary navigation, force majeure or distress or for the purpose of rendering assistance to persons, ships or aircraft in danger or distress.

10 영해에서 잠수함(submarines)그리고 수중에서 다니는 탈것(underwater vehicles)은 기를 보여주기 위해 수면에 올라와서(on the surface and to show their flag) 항해해야 한다.

11 Vessel making-way는 기관을 사용해서(using engine) 항해중인 선박이다.

12 해사영어에서 선박의 높이란 수선위에(above water line) 선박의 가장 높은 지점까지이다.

13 vermin & rodents (해충, 쥐)를 박멸하는 것은 소독(fumigation)이다.

14 ⓓ 배타적 관할권(exclusive jurisdiction)은 공해(high sea)에서 행사된다.
ⓘ 임검권(right of visit)은 공해(high sea)에서 행사된다.
추적권(right of hot pursuit)은 접속수역 이내에서는 발동될 수 있으므로 영해에서 행사될 수 있다고 볼 수 있다.

15 탱크아래 남은 잔유물(residue)에 대한 설명이다.

16 모두 옳음

17 (ii)The duration of each flash shall be about ⓐone second, the interval between flashes shall be about ⓑ one second, and the interval between successive signals shall be not less than ⓒten seconds.

(iii) the lights used for this signal shall, if fitted, be an all-round white light, visible at a minimum range of ⓓ5 miles, and shall comply with the provisions of Annex I.

18 해도(chart)나 등대표(light list)는 최신의 항행통보(Notice To Mariner)를 통해 수정되어야 한다.

19 여객선의 퇴선훈련은 매주(weekly) 실시된다.

20 ⓑ Course made good : That course of which a vessel makes good over the ground after allowing for the effect of currents, tidal streams, and leeway caused by wind and sea.

19회 | 모의고사

1	2	3	4	5	6	7	8	9	10
③	④	①	②	②	②	③	②	④	②
11	12	13	14	15	16	17	18	19	20
②	④	③	②	④	②	①	②	③	③

01 ⓐ Flooding
ⓑ Fume
ⓒ Muster list

02 – Received your (MAYDAY).
귀선의 조난통보를 수신하였다.
–I will (abandon) vessel at 1200UTC.
본선은 세계시 1200에 퇴선 할 것이다.
–(stand by) on VHF channel 16.
VHF 채널16에서 대기하고 있어라.

03 영해의 경계를 정하는 목적에 있어서, 가장 바깥 지점에 있는 부두 시스템의 필수적인(integral) 부분을 형성하는 영구적인 항만 시설은 해안의 일부를 형성하는 것으로 여겨진다. 해상설치물(off-shore installations)과 인공섬(artificial islands)은 영구적인 항만 시설로 여겨지지 않는다(shall not).

04 편의치적 선(flag of convenience)에 대한 설명이다. 편의 치적선은 선주가 자국의 비싼 세금을 피하고, 저렴한 노동력을 고용하고, 경제적 이점을 얻기 위해 자신의 국가가 아닌 타국에 선박을 등록한 선박을 말한다.

05 Cardinal buoy에 대한 설명이다.

06 —The drills of the crew shall take place within ⓐ 24h of the ship leaving a port if more than 25% of the crew ⓑhave not participated in abandon ship and fire drills

on board that particular ship in the previous month.
-When a ship enters service for the first time, after modification of a major character or when a new crew ⓒ is engaged, these drills shall be held ⓓbefore sailing.

07 평행항적수색법(parallel track search)에 대한 설명이다.

08 ⓐ Secured checked all derrick booms & other fittings.
ⓔ Started to heave let go port anchor.

09 선수미 부근에 두 개의 파도가 와서 선박의 중심은 반대방향으로 휘어지는 외력 Sagging에 대한 설명이다.

10 (b) A vessel of less than ②20 metres in length or a sailing vessel shall not impede the passage of a vessel which can safely navigate only within a narrow channel or fairway.

11 ⓐ be capable of throwing a line with accuracy
ⓑ include not less than 4 projectiles each capable of carrying the line at least 230m in calm weather

12 ④ shall not be exhibited.

13 (a) A vessel at anchor shall exhibit where it can best be seen :
(i) in the fore part, ⓐan white all round light or one ball
(ii) at or near the stern and at ⓑa lower level than the light prescribed in sub-paragraph(i), ⓒan all round white light.
(b) A vessel of less than ⓓ50metres in length may exhibit an all-round white light where it can best be seen instead of the lights prescribed in paragraph (a) of this Rule.

14 Great Circle(대권), abandoned(퇴선)

15 a number of lifejackets suitable for children equal to at least ③10% of the number of passengers on board shall be provided or such ④greater number as may be required

16 주권적 권리(sovereign right)는 해저에 인접한 수중, 해저, 그리고 해저의 하층토에 있는 무생물이거나 생명 자원의 탐험, 개발, 보존, 관리의 권리이다. 그리고 이것은 경제적 개발과 탐사를 위한 경제 활동과도 연관이 있는데 이것은 파도, 조류, 바람 등으로 부터 생산되는 에너지와 같은 것을 말한다. 배타적 경제수역(exclusive economic zone)에 대한 설명이다.

17 닻이 해저에서 떠난 상태(Anchor is clear of the bottom)

18 ⓒ williamson turn에 대한 설명이다.
ⓓ one turn은 원래 항적으로 돌아가지 않는다.

ⓔ 복원성(stability)과는 큰 관계가 없다. 선회성(turning characteristics)과 관련이 있다.
ⓕ 상당한 출력(considerable power)을 갖은 선박에 유리하다.

19 여객이 24시간 초과하여 항해하는 선박인 경우 새로 탑승한 여객은 출항 전, 혹은 직후에(prior to or immediately upon departure) 집합(muster)하여야 하고 구명조끼의 사용법과 비상시 행동에 대해 교육 받아야 한다.

20 ARPA : Automatic Radar Plotting Aids

20회 | 모의고사

1	2	3	4	5	6	7	8	9	10
①	②	③	③	②	①	②	②	②	④
11	12	13	14	15	16	17	18	19	20
④	②	③	①	①	③	②	④	③	①

01 ⓐ Tension winch
ⓑ Standing Order
ⓒ Way point

02 선박이 허리케인의 눈을 통과했고 소강(lull)을 마주했다. 일시적으로 비가 멈추고 그리고 바람이 약해졌다.
소강은 순간적으로 잔잔해지는 상태를 말한다. 잔잔한 기간(calm interval)이 올 수 있다.

03 특정 선박이 다른 특정선박을 추월한다는 객관적 사실에 대해 말하고 있기 때문에 Information 통신부호가 올 수 있다.

04 벌금이 외국 선박에 부과(levied)될 수 있다.
1. 외국 선박이 영해를 통과했다는 이유만으로는 요금을 부과(levied)할 수 없다.
2. 선박에 제공된 특정 서비스를 이용한 경우 영해를 통과하는 외국선박에 요금을 부과(levied) 할 수 있다. 그러나 차별없이(with out discrimination) 부과(levied)되어야 한다.

05 (a) if the consequences of the crime extend to the ⓒcoastal state;
(c) if the assistance of the local authorities has been requested by the master of the ship or by a diplomatic agent or consular officer of the ⓓflag state; or

06 RSC : Rescue Sub Centre

07 접속수역(contiguous zone)에서는 관세(customs), 재정(fiscal), 출입국(immigration)에 관련된 법의 위반을 방지하기 위한 통제를 할 수 있다.

통항(passage)은 해당사항 없음.

08 ⓐ 비상시에 긴급한 위험을 피하기 위해
ⓓ 분리대내에서 어로에 종사하기 위해

09 <u>방위분해능(bearing resolution)</u>은 같은 거리에 다른 방위에 있는 두 물체 사이를 분리하는 능력이다. 이것은 물표가 위치한 거리에 영향을 받고, 수평의 <u>빔폭(pencil beam width)</u>에 영향을 받는다.

10 옳은 것:
① 연료 제거
② 냉각 (화점 아래까지)
③ 화학억제

옳지 않은 것:
④ 화재 시 산소를 포함 시키는 것은 적절치 않다.
inclusion : 포함

11 VHF채널로의 대기 등은 일반적으로 <u>ADVICE</u>로 한다.

12 (b) A vessel using a traffic separation scheme shall:
(i) proceed in the appropriate traffic lane in the ② <u>general direction</u> of traffic flow for that lane;

13 옳지 않은 것:
ⓐ Assembly station
ⓒ Station
ⓔ Lifeboat station

14 선박의 전원이 나간 상태 <u>Deadship condition</u>에 대한 설명이다.

15 SART에 대한 설명이다.

16 INSTRUCTION은 법적으로 강제력 갖는다. 권한이 있는 대상만이 사용할 수 있다.
가. VTS station
마. 완전한 권한을 갖은 인물이나 직원
라. 해군 선박

17 1. 모든 여객선은 여객 집합 장소를 가져야 하는데 이 장소는 탈출 장소 주변에 있어야하고 탈출 장소에서 접근할 수 있어야한다.
2. 또한 한 사람당 적어도 <u>0.35m²</u> 공간이 확보 되어야한다.

18 ⓑ ~~passenger~~ cargo ships of less than 500 tons gross tonnage.
ⓔ Pleasure yachts <u>not</u> engaged in trade.

19 위도 43°N에서 서경으로 <u>날짜변경선(International Date Line)</u>을 넘어갔다. 6월 12일이 <u>반복되었다(repeated)</u>.
날짜변경선을 기준으로 동경으로 넘어가면 하루가 생략(skip/permit)되며 서경으로 넘어가면 반복(repeat)된다.

20 당직인수사관(relieving officer)은 인수멤버가 당직업무를 수행하는 것이 완전히 가능한지를 확인해야 한다. 특히 <u>야간시야(night vision)</u>의 적응을 염두 해야 한다. 인수사관은 그들의(멤버들) <u>시야(vision)</u>가 조명상태에 완전히 적응할 때까지 당직을 인수해서는 안 된다.

21회 | 모의고사

1	2	3	4	5	6	7	8	9	10
①	②	②	②	②	①	④	③	①	③
11	12	13	14	15	16	17	18	19	20
③	②	②	④	①	④	①	③	③	④

01 사고(casualties)의 위험을 감소시킬 목적을 갖는 한 개 이상의 교통방식의 체제를 말한다.

02 ⓑ <u>Dragging anchor</u>에 대한 설명이다.
ⓓ <u>Over flow</u>에 대한 설명이다.

03 ⓐ Track
ⓑ Traffic lane
ⓒ Say again *수신자가 송신자의 메시지를 잘 못 들었을 경우 사용한다. Repeat은 송신자가 강조를 위해 반복할 경우 사용하는 표현이다.*

04 ⓐ <u>Muster list</u>에 대한 설명이다.
ⓒ <u>Disembark</u>에 대한 설명이다.

05 <u>닻이 해저에서 떠난</u> Anchor aweigh에 대한 설명이다.
닻의 격납은 Secure를 사용한다.

06 ⓐ (안개 등이) 끼다. : <u>set in</u>
ⓑ (안개 등이) 걷히다. : lifted or <u>got cleared</u>
ⓒ 견시를 철저히 하다. : keep a <u>sharp</u> look out

07 ⓑ I am making way through the water.
→ 본선은 <u>대수속력</u>이 있다.
ⓒ Tide is setting in direction NE.
→ 조류는 북동 <u>방향으로 흘러가고 있다.</u>
ⓓ 풍속계가 작동하지 않는다.
→ <u>Anemometer</u> is not working
ⓔ Tanker Amoco, I am now making <u>call sign</u>.
→ 탱커 Amoco, 나는 지금 호출부호를 보내고 있다.

08 ⓐ ACO - Air craft <u>coordinator</u>
ⓔ VTS - Vessel Traffic <u>Service</u>

09 평행항적수색법(parallel track search)진행 시 가장 느린 선박의 가장 빠른 속도로 수색을 진행한다. (The maximum speed of the slowest ship present)

10 ⓐ Waters on the landward side of the baseline of the territorial sea are part of the internal water(내수) of the State.

ⓒ No state may validly purport to subject any part of the high seas(공해) to its sovereignty.

ⓓ The normal baseline for measuring the breadth of the territorial sea is the low-water(저조선) line along the coast as marked on large-scale charts officially recognized by the coastal State.

11 보기는 추적권(Right of hot pursuit)에 대한 설명이다. 추적권은 상대 선박이 연안국의 법을 위반했다는 좋은 증거가 있다면 실시될 수 있는데, 상대선박이 접속수역 이내에 있어야한다. 접속수역 이내에 포함되지 않는 수역으로는

마. the hight seas(공해),

바. the exclusive economic zone(배타적 경제수역)이 있다.

12 ⓐ 찬물에 있는 사람의 체온감소를 줄여주는 보호복

Immersion Suit

ⓑ 낮은 열전도율의 방수재질로 만들어진 옷이나 가방

Thermal protective aid

13 다음은 당직자(watch)들을 위한 구명조끼(lifejacket)에 대한 규정이다.

충분한 구명조끼의 수가 당직자들과 멀리 떨어진 생존정답승장소에 구비되어야 한다. 구명조끼는 ⓐ선교(bridge)와 ⓑ기관실(engine control room) 그리고 사람이 당직을 서는 장소에 비치 되어야한다.

14 ⓐ The normal equipment of every lifeboat shall consist of four rocket parachute flares complying with the requirements of regulation.

ⓑ The normal equipment of every lifeboat shall consist of six hand flares complying with the requirements of regulation.

ⓒ The normal equipment of every lifeboat shall consist of two buoyant smoke signal complying with the requirements of regulation.

15 ⓐ Criminal jurisdiction은 공해에서의 범죄혐의에 대해 규제한다.

ⓑ Right of transit passage는 국제 항해를 위한 해협(strait)통과에 대한 규정이다.

ⓒ Right of visit은 공해에서의 특정 혐의에 대해 규제한다.

16 ⓑ 선장이 선교에 올라오더라도 당직이 선장에게 이전(transfer)되는 것은 아니다.

ⓒ 견시원(the look out)과 타수(helmsman)의 업무는 분리되며(separated) 타수는(helmsman) 조타 중 견시 중인 것으로 여겨져서는 안 된다(shall not be considered).

ⓓ 항해사는 당직 중 안전하게 선박을 운항하기 위해 물리적으로 선교에 있어야한다. 객실(cabin)은 해당되지 않는다.

17 steady as she goes에 대한 설명이다.

18 ⓐ hampered vessel에 대한 설명이다.

ⓑ Muster에 대한 설명이다.

ⓒ Roll call에 대한 설명이다.

19 A vessel at anchor shall at interval of not more than ⓐ1minutes ring the bell rapidly for a bout ⓑ5seconds. In vessel ⓒ100meters or more in length the bell shall be sounded in the fore part of the vessel and immediately after the ringing of the bell the ⓓgong shall be sounded rapidly for ⓔ5seconds in the after part of the vessel.

20 정박선은 제한시계(restricted visibility) 내에서 추가신호로 1회의 단음, 1회의 장음, 1회의 장음(one short, one prolonged and one short blast)의 기적신호를 울려주어 접근 중인 타 선박들에게 위치에 대한 경고와, 충돌위험에 대한 경고를 해줄 수 있다.

22회 | 모의고사

1	2	3	4	5	6	7	8	9	10
②	②	④	①	③	③	①	①	②	①
11	12	13	14	15	16	17	18	19	20
②	④	④	②	②	③	②	③	①	④

01 선박이 VTS에 위치를 알리기 위해 보고해야하는 지점이나 장소를 보고지점(Reporting point)라 한다.

02 ⓐ ITZ(연안통항대)에 대한 설명이다.

ⓓ Precautionary area(경계수역)에 대한 설명이다.

03 조난에 빠진 선박, 항공기 혹은 사람을 찾는 것은 locating 이다.

04 ⓐ 조류가 북동쪽으로 흐르고 있다.(setting)

ⓑ 본선은 대수속력을 내고 있다.(making way through the water)

ⓒ 포항만 주변에 거리를 둘 것을 권고한다. 수색구조작업이 이루어지고 있다.(in operation)

05 선박이 선박과 같은 속력의 조류를 역조로 받고 있다. 선박은

항해중이나 대지속력은 0이다.(under way but not making way over the ground)
*대수 속력은(STW) 기관을 사용해 내는 속력이며 대지속력(SOG)는 외력의 영향을 모두 포함하여 나오는 선박의 이동 거리를 통해 계산한 속력이다. 선박이 대수속력은 내고 있으나 역조류의 영향으로 정지해 있는 것처럼 보이므로 대지속력은 없는 상태라고 볼 수 있다.

06 ⓒ A/CO – Alter Course 변침
ⓔ K.O – Knock off 작업중지
ⓕ S/Co – Set course 정침

07 ⓑ My present speed is one two knots
ⓓ Port fifteen

08 ⓓ Disembark에 대한 설명이다.
ⓕ Cardinal point에 대한 설명이다.

09 ⓓ single turn(one turn)에 대한 설명이다.

10 ⓔ 어로 종사중인 선박은 따로 분류 된다.
ⓕ 항해장비가 손상된 선박은 조종 제한선으로 분류되지 않는다.

11 ⓒ 해수의 밀도(the state of density of seawater)는 안전속력(safe speed) 정할 때 고려할 사항이 아니다.

12 용어 '가장 가까운 육지로부터(from the nearest land)'는 영해기선(baseline from which the territorial seas is established)을 의미한다.

13 ⓔ 정박지에 기항하는 것(calling at roadstead)은 유해하다고 판단하지 않는다.
ⓕ 내수로 항해하는 것(proceeding to internal water)은 유해하다고 판단하지 않는다.

14 ⓐ Security level 1 : The level for which (minimum appropriate) protective security measures shall be maintained at all times. : 최소한의 보호 보안 조치가 유지되는 단계
ⓑ Security level 2 : The level for which (appropriate additional) protective security measures shall be maintained for a period of time as a result of heightened risk of a security incident. : 절절한 추가적인 보호 보안 조치가 유지되는 단계
ⓒ Security level 3 : The level for which (further specific) protective security measures shall be maintained for a limited period of time when a security incident is probable or imminent, although it may not be possible to identify the specific target. : 보다 구체적인 보호 보안 조치가 유지되는 단계

15 ⓐ 가라앉은 선박에서 자동으로 방출되게 되는 진수방식인 float-free launching에 대한 설명이다.

16 Every officer in charge of a navigational watch serving on a seagoing ship of (500)gross tonnage or more shall hold an appropriate certificate. Every candidate for certification shall
– be not less than (18)years of age
– have approved seagoing service of not less than (12)months as part of an approved training programme which includes on-board training which meets the requirements of section A-11/1 of the STCW Code and is documented in an approved training record book, or otherwise have approved seagoing service of not less than (36)months.
500+18+12+36=566

17 조난에 빠진 선박, 항공기 사람을 알리기 위한 목적이 아닌 국제 조난신호의 사용과, 국제 조난신호에 혼란을 야기할 수 있는 신호의 사용은 금지된다(prohibited).

18 X-band radar는 동일 조건의 S-band radar에 비해 연안항해 시 좀 더 지도와 비슷한 화면을 보여준다(display more maplike presentation for inshore navigation).

19 조류의 방향은 진북기준(true)이지 자북기준(magnetic)이 아니다. 그리고 조류의 방향은 흘러가는(toward) 방향이며, 반면에 바람은 불어오는(from) 방향이다.

20 평균보다 낮은 저조를 갖고, 평균보다 높은 고조를 갖은 조석은 대조(Spring tide)이다.

23회 | 모의고사

1	2	3	4	5	6	7	8	9	10
③	②	②	③	②	①	①	②	③	①
11	12	13	14	15	16	17	18	19	20
④	②	②	②	③	③	①	①	①	②

01 권고항로(recommended track)는 특별 조사가 이루어져서 최대한 위험(dangers)이 없다는 것이 확인된 항로이며 선박의 항해가 권고되는(advised) 항로이다.

02 ⓐ steady에 대한 설명이다.

03 TSS를 횡단(cross)할 경우 일반적(general) 교통의 흐름에 직각(right) 방향으로 횡단해야한다.

04 보조 조타장치는 타를 한쪽 현 15도에서 반대 현 15도까지 ⓑ60초 이내로 들어오게 해야 하고 이때 선박은 최대만재흘수, 그리고 ⓒ최대속력 절반속도(one half)와 ⓓ7노트 중 더

큰(greater) 쪽의 속도로 항해하고 있어야 한다.

05 ⓐ Transshipment(항만 밖에서 선박과 선박 간 화물을 옮겨 싣는 행위를 말한다.)에 대한 설명이다.
ⓑ Abandon ship 퇴선에 대한 설명이다.

06 ⓐ 출항을 위해 핵심 계류 줄을 제외한 모든 줄들은 선내로 끌어 올리라는 명령어 Single up 에 대한 설명이다.
ⓑ 표준해사영어 단어 상 선박의 높이라 함은 수선 위(above the waterline)로 선박의 가장 높은 지점까지의 높이를 말한다.

07 항해속력(sea speed) 중의 시간을 말하며 달리 말하면 Rung Up Engine부터 목적 항 입항 전 Stand By Engine 사이의 시간을 말한다.

08 ⓐ "Search and rescue region" — An area of defined dimensions within which search and rescue services are provided.
ⓒ "Alert Phase" — A situation wherein apprehension exists as to the safety of a vessel and the persons on board.

09 평행 항적 수색 법(Parallel Sweep Search)에 대한 설명이다.

10 선박 간 상호시계 내인 경우 타선박의 동작이해에 실패했거나 타선박의 동작에 ㉠의심(doubt)이 있는 경우 ㉠의심(doubt)을 갖은 선박은 그 ⓑ의심(doubt)을 급속하고 ⓑ최소 5회의 단음을(at least five short) 울려줌으로 표시해주어야 한다.

11 배타적 경제수역에서 대한민국 정부는 해저에 인접한 수역, 그 해저, 그 하층토로부터 천연자원을(생명체든 무생물이든) 탐험하고, 개발하고, 보존(conserving) 그리고 관리(managing)할 주권적 권리를 갖는다.

12 ⓐ 항해 중(underway) 이란 선박이 정박(anchor)하지 않고, 계류(made fast)하지 않고, 좌초(aground)되지 않은 상태를 말한다. 대수속력이 없더라도(not making way through the water) 위의 세 가지에 해당하지 않는다면 선박은 항해 중 상태이다.

13 ⓑ Security Level에 대한 설명이다.
ⓒ Security Incident에 대한 설명이다.

14 좌초선은 주간 수직선상의 3개의 흑구 혹은 그와 비슷한 형상을 가장 잘 보이는 곳에 달아야 한다.

15 상호 시계인 경우(in sight of one another) 우현 변침 중인 선박은 1회(one) 단음을 울려주며 좌현변침 중은 2회(two), 후진중은 3회(three)를 울려준다.

16 특정 날의 고조면(water surface at high)과 저조면(that at low water)의 수직의 높이 차이를 조차(tidal range)라 한다.

17 선박을 jetty나 dock등에 나란히 놓는 행위를 접안(berthing)이라고 한다.

18 모두 옳음.

19 SOLAS에 의거하여 구명 자켓(life jacket)은 24시간 청수(fresh water)에 잠긴 이후에도 부양성(buoyancy)을 5%보다 더 잃어서는 안 된다.

20 유탱커의 기름 배출시 가장 가까운 육지로부터 적어도 50해리 밖에서 배출해야한다.

24회 | 모의고사

1	2	3	4	5	6	7	8	9	10
④	④	①	②	③	④	①	③	④	③
11	12	13	14	15	16	17	18	19	20
②	③	②	④	④	③	①	②	①	②

01 조난신호는 완전한 우선권(priority)을 모든 다른 통신 위에 갖게 된다. 이런 조난신호를 수신한 경우 다른 송신들은 모두 중단(cease)되고 이를 청취(listen in)해야 한다.

02 STCW코드는 각국 정부에게 당직중의 선박직원의 혈중 알콜 농도 0.05%를 최대로 할 것을 권고한다. 또한 당직 시작 전 4시간 이내의 알콜 섭취를 금지한다.
이는 STCW에서 요구하는 사항이다. 국내법에서는 이보다 엄격한 0.03%를 최대로 본다. 해사법규에서 제시하는 숫자와 STCW에서 제시하는 숫자가 다르므로 조심도록 한다.

03 ⓑ APRA : Automatic Radar Plotting Aids
ⓓ VHF : Very Heigh Frequency

04 ⓐ Hogging은 선박의 용골 혹은 선체가 받는 스트레스로, 선박의 중앙부가 위로 밀리는 것을 말한다.
ⓑ 선박의 선수가 처음 좌현으로 밀리고 나서 우현으로 밀리는 때, 선박은 Yawing을 하고 있는 것이다.

05 ⓑ S/B eng. for entering harbour area : 항만 접근을 위해 기관사용 준비
ⓓ pilot on board : 도선사 승선
ⓐ first line to pier : 첫줄을 부두에 연결함
ⓒ made her fast on pier : 부두에 선박 계류를 하였음

06 ⓑ Made fast port side to pier. F.W.E.
→ 좌현 안벽 접안을 완료했다. 기관사용 종료
ⓒ Made her stern fast to pier.
→ 부두에 선미 계류함
ⓓ The flood tide, it is one hour after low water.

→ 조류가 올라가고 있다. 저조 한 시간 후이다.

07 침로(course)는 각도이다. 선박의 중심선이나 용골이 자오선과 만든

08 A vessel engaged in fishing, other than trawling shall exhibit :
i) two all-round light in a vertical line, the ①upper being red and the lower white, or a shape consisting of two cones with apexes together in a vertical line one above the other.
ii) when there is outlying gear extending more than ②150 metres horizontally from the vessel, an all-round ③white light or a ④cone apex upward in the direction of the gear.
iii) when making way through the water, in addition to the lights, prescribed in this paragraph, sidelights and a stern light.

트롤링이 아닌 어로에 종사중인 선박은 상방에 홍색등 하방에 백색등을 점등하는데, 만일 어구가 한쪽 현으로 수평 150m를 초과하여 나가 있다면 해당 방향에 백색의 전주등을 점등하거나 정점이 상방을 향하는 원추형 형상물을 걸어야 한다.

09 모두 해당함

10 ⓐ A/CO : 변침
ⓔ SMC : 수색구조임무조정관

11 항해중 선박의 로그북 기사를 찾아야 하므로 운하를 통과하여 Rung Up engine을 했다는 기사가 적절하다.

12 ⓐ Immersion suit에 대한 설명이다.
ⓑ Thermal protective aid에 대한 설명이다.
ⓔ Retrieval에 대한 설명이다.

13 A. 군도기선(archipelagic baselines)의 길이는 100해리를 초과하면 안 되나 군도를 둘러싼 전체 기선의수의 ②3%까지는 최대 길이 125해리까지 초과 할 수 있다.
B. 그런 기선을 그리는 것이 해당 군도의 ④일반적 윤곽(general configuration)을 현저히 확장하는 정도로는 동떨어져서는 안 된다.

14 On a ship engaged on a voyage where passengers are scheduled to be on board for more than 24h, musters of newly-embarked passengers shall take place prior to or immediately upon departure. Passengers shall be instructed in the use of the lifejackets and the action to take in an emergency.

여객이 24시간을 초과하여 항해하게 되는 선박에서는 새로운 승선 여객은 (출항 전 혹은 출항 직후) 구명조끼 사용법과, 비상시 행동요령을 교육받기 위해 집합해야 한다.

15 ⓐ 다른 선박을 추월하는(overtaking) 모든 선박은 피 추월선(overtaken vessel)에게 길을 비켜 줘야한다.
ⓑ 안전속력(Safe speed)은 선박이 충돌을 피하기 위해 적절한 동작을 취하고 적절한 거리 이내에서 멈출(stopped) 수 있게 최대한의(maximum) 시간을 벌게 해주는 속력이다.

16 각 주관청은 피로를 예방할 목적으로 당직 시스템이 잘 배치되어서 개인의 당직 효율이 피로에 의해 저하되지 않고, 당직 시스템이 잘 조직화 되어서 출항 후 첫 당직자 혹은 그 이후의 인수 당직자가 충분히 휴식(sufficiently rested)을 취할 수 있게끔 요구를 해야 한다.

17 일반비상경보는 7회단음 이후 따라 나오는 1회의 장음이다. (seven short, one prolonged)

18 비상집합 장소(muster stations)는 탈출 장소 근처에 있어야 하고 각 집합 장소는 해당 장소에 집합하도록 할당된 각 사람을 충분히 수용할 수 있는 충분한 갑판 공간을 갖추어야 한다. 그러나 이 장소는 한 사람당 0.35m² 이상이어야 한다.

19 ⓐ 지구의 양극을 지나는 대권, 자오선(Meridian)에 대한 설명이다.
ⓑ 저조는 평균보다 높고 고조는 평균보다 낮은 조석인 소조(Neap)에 대한 설명이다.

20 모든 침로와 속도의 변침은 상황이 허락하는 한 시각적으로(visually), 레이더로 관찰중인 다른 선박에게 바로 ⓑ명백(apparent)하도록 충분히 커야한다(large)
즉 ⓓ소각(small)도 변침의 연속은 피한다.

25회 | 모의고사

1	2	3	4	5	6	7	8	9	10
④	④	①	③	③	②	③	②	②	①
11	12	13	14	15	16	17	18	19	20
①	②	②	②	②	②	④	①	①	②

01 보기의 내용은 본선이 선체를 바람과 파도가 있는 쪽으로 두어 조난에 빠진 선박을 보호하겠다는 내용이므로 본선이 권선을 "풍하측에 오게 하겠다"의 I will make a lee for you가 적절하다.

02 ⓐ선장이 선원들에게 해상 사고 시 내릴 수 있는 최후(last)의 명령은 퇴선(abandon ship)이다.
ⓑ조타의 자동에서 수동모드로의 전환 혹은 그 반대의 전환은 당직 항해사(responsible office)의 지휘 아래에서 이루어져야한다.

03 ⓑ backing(반전)에 대한 설명이다.

04 조종 제한선이 준설작업이나 수중작업을 하고 있는 경우 조종 제한선 등화에 추가하여 물체가 있는 현 쪽에 다음의 등화를 달아야 한다.
  1. 장애물이 존재하는 현(obstruction exists)에 **홍색 전주등 두 개(two all round red lights)** 혹은 흑구 두개를 수직선상에 달아야 한다.
  2. 선박이 통과 할 수 있는 현(vessel may pass) **녹색 전주등 두 개(two all round greed lights)** 혹은 마름모꼴 두 개를 수직선상에 달아야 한다.

05 유지선이 충돌을 피하기 위해서는
  (A) 상황이 극적이라면 피항 해야 한다.
  (B) 피항선(give-way vessel)이 규정에서 요구하는 동작을 취하고 있지 않다는 것이 명백해진다면 침로를 변경 할 수 있다.
  즉 A와 B 둘 다 옳다.

06 ⓑ **CSP(Commence Search Point), 수색시작지점**에 대한 설명이다.
  ⓓ **Rscue(구조)**에 대한 설명이다.

07 안전 속력을 정하는 데에 **선원의 능력(the competency of crew)**는 고려하지 않는다.

08 There are enough LSA(life saving appliance) for everyone on board.
  -> 선상의 모든 사람에게 충분한 **구명 설비**가 있음.

09 ⓑ **Advance**에 대한 설명이다.
  ⓒ **Walk out**에 대한 설명이다.
  ⓓ **ANSWER**에 대한 설명이다.

10 접근하다의 의미를 가지므로 **approaching**으로 대체 할 수 있다.

11 선박이 위험하고 즉각적인 원조를 요청하는 것은 Mayday 조난 신호이다.

12 닻줄이 팽팽하다(tight)하다고 대답했으므로 질문으로는 장력을 묻는 것이 적절하다.
  >> How is the cable **growing**?

13 ⓐ **Recommended area**에 대한 설명이다.
  ⓒ Inshore Traffic Zone : A routing measure comprising a designated area between the **landward** boundary of a traffic separation scheme and the adjacent coast, intended for local traffic.

14 **Filled** up A with B : A를 B로 채우다.

15 북태평양의 열대성 폭풍의 지역명은 **Typhoon**이다.
  *Atlantic Ocean : hurricane
  Indian ocean : cyclone
  Australian ocean : willy-willy*

16 제한 시계 내에서 대수속력이 있는 동력선(power-driven vessel making way through the water)은 **2분**을 넘지 않는 간격으로 **1회**의 장음(one prolonged)을 울려야 한다.
  2+1=3

17 계류 줄을 통과시킬 가장 최선의 방법은 계류 줄이 선박 측면의 **Fairlead**를 통과하는 것이다.

18 SOLAS에 의거하여 선원들은 **매달(every month)** 퇴선훈련과 화재훈련에 참가해야한다. 전체 승객인원의 **25퍼센트**를 넘는 인원이 전달 훈련을 받지 않았다면(매달 하는 퇴선훈련, 화재훈련) **24**시간이내에 해당 훈련을 받아야한다.

19 당직 항해사는 선장을 호출할 목적 때문이라도 선교를 떠나서는 안 된다.

20 동력선이 야간에(at night) 수평선상의 녹등과 홍등을 보았다면 이것은 현등(sidelights)이다. 또한 두 개의 수직선상의 백등을 보았다면 이것은 동력선의 마스트등이다.
  즉 head on situation으로 판단할 수 있으므로 규정에 따라 우현 변침(**alter course to starboard**)한다.

26회 | 모의고사

1	2	3	4	5	6	7	8	9	10
①	②	④	②	②	③	①	②	③	③
11	12	13	14	15	16	17	18	19	20
②	③	①	④	③	③	③	④	③	③

01 **명목적 광달거리(nominal range)**는 기상이 양호한 날 (주간 가시거리 10해리)등광을 볼 수 있는 최대거리를 의미한다.

02 시작지점으로 부터 방위나, 예상 거리를 통해 거리를 예측하여 얻는 위치를 말한다.
  천체나 전자 장비를 통해서 얻어지지 않으며, Gyro 인코더나, speed log를 통해 얻어진다.
  >>**Dead reckoning position (추측위치)**

03 ⓐ **파일럿 사다리(pilot ladder)**설치는 rig동사를 사용한다.
  ⓑ 내 보트가 귀선의 풍하측이 되도록 하여라.

04 Turn in cable은 **닻줄이 꼬이다**를 의미한다.

05 ⓑ ETA : Estimated Time of **Arrival**
  ⓓ FWT : Fresh **Water** Tank

06 ⓐ I am in danger of **sinking(침몰)**
  ⓑ What is your **Call sign(호출부호)**
  ⓒ **From(~로부터)** what direction are you approaching?

ⓓ What was your last port of call(호출부호)?

07 ⓐ Roll은 종방향 축의 회전운동이며 **복원성(Stability)**에 관련이 있다.
ⓑ Pitch는 횡방향 축의 회전운동이며 **트림(trim)**에 관련이 있다.
ⓒ Yaw는 수직 축에 대한 회전운동이며 **침로안정성(course keeping ability)**에 관련이 있다.

08 좌초선(vessel ground)의 등화는 선수 선미에 백등 전주등 하나씩을 점등하며(선미부의 것을 더욱 낮게) ⓒ**수직선상 두 개의 홍등(two all round red light in vertical line)**을 추가로 점등해준다. ⓔ의 흑구 한 개는 정박선(anchor)의 주간 형상물이다.

09 통항분리대에 닻을 내리는 것은 옳지 않다.

10 ⓒ TSS를 사용하지 않는 선박은 TSS에 **충분한 여유(wide a margin)**를 두고 항해해야한다.
ⓓ 분리대는 긴급 상황 시 그리고 어로종사를 위해서만 진입할 수 있다.

11 A ship which sails under the flags of two or more States, using them according to convenience, may not claim any of the nationalities in question with respect to any other State.
두 개 이상의 기를 편의를 위해 사용하고 있는 선박은 자신의 국적을 주장 할 수 없다.

12 ⓓ 항공기와 선박이 각각한대씩 독립된 수색을 한다면 함께 사용될 수 있다. : An aircraft and a vessel may not be used together to perform independent sector searches of the same area.
ⓔ **확대사각수색법(Expanding Square Search)**에 대한 설명이다.

13 NAVTEX는 주파수대 518KHz에서 운용되며 **해사안전정보(Maritime safety information)**를 수신할 수 있다.

14 식별 : identification

15 선주(shipowner)가 편의치적(flag of convenience) 선박을 사용하는 이유는:
① 세금 면제를 위해
② 자국의 노동력보다 더욱 저렴한 노동력을 고용하기 위해
④ 비슷한 방식으로 재정적으로 이윤을 얻기 위해서이다.

16 다른 선박과의 충돌을 피하기 위한 동작은 안전한 거리(a safe distance)로 통과하는 결과를 갖는 것이어야 한다.

17 ⓐ 선박이 해수에서 청수로 들어간다면 건현은 **감소(decreased)**할 것이다.
해수의 비중은 1.025, 청수의 비중은 1.00으로 해수에서 선박은 더욱 잘 뜨게 되고 청수에서 가라앉게 된다. 해수에서 청수로 들어간 경우라면 선박이 가라앉아 흘수는 증가하고 건현은 줄어들게 될 것이다.
ⓑ 선박이 선수트림인 경우, 등흘수로 만들기 위해선 **선수(fore)peak tank**의 평형수를 배출해 줘야한다.
선수 트림은 선수 흘수가 선미 흘수보다 큰 상태를 말한다.

18 선박은 일반적 항로로 바로 항해해야하는데, 출항 항구에서 도착지까지 **이로(deviation)**나 불필요한 지연이 없어야한다.

19 hampered vessel은 조종 제한 선이다. 대수속력이 있으므로(making way through the water) 조종제한선 등화인 상부와 하부의 ⓐ**홍등(red)**, 중간의 ⓑ**백등(white)**을 비롯하여 ⓓ**현등(sidelights)**, ⓔ**선미등(stern light)** 그리고 ⓒ**정부마스트등(masthead light)**을 점등한다.

20 ⓐ **생존정 탈출장소(survival craft embarkation stations)**에 위치한 사다리 **탈출사다리(embarkation ladder)**에 대한 설명이다.
ⓑ 도선사 사다리, 승정 사다리, 기중기 등 도선사의 안전한 환승을 위한 모든 장비들을 **도선사 승정장비(boarding arrangement)**라 한다.

27회 | 모의고사

1	2	3	4	5	6	7	8	9	10
④	③	②	①	④	④	②	③	③	④
11	12	13	14	15	16	17	18	19	20
①	①	②	①	②	②	④	④	④	③

01 ⓐ Traffic lane : An area within defined limits in which (one way traffic) is established. Natural obstacles, including those forming separation zones, may constitute a boundary.
ⓑ Inshore Traffic Zone : A routing measure comprising a designated area between the (landward) boundary of a traffic separation scheme and the adjacent coast, where local special rules may apply, and normally not to be used by through traffic.
ⓒ Deep water route : A route within limit which defined limits which has been accurately surveyed for (clearance) of sea bottom and (submerged obstacles) as indicated on the chart.

02 두 대의 출항선이 방파제 입구에 있다고 하는 객관적 정보를 알려주고 있다. 통신부호는 Information이 적절하다.

03 선박의 용골(keel)이나 선수미선(center line)이 선박의 항적(wake of the vessel or track)과 만드는 각도는 풍압차

04 모두 옳다.

05 ⓐ SSAS가 작동되면 선박 대 육상 (ship to shore)송신을 시작한다.
ⓑ 다른 주변 선박에게 경보를 울려선 안 된다. (Not send)
ⓒ 선내에 알람을 울려서는 안 된다. (Not raise)
ⓔ SSAS는 선교에 한 개 그리고 그 외의 장소에 한 개 이상 설치해야한다.(The ship security alert system shall be capable of being activated from the navigation bridge and in at least one other location)

06 선박이 교차방위법, 혹은 육표, 장비를 통해 선위를 얻는 방식이다. 이것은 날씨가 안 좋아지면 사용 할 수 없다. ; 지문항해(geo-navigation)

07 나머지는 모두 파일럿 하선에 대한 표현이며 ①은 파일럿 승선을 의미한다.

08 ⓔ heave up 은 양묘로 닻을 올리는 동작이다.

09 오기를 작성한 경우 한 줄로 긋고 다시 작성한다.
Remove, Blot out, erase 등은 모두 지운다는 의미로 옳지 않다.

10 벌금 부과(imposing)는 ISPS 상. 선박이나 항만에 공격위험이 식별됐을 경우 연안국이 실시할 수 있는 항만 통제로 나와 있지 않다.

11 특별구역(special area)은 이곳의 해양학적이고 생태학적인 조건과 교통의 특수성과 관련하여 인지된 기술을 위해 해양오염을 방지하기 위한 특별한 의무적 수단의 채택이 요구되는 해역이다.

12 ⓐ윌리엄슨 턴은 즉각적인 동작(immediate action)에 사용되므로 해당 항목자체가 삭제되어야 한다.
(1) ⓑRudder hard over
(2) After deviation from the original course by ⓒ60 degree, rudder hard over to the opposite side.
(3) When heading ⓓ20 degree short of opposite course, rudder to ⓔmidship position so that ship will turn to opposite course.

13 ⓐ 노예무역(slave trade)은 공해의 자유에 해당하지 않으며 오히려 공해상의 임검권(right of visit)을 행사할 수 있는 사유가 된다.

14 외력의 영향 없이 침로와 항정만으로 구하는 위치는 추측위치(Dead reckoning position이다.)

15 rendez-vous position은 선박과 선박 간에 만나는 약속지점이다. 때문에 이후 두 선박은 선박과 선박간의 활동(ship to ship activity)을 할 것이다.

16 ⓒ 귀선을 위해 풍하측을 만들어주겠다.

ⓓ 선박 횡경사(list)를 막기 위해 화물을 투하할 수 있는가?
capsize는 전복

17 트림(trim)의 변화는 부면심의(center of floatation)을 기준으로 무게중심을 앞뒤로 이동시켜서, 혹은 무게를 앞이나 뒤쪽에 더하거나 제거해서 생겨난다.

18 TSS를 사용하는 선박은 양현에 일반적 교통 방향에 소각으로(at as small an angle to the general direction of traffic flow as practicable.) 진입해야 한다.

19 유해액체물질의 배출은 수선아래(under the waterline) 수면하배출구를 통해 이루어져야 한다.

20 ⓑ False Alarm에 대한 설명이다.
ⓒ Distress Alert에 대한 설명이다.
ⓓ Rescue에 대한 설명이다.

28회 | 모의고사

1	2	3	4	5	6	7	8	9	10
①	③	③	④	③	④	②	④	①	④
11	12	13	14	15	16	17	18	19	20
③	②	①	②	①	①	④	①	①	④

01 UNCLOS에 따르면 연안국(coastal state)은 외국선박의 영해를 통한 무해통항(the innocent passage)를 방해해서는 안 된다.(UNCLOS에 따른 예외사항 제외)

02 점장도(mercator chart)위에서 항정선(rhumb line)은 직선(straight line)으로 보인다.

03 군도국가(Archipelagic state)는 군도의 일반적 윤곽(general configuration)에 현저히 동떨어지게 기선을 그려서는 안 된다(shall not depart).

04 영해(high seas)는 모든 국가의 선박들이 자유를 갖는 해역이다. 때문에 열린 바다(open sea), 국제수역(international water)등으로 불릴 수 있다. 그러나 해양(marine sea)은 그 범주가 너무 넓다.

05 ⓐ All vessels are advised to keep wide (berth). 선박은 안전공간을 확보하는 것을 권고 받는다.
ⓑ The SMCP is divided into (external) communication phrases and (on board) communication phrases.

06 discharge the tank with 30 tons of ballast water to refloat.
→ 선박을 이초시키기 위해 평형수 30톤을 배출하시오.

07 ⓑ 얼마나 많은 샤클이 나가야 하는가? 라는 표현이 되므로 부적합하다.

08 ⓐ Waters on the landward side of the **baseline of the territorial sea** form the internal water of the state.

ⓑ Every State has the right to establish the breadth of its territorial sea up to a limit not exceeding **12** nautical miles, measured from baselines determined in accordance with this Convention.

ⓒ **No** State may validly purport to subject any part of the high seas to its sovereignty.

ⓓ Except where otherwise provided in this Convention, the **normal baseline** for measuring the breadth of the territorial sea is the low-water line along the coast as marked on large-scale charts officially recognized by the coastal state.

09 비상배치표(Muster list)그리고 비상 절차 표는 항해 선교(navigation bridge), 기관실(engine room), 그리고 **선원 거주구(crew accommodation spaces)**를 포함한 선박 전체에 눈에 잘 띄도록 배치해야한다.

10 자동인식시스템(Automatic Identification System, AIS)에 대한 설명이다.

11 ⓐ 어로종사는 공해에서 자유다.
ⓒ 인공섬 건설은 공해에서 자유다.
ⓔ 과학 조사 활동은 공해에서 자다.

12 (**chart and light list**) should be checked to see that they have been corrected through the latest (**notice to mariners**). 해도와 등대표는 가장 최신의 항행통보를 통해서 이것이 최신의 것인지 확인해 줘야한다.

13 해당 선박의 침로가 좌측 경계에 너무 가까운 상황이기 때문에 VTS는 **INSTRUCTION** 통신부호를 통해 **우현변침(starboard)**을 지시하는 것이 적절하다.

14 배타적경제수역내에서 대한민국 정부는 (무생물이든 생물이든 해저에 인접한 수역, 그리고 해저, 그리고 그 하층토의) 천연자원을 탐험(**exploring**), 개발(**exploiting**), 관리(**managing**), 보존(**conserving**) (그리고 조류 바람 파도로부터의 에너지 생산 활동과 같은 경제 개발, 탐험을 위한 활동에 대해) 할 수 있는 주권적 권리(sovereign rights)를 갖는다. *charging은 벌금, 요금 등을 부과한다는 의미이다.*

15 ⓐ **유해 물질(harmful substance)**에 대한 설명이다.
ⓑ 총톤수 10,000톤 이상의 선박은 오일필터링장치(oil filtering equipment)와 배출액의 유분이 **15ppm**을 넘는 경우 자동 알람과 경보를 해줄 수 있는 설비를 갖추어야 한다.

16 승무원과 여객은 선박의 이 장소에 머물고, 쉬고 먹는다. 어떤 선박들은 수영장이나 농구장을 갖추고 있기도 하다.
***거주구(accommodation space)**에 대한 설명이다.*

17 ⓒ "**Variation**" means angle caused between the magnetic meridian and true meridian.

ⓓ The action of bringing your vessel alongside a jetty or dock is called "**berthing**".

ⓔ "**Line of position**" is an imaginary line on which a ship at sea must lie to satisfy certain data obtained by the observation of terrestrial or celestial object.

18 Every officer in charge of a engineering watch in a manned engine-room or designated duty engineer officer in a periodically unmanned engine-room on a seagoing ship powered by main propulsion machinery of (**750**)KW propulsion power or more shall hold an appropriate certificate. Every candidate for certification shall
- be not less than (**18**) years of age.
- have completed not less than (**6**) months seagoing service in the engine department in accordance with section A-III/1 of the STCW code

750+18+6=774

19 ⓐ The master of every ship is bound to ensure that (**watchkeeping arrangements**) are adequate for maintaining a safe navigational watch.

ⓑ Under the master's general direction, the officers of the navigational watch are responsible for navigating the ship safely during their periods of duty, when they will particularly concerned with avoiding (**collision and stranding**).

ⓒ The duties of the look-out and helmsperson are (**separate**).

20 Garbage는 선박 운항 시 생성되고, 지속적으로 정기적으로 배출되기 쉬운 모든 종류의 음식물, 가정, 작업 중 나오는 쓰레기들을 의미한다. (신선한 생선이나 그 생선의 일부분은 제외)

29회 | 모의고사

1	2	3	4	5	6	7	8	9	10
③	④	②	③	③	②	③	①	③	②
11	12	13	14	15	16	17	18	19	20
②	①	④	③	①	③	①	①	②	②

01 ⓒ Veering : When the wind direction moves clockwise.
ⓓ Hogging : A stress which a ship's hull or keel experiences that the middle of the ship is pushed to bend upward.
ⓔ A cold front : Where a cold air mass moves under warmer air mass.

02 ① 수신감도를 확인하는 넘버는 1~5까지이다.
② I am bound for next port : 다음 목적 항으로 향하는 중이다.
be bound to 는 ~을 할 의무가 있다 로 해석되기 때문에 해석상 어색한 문장이 된다.
③ SMCP 상 Can, May, Might등 애매한 표현으로의 질문은 피해야한다.

03 ⓑ Reporting point : a mark or place at which a vessel is required to report to the local VTS-Station to establish its position.
ⓕ List : Inclination of the vessel to port side or starboard side.

04 닻이 끌리고 있는가? : Are you dragging anchor?

05 ㉠ Damage control team : A group of crew members trained for fighting (flooding).
㉡ Refloat : To pull a vessel off after (grounding) ; to afloat again
㉢ Beach : To run a vessel up on a beach to prevent its (sinking) in deep water

06 가. I picked (up) in position .... 본선은 ... 위치에서 사람을 인양하였음
나. Person picked (up) is crew member of MT... 인양된 사람은 유조선 ...호의 승무원임.
다. Picked (up) two river pilot at 1230LT 지방시 12시30분에 두 명의 강 파일럿을 태웠음.
인양하다, 태우다 등은 pick up 동사로 표현할 수 있다.

07 Isolated danger marks는 고립장해표지에 대한 설명이다. 침선표지의 영문표기는 Emergency wreck marking mark(buoy)이다.

08 ② growing은 장력을 의미한다.
③ turn in cable은 닻줄이 꼬였음을 의미한다.
④ Fairway speed는 항로내 제한속력이다.

09 ⓒ는 Meridian에 대한 설명이다.

10 If suspicion remains after the documents have been checked, it may proceed to a further examination on board the ship which must be carried out with all possible consideration. 모든 문서를 조사한 이후 혐의가 남아있는 경우 조사를 정지하는 것이 아니라 추가적으로 선내 조사를 할 수 있다.

11 가. REQUEST. 예인선 두 대를 수배해 달라.
나. A steering order to reduce swing as rapidly as possible is Steady

12 방위는 분리해서 불러준다.

13 ⓐ 현등은 수평의 호 112.5도를 비추고, 범위는 정선수부터 정 횡 후방 22.5도까지이다.
ⓑ 섬광등은 분당 120회 이상 점멸하는 등화이다.

14 항내(harbour area)에서는 선속을 낮춰야한다. sea speed는 조종속력에서 보다 올라간 속도이다.

15 To reduce the oxygen in a tank by (inert) gas to avoid an explosion atmosphere.
폭발성 환경을 피하기 위해서는 탱크 내에 불활성가스(inert gas)를 주입해주어 산소농도를 낮추어야 한다.

16 - A passenger ship safety certificate shall be issued for a period not exceeding (12) months. A Cargo Ship Safety Construction Certificate, Cargo Ship Safety Equipment Certificate and Cargo Ship Safety Radio Certificate shall be issued for a period specified by the Administration which shall not exceed (5) years.
- A life jacket shall have buoyancy which is not reduced by more than (5)% after 24h submersion in fresh water. (12+5+5=22)

17 선박이 Quarantine anchorage(검역묘박지)에 들어가기 전에 검역증을 받기위해 모든 선원의 건강상태와 선박의 진반적인 위생상태를 확인해야한다.

18 음향신호 2회의 단음은 선박이 좌현변침 하고 있다는 것을 의미한다.

19 SMCP 상 거리는 해리(nautical miles)와 cables로 표현되며 단위(unit)은 생략되어서는 안 된다.

20 ⓐ Ah'd - 선수 방향 ⓔ NUC - 조종불능선

30회 | 모의고사

1	2	3	4	5	6	7	8	9	10
②	④	①	③	③	②	④	②	①	①
11	12	13	14	15	16	17	18	19	20
③	②	④	①	②	③	③	②	①	④

01 다. 침로가 출항선과 너무 가까이 붙어있으니 침로를 변경하거나 속도를 줄이라는 내용이 나오는 것이 적절하다.
라. Pease make a <u>lee</u> for my boat 본선을 <u>풍하측</u>으로 오게 해주시오.

02 Fog is set in (안개가 낌)

03 라. <u>Leeward</u>에 대한 설명이다.
아. <u>Muster list</u>에 대한 설명이다.

04 가. 좌현 닻줄이 물 안에 4샤클 있다고 되어있기 때문에 들어갈 수 있는 단어는 앵커가 완전히 박히다 의 <u>Brought</u> up 이다.
나. 부상자를 <u>회복(recover)</u>시키기 위해 즉각적인 동작을 취하라

05 옳지 않은 것 :
ⓓ Q.M : <u>Quarter</u> Master [SEP]
ⓖ G.T : <u>Gross</u> Tonnage [SEP] L
ⓗ L.S.T : Local <u>Standard</u> Time

06 가. <u>대축적지도(The largest-scale chart)</u> 가 연안 항해 시 오류를 최대로 줄이고 디테일을 보여주기 위해 사용되어야 한다.
나. 날씨 예보 상 날씨가 좋아진다고 되어있기 때문에 바람과 파도(wind and swell)는 약해질 것이다.<u>(eased)</u>. 그래서 선내 도선사가 접안을 동의 하였고 예인선을 붙이고 항진하였다.

07 <u>alloted</u>는 "할당된" 이라는 의미를 갖는다.

08 규정에 명시된 Check list를 통해서 선박 구명설비를 점검하는 것은 매달<u>(monthly)</u> 이루어진다.

09 <u>True course</u> : The angle between the ship's track and the true meridian. 선박의 항적과 진자오선이 이루는 각은 <u>진침로</u>이다.

10 훈련은 여객을 그들의 집합장소, 구명설비, 비상절차에 <u>친숙화(familiarize)</u> 시키기 위해 이루어진다.
familiarize A with B : A를 B에 친숙화 시키다.

11 물표로 선위를 알려주는 경우 물표로 부터의 방위와 거리를 불러준다. 괄호 안에는 거리에 대한 설명이 나와야 한다.
(<u>one decimal six miles</u>; 1.6마일)

12 (2) <u>유지선(stand-on vessel)</u>도 피항선이 피항 동작을 취하지 않는다는 것이 명백해진 경우 피항 동작을 자신의 동작만으로 해야 한다.
(b) 횡단상황에서 위와 같은 상황이 겹친 경우 유지선은 피항 할 때 좌현변침<u>(port)</u>을 하지 말아야 한다.

13 같은 말을 강조하기 위해 반복할 때는 <u>Repeat</u>이라고 말한 후 문장을 반복한다.

14 SOLAS에 의거하여 (<u>AIS</u>)는 자동으로 적절히 장비된 육상국, 타선박, 항공기에게 선박의 식별, 선종, 위치, 침로, 침속, 항해상태 그리고 다른 안전에 관련된 정보들을 포함한 정보들을 제공해야한다.

15 바. 조난 통신 시 구조선의 위치(<u>Location of the rescue vessel</u>)는 조난선에서 알 수 없다.

16 다. An instrument for measuring wind force or speed is a "<u>Anemometer</u>".

17 선박의 위치(position)는 (가)<u>좌표</u> 혹은 (라)<u>물표로부터의 거리와 방위로</u> 알려 준다.
<u>Way point(변침점)</u>의 경우 실제적으로 선위를 알려줄 때 사용하기엔 부적합하다. way point(변침점)은 항해상 2등 항해사가 해도 상에 표시해두는 변침해야하는 지점이므로 각 선박마다 상이한 way point를 가지고 있을 수 있다. 그러나 해당 문제는 기출문제로, way point를 선위 표시에 사용할 수 있다고 답이 나왔었다.

18 가. <u>Wing tank</u>에 대한 설명이다.
다. <u>Oil</u>에 대한 설명이다.

19 태풍(tropical cyclone)을 만난 경우 바람이 북반구 (Northern Hemisphere)에서 우전하면, 그리고 남반구 (Southern Hemisphere)에서 좌전하면 선박은 위험반원 (<u>dangerous semicircle</u>)에 있는 것이다.

20 이것은 화물창이나 탱크에 물이나 기름이 가득차지 않아서 야기되며 선박의 롤링이나 피칭에 따라서 예기치 못하게 발생한다. 이것은 선박 복원성(stability)에 좋지 않은 영향을 주고 선박 전복 (capsize down)을 야기한다. : <u>자유표면 효과 (free surface effect)</u>

memo

memo